BUCKMINSTER FULLER AT HOME IN THE UNIVERSE

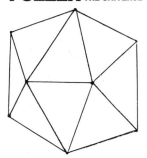

Books by Alden Hatch

General Ike (General Dwight D. Eisenhower)
General in Spurs (General George S. Patton)
Franklin D. Roosevelt
American Express
Red Carpet for Mamie (Mamie Eisenhower)
Ambassador Extraordinary (Clare Boothe Luce)
The Circus Kings with Henry Ringling North
Crown of Glory (Pope Pius XII)
A Man Called John (Pope John XXIII)
Apostle on the Move (Pope Paul VI)

Family Histories

The Wadsworths of the Genesee
The Mountbattens
The Byrds of Virginia
The Lodges of Massachusetts

BUCKMINSTER FULLER AT HOME IN THE UNIVERSE

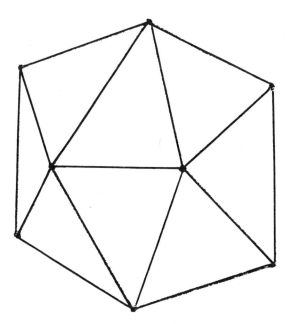

by Alden Hatch

Crown Publishers, Inc., New York

Design: Michael Perpich

CONTENTS

FOREWORD

Books and articles about Buckminster Fuller are always about his ideas and inventions, never about the intellectually complex, emotionally simple, mystical technocrat who is known to so many passengers on Spaceship Earth as "Bucky." He prefers it that way. For to him the persona is nothing, the weightless, metaphysical ideas everything. Nevertheless, to peer at a disembodied mind is no way to understand the man himself and how he got that way.

This book, written by one who has known Bucky in gaiety and sorrow, defeat and triumph for over fifty-eight years, is an attempt to illuminate the very human being that he is, with all his faults and virtues, strong emotions, intense loyalties, outrageous egotism, and unexpected humility; his intellectual sophistication and incredible naïveté, his heterodox thinking and his very orthodox, almost puritanical mores; all the delightful paradoxes that make his personality so interesting.

So my story goes back to the cross-eyed, typhlotic little boy who discovered the beautiful world through his first pair of glasses and has never ceased to wonder at it. It takes him from extraordinarily callow youth to splendid maturity in a life that has held far more attainments and defeats, adventures, and ordeals, delight and tragedy than most men know.

Of course, no one can write about Bucky without describing his transcendental philosophy and his futuristic inventions, because they are his very reason for being, so I have endeavored to explicate them as best I can. But my real purpose will be served if the reader enjoys the remarkable and fascinating experience of *knowing* him.

If my endeavor is successful I have to thank first of all Bucky himself who has talked uncounted hours with me at his usual rate of 7,000 words an hour. In addition I owe much to Norman Cousins, E. J. Applewhite, Leslie Larned Gibson, Rosamund Fuller Kennison, K Hally, Donald Moore, Mrs. William H. Osborn, Glenn A. Olds, William Wasserman, and, especially, to members of that happy Hewlett tribe, Anne Hewlett Fuller, Roger Hewlett, Hope Hewlett Watts, Hester Hewlett Stearns, and James B. Stearns. I thank my wife, Allene G. Hatch, for many of the drawings in the text.

Alden Hatch
Quartermile, Germantown, N.Y.
September, 1973

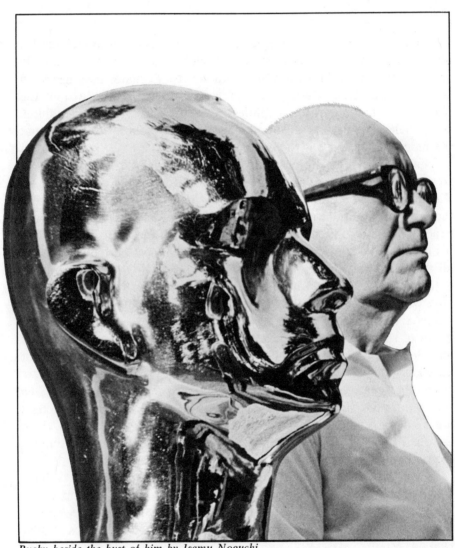

Bucky beside the bust of him by Isamu Noguchi.

CHAPTER I

A RAGING OPTIMIST

APART from the temporary notoriety of a few high government officials and some athletes like Muhammad Ali and Mark Spitz, Buckminster Fuller is probably the best-known American in the world outside of the United States. This is certainly true of the population under thirty. Nor is he without honor among the youth of his own country. Though some mathematicians, savants, and other ivory towerites still sneer gently at the intellectual pretentions of a man whose only scholarly degrees are honorary ones, young people worship him with a fervor they accord to no one else above their arbitrary cutoff age of three decades. At seventy-eight he is the Pied Piper of the twentieth century whom the children follow in their multiracial millions; the prophet of that Supreme Intelligence who designed the exquisitely balanced, ever-regenerative entropic-antientropic, nonsimultaneous, technological-metaphysical synergetic system, which Bucky calls Universe.

The reasons for his hold upon the young are quite simple. They believe in him because he believes in them, believes that their uncluttered, tradition-spurning minds will lead humankind out of the wilderness of fallacious reasoning and outworn concepts into a glorious era of new enlightenment when, by the intelligent use of never-diminished energy and by ephemeralization—doing ever more with less—all men will enjoy a standard of living as high or higher than the most fortunate 5 percent of now-living people. In short, among the clamorous voices of doom and gloom he alone gives them hope and a reason for being and striving.

For Bucky is a raging optimist, often overhopeful, but frequently magnificently right. This facet of his character is acutely expressed in an adjuration his brother-in-law, Roger Hewlett, addressed to Bucky's ever-loyal wife, Anne Hewlett Fuller, at a time when the Fullers were, as usual in those early days, almost flat broke:

> Lady Anne, Lady Anne,
> Keep the coffee hot,
> Bucky's found a sixpence
> And he's off to buy a yacht.

Many years later when Bucky and Anne came to visit the author in Florida, I asked him what he would like to do the following day.

"I think I'll run up to St. Petersburg and buy a yacht," said he.

"Dear Bucky, thank God you haven't changed," I said.

Though Bucky confides the future of the passengers and crew of Spaceship Earth to ever-increasing technology and intelligent industrialization, he is above all a mystic. He believes that the great discoveries of general principles by which the mind of mankind has suddenly leaped forward are not entirely due to the laborious piling up of data upon data until a general principle becomes clear, but are sudden flashes of intuition that come as some exceptionally gifted mind meshes briefly with a Greater Intelligence to obtain a revelation of Truth, later to be proved by conventional pragmatic experimentation. Such was the discovery of the law of gravity by Sir Isaac Newton, such also Einstein's basic law of physics—$E = MC^2$. Though such a mind must have the rigorous training and profundity which enables it to grasp the suddenly revealed truth, such truth could not be discovered by ratiocination, since it is a matter of synergy, which means the behavior of a whole system which is not predictable by the behaviors of any of the system's components taken separately. As Bucky puts it: "Mind relates to the generalized principles, and mind alone can discover them. The mind makes contact with the eternal in these moments of discovery." [1]

Bucky has had several such insights himself. One was the discovery that the tetrahedron was the basic building block of Universe, and another the fact that Nature—which he capitalizes—deals always in beautifully coordinated whole numbers. In his new synergetic geometry, which has revolutionized mathematical thinking, there is no such thing as pi—that awkward, irresolute expression for the circle that is never truly squared, but wanders off the page in a gaggle of digits carried to

[1] Buckminster Fuller to the author.

infinity. He proves it in a series of calculations far too complex for the purposes of this book.

Bucky's most recent glimpse of Truth occurred in 1971 as he was sitting on the end of his dock at Bear Island in Penobscot Bay, Maine, waiting for Norman Cousins to arrive in a chartered schooner. Delayed by adverse winds and tides, Bucky's guest was an hour or more overdue, which gave him a precious period for meditation. Cousins tells how he rowed ashore full of apologies to be greeted by Bucky with a great bear hug. Then, "with his eyes blazing behind his large, thick glasses like watermelon seeds in an agitated bowl of olive oil, just flashing back and forth, Bucky exclaimed, 'Something wonderful has happened!' "

"What is it, Bucky?" Cousins asked.

"I've just discovered the coordinates of Universe."

"I'm sure he had," says Cousins. "That night at dinner and long afterward, Bucky explained it; and once again all the people there were privileged to have a share in the discovery, and they'll never forget it.

"They'll never forget hearing about it though neither they nor I would be able to tell you what the coordinates of Universe are. What I am trying to say is that you don't have to know what Bucky is talking about in order to get the impact of it; which is especially true when he's saying it; less so when he's writing it. Then one gets bogged down in a flow of prose. Oh, he has to say it, because it parses beautifully as he says it. It's an act of creation, you see, because he never says it the same way twice. He's just a lovely human being.

"Bucky's amazing range, his inventiveness, his ingenuity are inexhaustible and infinite; within five minutes after telling you about the coordinates of Universe, he will tell you that he invented a new dance step and demonstrate it." [2]

Though Fuller became well known through his inventions—"the House on a Pole," the Dymaxion car, the Dymaxion map, and, above all, the Geodesic Dome, which encloses more space with far less material and expense than any other form of structure known to man—he does not think of himself as an inventor but rather a discoverer of general principles. For all of his remarkable contributions to technology are simply fallout from those principles. He is a philosopher,

[2] Norman Cousins to the author.

some of whose revelations happen to have a practical application. Previously, the enormous publicity which he has received has been beamed on things—the Dome and so forth. Now, at last, to his great delight, people are talking and writing about his *ideas*, because, as he believes, their time, and his, has come.

In the beginning, after some sad experiences with "practical" people hedged in by traditional concepts, Bucky did some calculating. He figured that the time lag between the inception of a new idea and its practical application varied in different industries. In electronics it was two years, in the aircraft industry about four years, in railroading fifteen years, and in the most backward of all, the construction industry, approximately forty-two years. So he said to himself: "If I aim to be fifty years ahead of my time I shall be safe. No one will interfere with me because I'll be so far ahead that I will pose no threat to all the people who have a vested interest in opposing progress. They'll just call me a nut."

Which, of course, they did.

His ever-increasing fame brings constantly intensifying pressures upon Bucky. Millions of people from Osaka to Leningrad, from Reykjavík to Cape Comorin want to see him and to listen to his complex but inspiring message of hope. In addition, he must find time to write the books in which he expresses his ideas in more detail, and for meditation to enlarge his understanding of Universe and open his mind to further flashes of intuition.

Bucky takes his responsibilities to humanity very seriously indeed. He is driven by a fierce compulsion to accomplish an enormous amount of work in whatever time he may have left, and to express the truth, as he sees it, to the greatest possible number of people, especially young people. His schedule is Homeric, strenuous enough to destroy an ordinary man forty years younger. An example was his itinerary for the summer of 1972:

> June 7, Wednesday. Speak at 3M Company, St. Paul, Minnesota. Lunch with technical directors.
> June 8, Thursday. Speak at 6th Conference of the International Work Simplification Institution, Boston, Massachusetts.
> June 9, Friday. Speak at Taft School, Watertown, Connecticut.
> June 10, 11, and 12. Burr wedding. Lloyd's Neck, Long Island.

June 12, Monday. Confer with biographer Alden Hatch.

June 13, Tuesday. Fifty-fifth Reunion Class of 1917, Cambridge, Mass.

June 17, Saturday. Fly to London, confer with dons on plan for theater at Cambridge.

June 20, Tel Aviv, Israel.

June 24–27, Carbondale, Illinois.

June 28. Meet with president and directors of Design Science Institute, New York.

June 29. Fly to Spoleto, Italy.

June 30–July 6. Spoleto Festival.

July 7 and 8. Speak at the Aegina Art Center, Aegina Island, Greece.

July 9. Gathering on Philopappas Hill, Athens, Greece.

July 10–17. Doxiadis cruise.

July 18. Fly from Athens to New Delhi, India.

July 19–31. India (working on plans for new airports at New Delhi, Bombay, Madras).

August. Reserved. [For Bear Island, Maine].

Bucky did not, in fact, arrive in Maine until August 21, having been delayed by unexpected difficulties in India and by stopping on his way back around the world to make a speech in Seattle.

Bear Island! That is Bucky's Shangri-La, his Blessed Isle, his Eden. For eleven months of the year he is truly a world citizen, uncaring, hardly even noticing, whether he is in Carbondale or Moscow, New Delhi or Tokyo. On the twelfth month he touches earth, like Antaeus to renew his strength. Touches the earth where he spent his happiest boyhood days; where his family gathers around him; where he escapes the stress of modern life and the complexities of the technological civilization he so ardently endorses.

For Bucky has seen to it that Bear Island remains just as it was when he was a boy seventy years ago. This prophet of industrialization, whose aim is to harness the energy of the sun and the stars in the service of mankind, will not allow so much as an electric generator on his beloved island. There are no telephones or radios. You haul water from a well in a bucket—not even a hand pump—and go to the toilet in the rain.

In 1953, Bucky wrote about the island in his most poetic vein—he is a poet, too, who once held the Charles Eliot Norton Chair of Poetry at Harvard.

"Took 543 photographs of Bear Island, which alone, in my forty-nine years' memory of it, remains unchanged in an otherwise all-changed physical world. All that was inherited from the past, all that was first found wonderfully good in life, here remains vividly alive, and how dearly I love it, and what strength it gives!"

"R B F."

With his faith in an Omniscient Intelligence that designed and is embodied in the exquisitely ordered complexities of Universe, which he sometimes calls Nature, sometimes the Supreme Intelligence, and occasionally God, Bucky is a latter-day transcendentalist. William H. Channing, whose brother, William Ellery Channing, cofounder of the Unitarian Church, married Bucky's great-aunt Ellen Fuller, described the transcendentalist movement, which dawned brilliantly over New England in the summer of 1839, as an "assertion of the inalienable integrity of man, of the immanence of Divinity in instinct." It was, he said, "grafted on the somewhat stunted stock of Unitarianism. . . . Transcendentalism, as viewed by its disciples, was a pilgrimage from the idolatrous world of creeds and rituals to the temple of the Living God in the soul. It was a putting to silence of tradition and formulas, that the Sacred Oracle might be heard through intuitions of the single-eyed and pure-hearted. . . ." The transcendentalist believed in "perpetual inspiration, the miraculous power of will, and a birthright of universal good. . . ." Channing says of the ideal transcendentalist, "His work was to be faithful, as all saints, sages, and lovers of man had been, to Truth as the very *Word of God*." [3] By that definition Buckminster Fuller is a transcendentalist.

Should he not be with his heritage! For the Fullers were of that New England strain who led and nurtured the first intellectual blooming of America, and Bucky's great-aunt, Margaret Fuller, was the original liberated American woman, with an intellect so profound that it dazed the members of her own sex and even daunted the men who were then the leaders of American literature and learning. She it was who first published Ralph Waldo Emerson, the high priest of transcendentalism, in *Dial,* a magazine she founded with him for the purpose of encouraging a native American literature untrammeled by subservience to foreign

[3] *Memoirs of Margaret Fuller Ossoli,* edited by R. F. Fuller. Phillips, Sampson and Company, Boston, 1852.

culture. "Books which imitate or represent the thoughts and life of Europe do not constitute an American literature," she wrote.

While she was editor of *Dial* she also published Nathaniel Hawthorne and Edgar Allan Poe, and she was the first editor to publish Henry Thoreau. Though she is described as extremely ugly, these men, with the exception of Hawthorne, who disliked her intensely, and their contemporaries of that small brilliant coterie, were dazzled and enthralled by her learning and wit, though sometimes disturbed by her blunt unfeminine manner of expressing the truth as she saw it, and at others embarrassed by her all-too-feminine desire to be loved.

One can picture her in Emerson's book-cluttered library in Concord, arguing about esoteric enigmas of German philosophy (which, by the way, she introduced to Harvard by her translations of Goethe and Schiller), her eyes flashing with excitement, her head on her abnormally long neck darting this way and that like an angry swan, while the Sage listened with a mixture of admiration and discomfort. When Margaret met her tragic death in a shipwreck off Fire Island in 1850, it is said that Thoreau combed the sands for days in the hope that some fragments of her monumental biography of Goethe would be washed ashore among the flotsam.

Margaret Fuller was as far ahead of her time as Bucky has been of his, and he is the first to acknowledge his debt to her, even reprinting part of one of her essays in his autobiographical *Ideas and Integrities,* as foreshadowing his own thoughts.

The sublime self-assurance, which for years enabled Bucky to maintain his ideas against an almost universal chorus of derogation, is not unlike the intellectual arrogance of his great-aunt who once said to Emerson, "I now know all the people worth knowing in America, and I find no intellect comparable to mine." [4]

Though Bucky intellectually regards race as a dirty word and considers that all types of human beings are of equal value and native ability, he is, paradoxically, extremely proud of his ancestry—a man of many paradoxes he, and the greater for that fact.

The first of the family to come to Massachusetts was Lieutenant Thomas Fuller of the British Army, who in 1638 took a year's leave to have a look at the tiny colony on Massachusetts Bay, the talk of whose exploits and religious dedication had excited his curiosity. In

[4] R. W. Emerson in *Memoirs, ibid.*

Cambridge, the preaching of eloquent Reverend Thomas Shepard so moved him that he abandoned all thoughts of returning to England and decided to live among the Puritans in "the forest aisles where God might be freely worshiped." [5] He bought a large tract of land in Middleton, Massachusetts, married three times, buried two wives, and raised a family of three daughters and five sons.

The Fullers, like their progenitor, were exceedingly devout. One Biblical injunction which they strenuously followed was "Go forth and multiply." Thomas's favorite son, Jacob, to whom he left the Middleton farm, had six children, and his son, also named Jacob, had ten children, of whom Timothy Fuller set the style and tradition of Bucky's direct line.

Timothy was the first Fuller to be graduated from Harvard—the Class of 1760. He "applied himself to theology," and was ordained the first minister of the town of Princeton, Massachusetts, in 1767. He was a successful, though controversial, preacher, being very independent in his thinking. He married Sarah Williams, the daughter of the Reverend Abraham Williams of Sandwich, Massachusetts, and his wife Anna Buckminster, daughter of Colonel Joseph Buckminster of the British Army, who left it to join the Revolutionary Army under Washington. When Timothy Fuller died, "He left a widow and ten children to mourn him."

None of these children went to school regularly. Strong-minded Timothy trusted not in other people's pedagogy but educated his sons and daughters himself until the former were ready to go to Harvard. Timothy, Jr., made even more of a mark than his father. He was graduated second in his Class of 1801 at Harvard, and of course would have been first had he not been set back by participating in a student rebellion against certain oppressive and unjust rules of the college. All his life he was hot for freedom and the rights of man—a Jeffersonian Democrat among Federalists.

After graduation he studied law and went into politics, becoming successively a Massachusetts senator, a United States congressman, Speaker of the Massachusetts House of Representatives, and a member of the Executive Council.

However, the most important thing he ever did was to sire Margaret Fuller and force-feed her education so that she read Latin at six and

[5] "Thomas Fuller and His Descendants," *New England Historical and Genealogical Register,* October 1859.

learned Greek, French, German, and Italian. By the time she was in her teens she had read many of the classics in all those languages. It was pretty tough on Margaret, but it made her the outstanding woman of her era.

Another important accomplishment of the Honorable Timothy in the progenitive field was to father Bucky's grandfather, Arthur Buckminster Fuller, and educate him. When Timothy died of Asiatic cholera in 1835, at the age of forty-three, Margaret took over the education of Arthur and his next younger brother, Richard Frederick Fuller, and poor though she always was, having to earn her own living, sent them both through Harvard. Arthur was graduated in 1843 and Frederick in 1844.

At Harvard, Arthur "united with the church connected with the university" (Unitarian). Soon after graduation he became a member of the Illinois Conference of Christian and Unitarian Ministers and was licensed by them to preach. He preached his first sermon in Chicago in 1843, in the Reverend Joseph Harrington's Unitarian Church. When he returned to New England, he studied at Harvard Divinity School, and then became pastor of the Unitarian Society in Manchester, New Hampshire, where he was ordained in 1848. In 1853, he was called to the New North Church on Hanover Street in Boston. He was also elected Chaplain of the Massachusetts Senate in 1858.

Arthur and Frederick, who became a lawyer, were the closest to each other of the whole family. They both married, Arthur having two children, and Frederick four by their first wives. When both brothers lost their wives, Frederick married Adeline R. Reeves, a widow, in 1856. Two years later Arthur married her sister, Emma Lucilla Reeves, who was also a widow. Then the two brothers bought a house at 13 Hilliard Street in Cambridge and formed an extraordinarily loving joint household with their wives, their children, and their stepchildren, to whom were soon added the children of their second marriages, two sons in Arthur's case while Frederick contributed three sons and two daughters. Forty years later members of both families were still living at 13 Hilliard Street.

Arthur's son, Richard Buckminster Fuller, Bucky's father, was born on February 13, 1861. He never knew his father. Though Arthur had resigned his pastorate of the New North Church in 1859 because of poor health, the onset of the Civil War stirred him to action. So ardent was his patriotism, so strong his hatred of slavery, that he felt impelled by his conscience to take part in the war. In August 1861, he was commissioned chaplain of the 16th Massachusetts Volunteer Infantry. While serving with them he also acted as a war correspondent for the Boston *Herald,* the *Journal,* the *Christian Enquirer,* and the New York *Tribune,* for whom he wrote a vivid eyewitness account of the battle between the *Monitor* and the *Merrimack.*

One would think that this man of forty had done enough by leaving his pleasant home, his wife and children for the rugged conditions of army life and the heartbreaking business of ministering to the dying and wounded, but a New England conscience is a powerful propellant. In December 1862, the Federal Army was encamped at Fredericksburg on the road to Richmond. Bewhiskered General Ambrose E. Burnside conceived the preposterous plan of crossing the Rappahannock River to attack General Robert E. Lee's Army of Northern Virginia, impregnably entrenched on the heights beyond. Early in the morning of December 11, a pontoon bridge was flung across the Rappahannock and the 16th Massachusetts was ordered to cross it. In view of the murderous fire of Confederate rifles and artillery from the commanding heights, they very sensibly hesitated. Whereupon Arthur Fuller, with deep faith that he was doing the Lord's work, led them onto the bridge. Halfway across he was killed by a Confederate bullet, thus becoming one of the first casualties of that bloody Union defeat.

Though Arthur's infant son, Richard Buckminster Fuller, grew up to be a charming gentleman, he never displayed the intellectual strength of his father nor did his life involve such dramatic incidents. The most important thing he did was to father Richard Buckminster Fuller, Jr.

CHAPTER II

BELOVED ISLAND

WHEN Richard Buckminster Fuller, Jr., was born on July 12, 1895, in the Fullers' big, rambling wooden house in Milton, Massachusetts, his father was at the peak of his business success, and life was very comfortable. The Fullers could afford a number of servants and a yard-man—not an extravagant household since a good cook was paid twenty or twenty-five dollars a month and the maids proportionately less.

Until he was four years old Bucky's world was confusingly nebulous. His eyes were crossed and completely unfocused so he saw only masses of color with no distinct outlines. He did not know what his father or mother, his older sister Leslie, or his baby brother Wolcott, looked like. They were mere shapes that he recognized by their size and their voices. Being a very loving child he was completely devoted to them and eager to please, but it was inevitable that he appeared annoyingly stupid and clumsy. Then he was fitted with a pair of glasses.

That was the moment of Bucky's first revelation, the beginning of his long love affair with Universe. He has said, "For the first time I saw leaves on a tree, small birds, and lovely butterflies; I saw the stars and the shapes of clouds and people's faces. It was a time of utter joy as though all these things had been newly created just for me; in a way they belonged to me.

"I was filled with wonder at the beauty of the world and I have never lost my delight in it." [1]

Once equipped with glasses, Bucky soon showed that, whatever his other failings, he was not stupid. Indeed, from being rather slow he became irritatingly bright. He was immensely curious and unwilling to take things on a grown-up's say-so; he always wanted to know the

[1] Buckminster Fuller to the author. All unattributed quotations from Fuller were made to the author in a series of interviews.

reasons for everything, especially the things for which there were no good reasons except that they were traditional or customary. Thus he often appeared to be challenging adult wisdom and authority.

Bucky showed his inventiveness early. In the autumn of his sixth year he was sent to kindergarten where he was given some toothpicks and dried peas to play with. Working with intense concentration he used them to construct a tetrahedronal octet truss.[2] He had no idea why he did it or what good it was—he just knew it pleased him by its symmetry and strength. He remembers his teacher calling others to come and admire it.

Bucky at Wiscasset, Maine.

[2] Three squares combined to make eight triangles, patented in 1961 by R. Buckminster Fuller as the Octetruss.

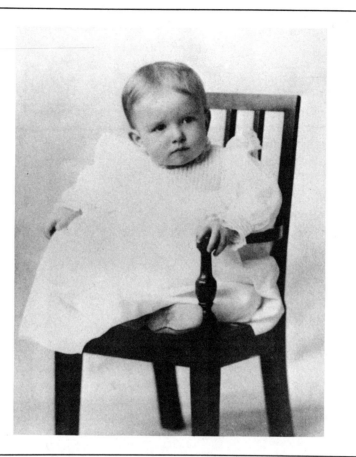

Bucky, age one.

Bucky must have been a very sensitive child, perhaps hypersensitive. His eagerness to please, his intense need for approval and love, were in conflict with his stubborn independence of mind which put people off. In addition, the thick lenses of his glasses magnified his hazel eyes to owllike proportions, giving him an air of precocious wisdom which could be annoying. Thus his attempts to win affection and praise were frequently rebuffed.

For example, Leslie, who was three years older, consistently tried to suppress him. Until Bucky came along, she had been the focus of love and attention in the household; suddenly she was displaced by a newcomer—and a boy at that! In those days almost nobody made an effort

Bucky with his older sister, Leslie, who consistently tried to suppress him.

to disguise the fact that boys were more important than girls. Looking back on it Bucky feels that his sister's concealed or unconscious hostility was perfectly natural. Her assumption of superiority, as when she would say, "Bucky, when I was in first grade I was able to do the work very easily, but you will find it hard," was, he realizes, purely defensive. But when he was five or six it crushed him. He says, "She had a very powerful influence on my life."

On the other hand, Bucky felt no sibling rivalry for his younger brother, Wolcott (known as Woolly), but loved him dearly. However, three years difference in age made real companionship impossible until they both grew up. Nor was Bucky very close to his mother, who never quite understood this changling child of hers, with his strange combination of mental precocity and emotional immaturity.

The object of Bucky's utter devotion was his father. Mr. Fuller was a lovable man. He had grown up in that heterogeneous household at 13 Hilliard Street, the youngest but one of all those brothers and sisters, half-brothers, half-sisters, stepbrothers, stepsisters, and double first cousins, so he had learned early to get along with people. The fact that his father died so young at Fredericksburg doubtless made him an object of special tenderness to his siblings and he returned their love.

Dick Fuller grew up to be a rather delicate young man. He entered Harvard with the Class of 1883, but his health gave way after two years, and he went to Arizona to recuperate. Though he never was formally graduated from Harvard, he was so well liked—and so well read—that on his return from Arizona he was voted his degree. During his brief time at Harvard, he made many staunch friends, as Bucky learned after his father's early death. "For love of him," he says, "they were willing to do anything they could for me, particularly when I was in trouble, which was quite often."

Though most of his progenitors had been ministers or doctors or lawyers, Richard Fuller had become a merchant, importing teas and fine leathers from India and the Argentine. Bucky thinks that he would have preferred to follow the family tradition, but he felt he needed to do something to refurbish the Fuller fortunes. Though he was a gentle person, totally lacking the flinty character supposedly necessary for business success in that time and place, he made a moderate fortune.

In 1891, Richard Fuller married Bucky's mother, Caroline Wolcott Andrews of Chicago. She, too, was of New England ancestry, being descended from Roger Wolcott, the Royal Governor of the Colony of Connecticut, and his son Oliver Wolcott, a signer of the Declaration of Independence, who became the first governor of the State of Connecticut. Oliver's grandson, Christopher Wolcott, went west and married the daughter of Colonel John Kinzie, commanding Fort Dearborn. This was the first marriage between Americans in Chicago. Their daughter, Caroline Wolcott, married John Andrews of Birchwood Farm on Lake Michigan about five miles north of the growing city. Bucky's mother was born there, and as a little girl watched the splendidly terrifying spectacle of the Chicago fire from the cupola of the farmhouse.

Bucky describes his mother as "very loving but extraordinarily devout." A high-church Episcopalian, she often took Bucky to the big Episcopalian church in Boston where the ritual was almost as elaborate as in St. Peter's.

On most Sundays Bucky walked to the Episcopal church in Milton with his father. Mr. Fuller had been brought up as a Unitarian, but had become an Episcopalian to please his wife, and was a vestryman of the Milton church. Bucky vividly remembers walking beside his father while the latter earnestly talked to him about God and urged him to become a minister when he grew up. "I remember how extraordinarily loving he was to me," Bucky says.

He also recalls going for Thanksgiving dinner at 13 Hilliard Street with all his ebullient relations. Even though the huge family had grown up and scattered, they all tried to return home for that great New England feast day.

When Bucky was five, in 1900, his mother took him to Chicago to visit her family at Birchwood Farm. There she showed him the land where her old house had been and from which she had watched the fire. Bucky stood there, enjoying the magnificent view of the lake with ore-laden steamers making white tracks on the blue water as they headed for the great inland port, and the creamy sails of fishing boats and yachts catching the sunset light. He loved ships more than anything.

Bucky went to Chicago again in the summer of 1903; by train to Buffalo and then on a big, white paddle-wheel steamer to Chicago; a most exciting experience. He and his mother stayed with the Rockwell Kings on Hawthorne Street. His Aunt Lucy King, his mother's older sister, was his godmother. "Uncle Rock" owned the Western Cold Storage Company with a plant he had built on Kinzie Street, a few blocks west of where his wife's great-grandfather had lived. Every weekday morning he drove downtown in his buggy, and sometimes took Bucky with him. The eight-year-old enjoyed the three-mile drive through the pleasant, quiet streets, for that part of the city was still almost like a country town. There was very little traffic, just a few delivery wagons and the smart carriages of the rich people who were building their big, ugly brownstone houses northward along Lake Shore Drive. When they reached the plant, Uncle Rock would tie the reins around the whip in its socket on the dashboard and give the horse a smart slap on the rump to find his way home alone.

Always interested in machinery, Bucky was fascinated by the big stationary steam engine—with its steel pistons slipping silently up and down in the tall, vertical cylinders—that supplied the power to drive liquid ammonia through miles of frosty pipes that cooled the storage rooms hung with the dressed carcasses of pigs and steers and sheep.

Most summers the Fullers spent a month or more at the seashore, at first in Marblehead, then in Wiscasset on the coast of Maine, where they took a cottage on Peache's Point. Bucky's father was frequently away on business trips—to the Argentine, which took four or five months, and once to India when he was gone a whole year. Bucky likes to point out the enormous advance in man's mobility that has taken place in his lifetime—now he goes to India four times a year.

Mr. Fuller's long journeys only served to increase his son's love for him; the world turned drab when his father left, radiant when he returned.

The summer of 1904 was a landmark in the life of Bucky Fuller and, indeed, in that of all his family. Grandmother Andrews came east with the Rockwell Kings and their seven children to join the Fullers in Boston, whence they took the Eastern Steamship Company's walking-beam side-wheeler, *City of Rockland,* to Rockland, Maine. There they chartered the small steam packet *Juliet* to take them to Eagle Island in the mouth of Penobscot Bay where they spent the entire summer in John and Hattie Quinn's boardinghouse. The children, and the adults, too, had a perfectly glorious time.

That part of the Maine coast is where the Appalachian Range, the spine of America's east coast, plunges at last into the Atlantic. Penobscot Bay is filled with dozens of small, rocky, tree-clad islands, which are, in fact, mountaintops rising above its surface. That summer Bucky, his siblings, and cousins explored and picnicked on almost every island, most of which were uninhabited. They were exhilarated by the strong, salt winds, which blew straight off the Atlantic, and loved swimming in the icy cold waters that lapped the stony beaches.

Their elders were so happy that Mrs. Andrews decided to buy an island in the bay, where the whole family could come together every summer.

She and the others unanimously decided on Bear Island,[3] the focal center of a microarchipelago consisting of Bear, Little Sprucehead, and

[3] It was then called Bare Island, but Mr. Fuller found its original name was Bear Island and so renamed it.

Compass islands, lying near the mouth of Penobscot Bay six miles north of Cape Rosier. It is nearly a mile long and from a quarter of a mile to a few hundred yards wide, bound and defended from the waves by rocky shores rising to a sixty-foot cliff at the seaward end. Rare in such an island, it has a deep, narrow harbor completely protected from the Atlantic gales by almost perpendicular bluffs and a natural rock breakwater.

Bear Island has probably been inhabited for hundreds of years. Norse fishermen may have dried their catch on its sun-hot rocks; certainly Indians had lived on it, for the soil is full of arrowheads. An eighteenth-century owner of Little Sprucehead found it so idyllic that he named his children Adam and Eve. In the nineteenth century Bear Island was taken over by Latter-Day Saints. Over a hundred years ago a sect of the Mormon Church interpreted scripture as indicating that, at a certain hour on a certain day, the end of the world would come. Their elder, Jonathon Eaton, further prophesied that the most favorable place to enter heaven was the highest point on Bear Island. At the appointed time Latter-Day Saints from far and near came to the island, in schooners, sloops, rowboats—anything that would float. Elder Jonathon Eaton, somewhat ungallantly, climbed the highest tree so as to be the first one through the heavenly portals. When nothing happened except a superbly chromatic Maine sunrise, most of the Saints went away disappointed.

But apparently not Elder Eaton, for Mrs. Andrews bought the island from the Eaton and Parson families, who then moved to Pulpit Harbor on North Haven Island.

Bucky says, "My grandmother acquired Bear Island in the hope that it would serve through many years to hold her family and descendants together. That was part of her dreaming, and of my mother's dreaming, and my father's. And so it has happened. After my grandmother died in 1906, my mother carried on powerfully, holding the island together. After that my little sister, Rosey, held it, which was hard because we had so little money then; and finally I have been able to help. We have made it into a company in which all the members of our families hold shares. Many of them come here still, a dozen of the younger generation, that is, my grandchildren, great-nephews, and nieces."

At the time Mrs. Andrews bought Bear Island, Bucky's father and Uncle Rock bought Little Sprucehead and Compass islands. Bucky now owns Little Sprucehead, having bought out the other heirs.

When Mrs. Andrews acquired Bear Island there were several wells and three cottages on it. In the spring of 1905, she had one of the cottages painted and improved to accommodate the family. Another was rebuilt to encompass the main dining room, kitchen with a big, iron wood-burning stove, storehouse, laundry, and servant quarters, with a toolhouse, woodshed, icehouse, and coalroom adjoining it.

The main house on Bear Island

Bucky always remembers the Fuller's first journey to what was now their own island because it set the pattern for all the subsequent trips he made as a boy. He and Woolly were awakened by the deep-toned whistle of the *City of Rockland* as she passed Owl's Head Light at the entrance to Penobscot Bay. They dressed quickly and went up on deck in the still darkness to watch the ship steam through the bay. She passed Rockland Breakwater Light about four A.M. and, with much shouting, backing and filling, and heaving of hawsers, tied up at the pier. The gangplank was rigged, and the boys ran down it to the dock to watch the long process of unloading the steamer. First came piles of luggage;

then many beautiful carriages with their teams and saddle horses were led ashore. They belonged to the rich summer "rusticaters," as the Maine people call them, who lived in the famous Maine resorts, such as Bar Harbor and Northeast Harbor, North Haven, Eagle Island, and Blue Hill.

The horses and the carriages were reloaded on the smaller steamers *Catherine, Juliet,* and *Sieur des Monts,* which fanned out from Rockland, while the big Boston boat went on to call at Camden, Bristol, and up the Penobscot River to Bangor. In the bright morning light, Bucky and Woolly could see all those steamers as diminishing, faraway, smoke-plumed silhouettes against the bright blue water.

In his unpublished memoir of Bear Island, Bucky wrote, "All of the, last seventy years of his life, the exquisite sensorial thrill of nine-year-old Bucky's receptiveness to the sight, sound and smell, and the touch of the wind on his skin, at that Penobscot dawn-moment has remained his most memorable concept of nature's beauty."

That summer on Bear Island was sheer delight to Bucky. Though the families were rather crowded in the low, two-story, white-painted house, it did not matter for there was plenty of room to roam on the island. The two older King boys, McGregor and Andrew, lived in the house down by the harbor, which became known as the Boys' House, and Captain John Johnson, Bear Island's first "captain," had another cottage. In those days the island was not as wooded as it is now. There were vegetable gardens, big hayfields, and workhorses to pull the plow and the big farm wagon. Captain Johnson farmed and fished for a living to supplement the money the family paid him to care for the island. There were, of course, no modern conveniences such as indoor plumbing, but deliciously cold water was hauled in buckets out of one of the wells. Later, cisterns were built at the corners of the houses into which rainwater ran down pipes from the roofs. This was used for washing.

At first Captain Johnson's fishing boat was the Bear Islanders' only means of reaching the mainland. Then came a sloop with one of the earliest auxiliary gasoline marine engines which required "gallons of sweat relevant to priming the engine, testing the spark and rolling the flywheel" to get her started. And soon the little harbor was filled by a fleet of small sloops and catboats belonging to various members of the two families. A bit later, Mrs. Fuller bought the *Wego,* a small cabin cruiser with a marine gasoline engine. In 1905, Bucky had a little sailing dinghy called the *Sea Bird* in which he rowed or sailed to Butter

Island or Eagle Island to get the mail. It was about a two-mile trip each way, an arduous row for a young fellow just ten years old, especially as there were strong tidal currents and frequent fogs which required navigation by compass.

This produced Bucky's first practical invention. He thought rowing with his back to where he was going, constantly looking over his shoulder to correct his course, a very inefficient way of moving a boat through the water. And he thought of the white jellyfish who shoved themselves through the sea by spurting out small jets of water. This led him to imagine and construct a "mechanical jellyfish" to push his boat along. It was a web-and-sprit cone mounted like an inside-out umbrella on a pole that could be pulled and pushed through a ring mounted on the stern board of his dinghy. When pulled through the water the cone would close, thus offering very little resistance; when pushed back it opened, giving the boat a powerful thrust ahead, driving her along far more quickly than the oars. Sitting in the stern shoving his boat through the sea, Bucky was always looking ahead, a thing he has done all his life.

Dick Fuller gave his son his first real boat in 1906. It was a lovely little keel sloop, eighteen feet overall, stone-ballasted, fast and able, built for him by Captain Johnson. When she was ready for launching Mr. Fuller asked Bucky, "What would you like to call her?"

"The *Cuspidor*," Bucky said eagerly.

Mr. Fuller was shocked by this piece of vulgarity on the part of his son. He furiously told Bucky that he did not deserve to have such a boat and almost took it away then and there. In tears, both at the prospect of losing his boat, and even more upset by having angered his father, Bucky explained that he did not even know what a cuspidor was. He had been thinking of the old sea chanty in which "the good ship *Cuspidor* sailed from Baffins Bay," so the word had a heroic sound to him. Mr. Fuller, delighted with his sort of innocence, was appeased. They conferred about other names and finally settled on *Ursa Minor,* the constellation of the Little Bear.

The crowded conditions that first summer, and the birth of Bucky's little sister Rosamund, made the Fullers decide to build a proper house on the island. During the winter of 1906, Dick Fuller's Harvard classmate, Henry Wadsworth Longfellow, Jr., known as Waddy, designed it for them. In the spring Mr. Sewell, a contractor from Cambridge in whom they had justifiable confidence, was engaged to build it. Sewell chartered the schooner *Polly,* a historic relic built in 1805, which had fought the British in the War of 1812. Into her he loaded all the lumber, nails, copper gutters, glass, hardware, and tools he needed together with his crew of carpenters and laborers.

On June 6, 1906, the *Polly* anchored off Dining Room Beach on Bear Island where she lay for three months, serving as a warehouse for the building materials and quarters for the workmen. The Big House, as it is called, was built on the edge of the high cliff on the southeast promontory of the island, close to where Elder Eaton climbed that tree. Mrs. Fuller supervised every stage of its construction. Bucky, fascinated by the technique involved in building the first house he had ever seen rise from bare earth, was constantly on hand.

When completed it looked quite grand; for it dominated the whole island before the shingles weathered to blend with the gray rocks, and friendly trees grew up around it. It was typical of the big summer cottages of the era; two stories tall with an attic under a hipped roof. One long living room with a big fieldstone fireplace, built by Mr. McDonald of Castine, dominated the ground floor with two bedrooms off it, one of which was occupied by Bucky's parents. Grandmother Andrews had the large southeast room on the second floor, and the Rockwell Kings had the big northwest room. Smaller rooms were assigned to Marjory King, Leslie Fuller, and baby Rosey. The southwest room, now used by Bucky and Anne Fuller, was the guest room, first occupied by the Ellery Sedgwicks of Boston. Bucky and Woolly had the whole unpartitioned attic. They often ran races around it, which, when done too early in the morning, brought frequent spankings.

Almost every room had a porch or balcony commanding superb, 360-degree views of the island-dotted bay and the Atlantic beyond. At night one could see six lighthouses flashing, each in its special time sequence for mariners' identification.

McGregor and Andrew King still lived down at the Boys' House, a good half mile away. Bucky was grateful for this arrangement, for the King boys, being three and six years older than he and strong and handsome, were lords of the island. They treated Bucky with friendly contempt, bossed him, and hazed him. Bucky says, "They were a very powerful influence on my life experiences as a kid. I don't think they thought very well of their eastern cousins, and my mother was eager for them to harden me up and make me into something they thought would be an acceptable character."

In fact, he was quite strong and resilient for a boy of his age; able on the sea and efficient at making things with his hands. When he was only thirteen he built a cabin for himself out of lumber and shingles left over from the Big House. He named it Birch Lodge and, considerably enlarged, it is used today to house some of the eager young people whom Bucky's fame and unbounded hospitality attract to the island. He also made various pieces of furniture for the Big House, and invented a record cabinet to hold Victor records upright in easily accessible divisions like those sold commercially many years later.

Bucky in his kayak at Bear Island.

Bucky thinks the King boys' rather contemptuous attitude was partly due to Midwesterners' general disposition to regard Easterners, and particularly New Englanders, as effete. Of course, this was a riposte to the Easterners looking on anyone from west of the Alleghenies as crude. "There was really a very strong feeling in those days between Chicago and the East," said Bucky. "It persisted for many years. When I first went to live in Chicago in 1925, it was still apparent. At the Sunday Night Club, which was a meeting place for out-of-towners, our Chicago hosts would sometimes get up and talk disdainfully about 'the effete East.' Later, when the King boys went to Harvard and used to come to our house in Milton for Sunday lunch, their attitude was modified considerably, though not entirely. However, they were extremely interesting people and played an important role in my life."

Those first happy days at Bear Island were soon clouded by family sorrow. Grandmother Andrews died in the winter of 1906, and in 1907 Bucky's father suffered a severe stroke. The medical profession had not yet learned of the preventive methods that make repetitions of such things less likely, and Mr. Fuller's first stroke was followed by others which rendered him progressively more helpless. To Bucky it was truly a heartbreaking experience. "It was a very extraordinary thing," he said, "having been so loved and really well looked after by this father, to suddenly have him have these strokes. My mother was determined that he should have the best possible care, and not be separated from us, so she simply fixed up a room in our house in such a way that he would not have to go to a hospital. This meant that for the years between ten and thirteen I was leading my own father around by the hand, and to have this man, whom I loved so much, be unable to remember things or to speak to me, was a very extraordinary matter."

So Bucky tells it, but the ever-ready tears gather in his eyes as he does so.

His father's illness and death threw heavy responsibilities on Bucky's shoulders. With the medical expenses and her income from the business cut off, Mrs. Fuller had to cut costs to maintain the kind of household she had been used to in Milton. Among the first to go was the handyman who tended the furnace in winter. Bucky inherited the job and other household chores. Stoking the fire, rolling out barrels of ashes, cutting grass, and raking driveways involved an enormous amount of muscular work. Bucky says, "The operation of a big house was a very prodigious matter; most people today have no memory of what it took to keep one of those big houses going. We did not have electricity because mother could not afford to install it. We used candles and kerosene lamps which had to be filled every day. I didn't object to these things at all; it was a very, very rich part of my life experience to learn so much about how houses were run. I imagine this must have affected a lot of my feelings about what needs to be done to make things work."

Thinking about those old-fashioned houses and his early experiences of them, Bucky observed that many people seem to relish the smell of old houses, the scent of decaying wood. "I did not like the way they smelled," he said, "and incidentally, the smell of schools I thought was absolutely awful. The teacher would go and open the windows sometimes, but the whole thing seemed to stink to me—and the smell of the lavatories and toilets!

"I was also bothered a whole lot by the way the houses looked when I was young. The white ones were pretty, but many others were painted drab gray, or brown and yellow. The General Grant style of architecture, those big, grand mansions, did not seem grand at all to me. I found them formidable. The people in them were not, I felt, as kindly as they could be—in fact, they were pretty hard. These were the people who were being successful, making money, and so forth. It was an era of considerable hardness and they were not gentle. I identify that with the looks, feelings, and smells of those buildings.

"As for the city itself; Boston, I thought it horribly stinky. Yet I was in awe of it, and I explored it and I wanted to know what it was about. I was not afraid of it, I just didn't like it but I was terribly eager to understand it.

"That is why I love Bear Island so much. I came here as a child of freedom. The island was so big you could get away from people—exploring beaches and wooded places. It has been a wonderful characteristic of Bear Island that mothers have never been afraid to let their children roam—a child doesn't just walk over a cliff; he doesn't make that stupid sort of blunder. So no child has ever gotten hurt here because of the boldness of it!"

Thus there was this great contrast in Bucky's young life between the city and its suburbs, which he felt to be so formidable as to adversely affect the very souls of the people who lived there, and the freedom and simplicity of the island life—"the goodness of life here compared to that other. . . ."

That, Bucky believes, was the beginning of his interest in improving housing; the spark plug of his desire to make it possible for people to dwell in houses which, instead of stultifying their characters, would enlarge their spirits and liberate their natural goodness.

CHAPTER III

NOT SO FAIR HARVARD

THE trauma of his father's illness and death was the first of several psychic shocks that distorted Bucky's youthful character, and led him at times to wildly irresponsible behavior. More than ever he needed love and approval; and when they were denied him he overreacted. For example, the Fullers' reduced circumstances shamed him unduly, and he magnified unintentional slights into deliberate insults, attributing them to his lack of means. Because he had so little money he set up a dichotomy concerning wealth, at one and the same time exaggerating its power for evil and trying to convince himself of its total unimportance. He succeeded so well in the latter endeavor that throughout his entire life he has treated his personal finances in a downright feckless manner.

Mrs. Fuller unwittingly contributed to this attitude. Determined that her children should have the best possible education, she scrimped and sacrificed to send Bucky as a day scholar to Milton Academy, one of New England's finest and richest preparatory schools. But it never occurred to her that he should have an allowance, no matter how small— some money of his own to budget and spend as he saw fit. Bucky says, "If my father had been there he would certainly have given me an allowance. As it was, I had to ask mother for everything I did or bought; and feel very badly about asking for it. Sometimes, really needing something and not quite daring to ask for it, I charged it. Then the bill would come in and things were messy."

Not only were they messy, but Mrs. Fuller began to feel that her son was thoughtless and irresponsible.

There was the incident of the football helmet. Milton had an excellent football team and Bucky went out for it. He was small, but he was a compact mass of muscle, and was speedy. His great ambition at this time was to make quarterback of the team. When he first began to play he told his mother he needed a helmet. What he had in mind was the regulation leather helmet of the period which all the other boys wore. Mrs. Fuller, struggling desperately to make ends meet, went to the ten-cent store, and bought him a cheap helmet made of a sort of Chinese quilting. Bucky thanked her politely enough, but when he wore it, as he had to in order to be allowed to play, he felt shamed. Sixty-odd years later he still mentally cringes at the memory. It all became very much a part of his attitude toward wealth.

Middlesex Football Team (Bucky lower left).

At Milton, though, Bucky had one thing no other boy had, and he gloried in it. In his senior year he was given a beautiful little kayak. He quickly learned to handle it with great expertise. Once he paddled all the way down the Charles River to Boston and out on the choppy water of the harbor itself. Though no great feat for a boy who had been nurtured on the tide-ripped, fog-bound waters of Penobscot Bay, it was considered a rugged and daring stunt by his fellows. Bucky basked in the glow of their admiration.

In fact, Bucky's record at Milton was very good. He was, of course, stubbornly independent in his thinking. When he began Euclidian geometry his teacher first made a dot on the blackboard which she explained was not a thing of substance but merely an imaginary point in space. She then made other dots and connected them by a line which she said did not exist either. A series of parallel lines made a plane which was also nonexistent, but when the planes were stacked up to make a cube, she said *that* existed. Bucky could not see how you could make something real out of nothing. He asked how much it weighed; this was considered impertinent. There followed a series of nonexistent triangles, and circles which could not be squared. Bucky's logical mind instantly rejected these fictitious objects, with no substance, and he voiced his doubts, which persisted until he invented his own synergetic geometry many years later. However, with the weight of authority pressing upon him, and the knowledge that he would get into trouble if he questioned traditional thinking, he "shut up." He decided to conform and play the game according to its illogical rules—for the time being. He played it so well that he got As in all his science and mathematics courses throughout his school career. He did not do as well in Classics, Latin, English Literature, and History because they bored him, but he managed good grades except in Latin, which he barely passed.

Bucky loved athletics, which he later rationalized in Fullerese as "an enthusiastically broad experience in the historically differentiated family of controlled physical principles, known as athletics, which greatly heightened what I call the intuitive dynamic sense, a *fundamental* I am convinced, of competent anticipatory design formation."

Anything Bucky liked, he did very well indeed. Despite his comparatively small size and the fact, which he did not then know, that one leg was three-quarters of an inch shorter than the other, he realized his ambition to become quarterback of the varsity football team.

All in all, his experience at Milton was a happy one—despite those awful stinks. So he came to Harvard in the fall of 1913, with a good scholastic and athletic record, and very high hopes.

Bucky's hopes were far too high. Based on his father's descriptions of Harvard and the reminiscenses of his father's friends, he had created a place as idyllically unreal as Tennyson's "Avilion; Where falls not hail, or rain, or any snow, Nor ever wind blows loudly."

As Bucky put it in an address to the Planning Committee of Southern Illinois University in 1961, "I was too puerilely in love with a special romantic, mythical Harvard of my own conjuring—an Olympian world of superathletes and alluring, grown-up, worldly heroes." He expected to become an equal and good companion of that exalted company. The reality was dismally different.

First off, due, he thinks, to the unequal length of his legs, he broke his knee at football practice, which ended his glorious dream of becoming Harvard's quarterback; the ranks of superathletes were closed to him forever.

Then, because he found mathematics too easy, he chose to major in "something really difficult like government or English." Since literature was not the love of his life, and politics and politicians soon became anathema to him, his college work seemed "a chore done only to earn the right to live in the Harvard community." The things he was taught and the way they were taught appeared to him either untrue or irrelevant, though he would not have used exactly that word at that time. To these disillusionments was added an unexpected and crushing rejection.

In 1913, Harvard was socially stratified by the clubs. Porcellian was the social pinnacle, followed by others in descending order. In the outer purlieus were barbarians who belonged to no club at all. As his first semester drew to a close Bucky was "shockingly surprised" by the looming prospect that he would not be invited to join any club.

In his speech at Southern Illinois Bucky said, "I soon saw that I wasn't going to be included in the clubs as I might have been if I had been very wealthy or had a father looking out for me; for much of the clubs' membership was arranged by the clubs' graduate committees. . . . I hadn't anticipated these social developments. I suddenly saw a class system existing in Harvard of which I had never dreamed. I was not aware, up to that moment, that there was a social class system and that

Bucky about the time he went to Harvard.

there were different grades of citizens. My thoughts had been idealistically democratic. Some people had good luck and others bad; but not because they were not equal. I considered myself about to be ostracized or compassionately tolerated by the boys I had grown up with. I felt that my social degradation would bring disgrace to my family. . . ."

This is Buckminster Fuller the egalitarian philosopher speaking, not Bucky Fuller the prep-school-educated son of Boston's best. It is typical of Fuller's habit of endowing his youthful self with the ideals he acquired through pain and compassion very much later. In 1913, Harvard was about as democratic as the court of Louis XIV, and it is difficult to believe that a boy brought up in the atmosphere and traditions of Harvard's elite should have been surprised and disturbed to discover that it was not an egalitarian society—he had heard talk about the clubs all his life. In fact, it is highly improbable that young Bucky, who up to that time had never thought seriously about the social condition of mankind, gave a hoot whether Harvard was democratic or not.

In his final sentence he unconsciously gives it away. *I felt that my social degradation would bring disgrace to my family.* There is the pith and substance of it; the dismaying discovery was not that there were social classes at Harvard, but that Bucky was not to be accepted into the upper class.

The reasons he gives for his "ostracism"—lack of wealth, no father to look out for him—are also a rationalization long after the fact. However deplorable Cambridgian snobbery may have been, wealth was not the key to acceptance. The clubs were very inexpensive and the richest boy in the world could not have bought his way in. Nor is there much more validity to the argument that lack of a father had a great deal to do with it. It is true that the graduate committees could bring a certain amount of pressure to bear on the undergraduate membership committees of the clubs, but the final decision was up to the boys themselves.

The plain truth is that Bucky was too individualistic, too much of an oddball in thought and appearance to meet the conformist standards of those young, so-sure-of-themselves aristocrats. He was short, carelessly dressed, with a head much too large for his body. His teeth, which had not then been straightened, were oddly arranged and those enormous magnifying lenses made his eyes look like big pools of amber liquid. Above all he was too vulnerable, too eager, and too emotional to be acceptable to young men who conformed to New England's mode of suppressing all emotion. His brother-in-law, Roger Hewlett, says, "As a young man trying to make an impression he went to excesses. If he went on a drunk it was a bigger drunk than it should be in that crowd, or if he went to a party he made too much noise. By trying too hard he managed to keep himself out of being in all the time."

So it must be concluded that Bucky was unloved for himself alone; another rejection and one most bitter.

This analysis is not to imply that Bucky was consciously sophistical in his speech at Southern Illinois. He believed it to be an accurate statement of fact.

Bucky was so deeply hurt and disillusioned that Harvard became hell to him. He wanted desperately to get away. As to the manner of his going he had, of course, several reasonable options. He could simply resign; he could leave without resigning; or he could stop studying and quietly and deliberately fail his examinations. The latter course was unthinkable because, to the "social degradation," it would add the stigma of mental incapacity, and, though he found his courses so uninteresting, by sheer perseverance he had maintained a better than the C average, which was all anybody expected of a Harvard man in those halcyon days. Nor did the other options appeal to him. Though he clearly did not think it out, they were much too undramatic. So he chose an imaginative if egomaniacal alternative.

In the depressing depth of a New England winter as midyear examinations approached, Bucky's desperation cracked the shell of reason and submerged filial feeling and even ordinary consideration of others. He drew from the bank a considerable sum of money which his mother had put there for his tuition, lodging, board, and other expenses, and headed for New York and one grand and glorious bust.

Even at his least rational no one could accuse Bucky of lack of enterprise. He put up at one of the great hotels, and the second night went to the Ziegfeld Follies. Of course he fell in love with Marilyn Miller. The next night he went again and sent Miss Miller a huge bunch of roses and five bottles of champagne with his card. So she let him come to see her backstage.

Bucky was, and is, one of the world's great natural salesmen. He induced Miss Miller and several of the other girls to come out to dinner after the show. He gave them a smashing party at Churchill's famous restaurant with champagne flowing like the Hudson River. By the time it all ended, Bucky had not only blown his entire capital, but run up some large bills which his family eventually had to pay. Harvard promptly expelled him for "irresponsible conduct," which was a Cambridge understatement.

One would not have liked to be present at Bucky's confrontation with his family. Despite the Fullers' very real love and loyalty for one another, when they had a disagreement they tightened up like piano wires. In those moments, in the words of one friend, they got along "like rheumatism and St. Vitus Dance. The things they said to each other were positively terrifying." Mrs. Fuller was a wonderful mother, who bailed Bucky out of many financial difficulties, but she could be venemous when she felt that one of her children had traduced her moral code. In this case she had good reason.

The family council decided that Bucky had disgraced them and should be sent as far away from Boston as possible. One of Mr. Fuller's loyal friends got him a job with the Connecticut Canada Textile Company as an apprentice mechanic at a new mill they were erecting in Sherbrooke, Canada. They all felt that such a rugged experience would teach him a lesson. It taught him several lessons that Bucky considers among the most valuable of his early life.

Sherbrooke was a small manufacturing town in the desolate hinterland of Quebec Province. When Bucky reached it on a bleak February day in 1914, he found the acme of discomfort amid a population who spoke the peculiar French-Canadian patois that even a Frenchman cannot understand. The new mill building, standing among raw piles of earth, dirty snow, and wooden crates of machinery in a freshly cleared field, was empty and ominous. The prospect before him was as bleak as the weather. And he thoroughly enjoyed the whole experience.

He never minded physical hardship and seems impervious to cold. Even in his seventies he could stand for hours in a chill wind in his shirt sleeves while other men were bundled in sweaters and windbreakers. Give him something to do with his hands, machinery to understand and work with, and he is totally at ease. In Sherbrooke there were none of the expectations or social pressures of Harvard; no need to deal with the patterns of arbitrary and unreasonable customs and bans by which people in Boston evaluated what he could not be. Here was just work to be done and a crew of Lancashire and German engineers and mechanics who knew how to do it. Here a man stood on his own feet with no one to care what he looked like or if he conformed, provided only that he was worth his weight in doing the job at hand. Fifty years later Bucky wrote: "I liked the people I met at work and I liked mechanics. I worked hard. . . ." The men liked him. He was accepted and appreciated.

The job was installing textile machinery, shipped over from England and France, in the new mill. Bucky quickly learned the techniques of assembling and installing the machinery, which was crated in disassembled parts, and running the belts and shafting throughout the building, big as a car barn, and aligning them exactly to the large stationary steam engine, much like that in his uncle's cold storage plant, in the powerhouse. He also gained "a dawning awareness of a major economic pattern factor," the addition of value by manufacture gained by the admixture of technology and energy.

Evaluating the big cotton-weaving machines, he found that those from Combers in France were superior in both metal quality and exact tolerances to those from Dobson and Barlow in England. The British-made parts were frequently damaged or broken in transit. Noting Bucky's keen interest and initiative, the chief engineer gave him the job of finding local facilities for repairing or replacing those parts. This gave Bucky a "self-tutored" course in the metallurgy, stresses, and function of each of the parts, as well as a very rich experience in the actual processes of manufacture in the small local forges and machine shops that he found in the vicinity. Just how he communicated with the French Canadians who manned them is something of a mystery, but he has always been able to communicate with people of other countries, mainly because of his genuine friendship and interest in them, and his total lack of any chauvinistic prejudice or even sense of their foreignness.

Because of this, and also because of his genius for unconventional solutions of mechanical problems, Bucky was extraordinarily successful in improvising the new parts. In some cases his inventive mind actually designed better-functioning parts than the original ones.

His friend, the chief engineer, advised Bucky to keep an engineering notebook complete with sketches of the work, which became a valuable resource, far more useful than any college notebooks. Bucky regards this whole experience as of basic importance in his education, a cornerstone of his self-taught engineering expertise, and he considers that his intimate association with engineers, foundry men, and mechanics was a vitally important preparation for his future career as well as a thoroughly enjoyable episode.

Typically, Bucky also credits himself with beginning to perceive a magnificent reorientation of mankind from the role of inherent failure to inherent success through experience-rich competence in design which transcendentally integrated man's conscious planning. In other words, physical laws and teleological necessity were, without man's deliberate intent, developing "an organic workable complex—industrialization—which would eventually liberate humanity from the old problem of scarcity and provide abundance for all."

In real fact he did nothing of the sort at that time—this is another transference backward of Bucky's later-developed philosophical insights. However, there is no doubt that remembrance of these highly educative experiences eventually played an important role in forming his fundamental theorem, just as the practical knowledge of metallurgy and engineering enabled him to apply the general principles he later discovered to concrete particulars in his inventions.

So happy was he at Sherbrooke that, when the work on the mill was done, he stayed on to oversee the start of operations and cope with any bugs that might develop.

In July, Bucky was back on Bear Island. He was also back in the good graces of his family. Reports of his good work in Sherbrooke had amazed and delighted them. He had proved that he could be a sane, responsible young man; he was rehabilitated.

In July, 1914, Europe was rushing down the steep declivity toward war with the suicidal abandon of particularly moronic lemmings, but the alarm bells were hardly heard on Bear Island. The inhabitants of Eden tend to ignore the news of the world lest it disturb their tranquillity. Even today there is not a radio on the island and the latest information concerning events beyond the azure horizon is contained in a two-day-old New York *Times,* which hardly anybody bothers to read. In the summer of 1914, only vague repercussions of earth-shaking events sounded dimly in their ears.

On August 3rd, the day England sent her final ultimatum to Germany and the huge new Krupp howitzers opened fire on the "impregnable" fortifications of Liège, Bucky packed a fantastically imagined fish costume into a suitcase and sailed *Ursa Minor* over a tranquil summer sea to Mount Desert Island. In the late afternoon he coasted around its forested cliffs, glimpsing the huge summer cottages through the evergreens, and eventually dropped anchor in Frenchman's Bay off Bar Harbor.

It was quite a feat to get into his costume in the narrow cockpit of *Ursa Minor*, and his appearance as he rowed ashore, with round thick glasses adding verisimilitude to his aquatic outfit, must have given thought to any Maine fishermen who happened to be on the wharf. However, it was not one of Bucky's fantasies, but a perfectly sane, sensible performance. He was on his way to the Herman Oelrichs' undersea masquerade ball.

At the ball Bucky had a splendid time. He loved parties, and though he was often somber and withdrawn, no one could be gayer and more fun when he was in the mood. He heard some talk of the war, but with all those pretty girls, Japanese lanterns, champagne, and an orchestra dashing off syncopated tunes and everyone doing the daring new dances like the Turkey Trot and the Bunny Hug, it was no time to discuss the end of a world *At six o'clock Bar Harbor time the British ultimatum had expired and in New York the newsboys were shouting, "Extra! Extra! England at war!"* But nobody in Bar Harbor knew or cared about that.

Some time before dawn Bucky made his way back to the wharf and rowed out to *Ursa Minor* where he curled up in the cockpit and went to sleep.

He was shaken awake by the immense vibrations of a big ship's whistle, followed by excited shouts on the dock and the rattle of great anchor chains. Grabbing his glasses Bucky looked seaward at a quite unbelievable picture. Just beyond the mouth of the harbor, filling the entire sea and blotting out the sky, was a great ocean liner with row upon row of portholes in her black hull and tiers of white superstructure, looking from water level as tall as New York's skyscrapers. Her funnels were painted in the colors of the North German Lloyd and from her stern, lit by the level sunlight, flew the flag of the German Merchant Marine. Bucky could only gaze in awe, and wonder what the devil she was doing in Frenchman's Bay.

Going ashore he found the town abuzz with rumors and eventually learned the facts. The ship was the *Kronprinzessin Cecilie,* which had sailed from New York over a week earlier with a full passenger list and a cargo of gold bullion in her hold worth thirteen million dollars. When war became imminent her captain had put about and headed for the safety of a neutral port, chased halfway across the ocean by French and British warships hungry to take the treasure she carried as a prize of war. It suddenly brought the war much closer to the coast of Maine.

Bucky was also rehabilitated at Harvard. Due to his excellent record at Sherbrooke, his previous good marks—until he flew the coop—and, doubtless, to the persuasive efforts of his father's influential and devoted friends, he was allowed to return in September, 1914. This time his tenure was even shorter. His excursion into the real world made the academic atmosphere seem even more phantasmagorical to him, and the old social dichotomy still troubled him. He was utterly wretched and bored, so he rapidly became unrehabilitated. This time Harvard fired him for "lack of sustained interest in the processes within the university."

While at Harvard, both times, Bucky had two really close friends —Lincoln Pierce and Pierce's roommate, Thomas Whitehall—Bucky roomed alone. Link Pierce—pronounced Purse in Massachusetts—had been Bucky's first and dearest friend, and remained so until he died in 1970. His father, Doctor Vassar Pierce, had attended Bucky's arrival on Spaceship Earth just six months before his own son was born. Link and Bucky both remembered being pushed by their nurses through the country lanes around Milton and scraping the mud off the wheels of their baby carriages with their hands, much to the dissatisfaction of their attendants. Link had grown up to be a strikingly handsome young man. He was graduated from Milton in Bucky's class.

Tommy Whitehall had also been graduated from Milton Academy. There, and in Harvard, he had straight As and was intellectually brilliant. Of him Bucky says: "He used to stimulate me more than all the other students I knew. In those days what the young men were talking about was of a pretty low order intellectually—mostly about athletics. They did not even talk very much about sex, because our parents had not allowed them to learn anything about that taboo subject and we were pretty much in a fog about it.

"Tommy was a tremendous freshman, superbly well read, he got me interested in doing my own reading—some very, very good books. And he really understood my reaching out, all of a sudden, for knowledge about the world and history. Most of us had no ideological challenges; we knew virtually nothing about social problems and economics. But Tommy knew a great deal about history and the way such problems had come about. I got much more from him than I did from my schoolbooks—he influenced me greatly, in big ways and small. For example, he was inclined to be an epicurean, so I became an avid epicurean. . . .

"Tommy was really a great joy to be with—he was so intellectually rich."

It is evident that Bucky's sojourn at Harvard was not entirely in vain, for he was thus awakened to what was to become his great preoccupation, the welfare of humanity.

After leaving Harvard, Bucky resumed what he called "his real lessons," though not without "deep anguish and shame at having brought hurt to my family." They, especially his mother, were about ready to write him off as a total failure. But he experienced an enormous sense of relief at working in the functioning economic pattern.

His new job was with Armour and Company, the great meat-packing house. During the next two years he worked in twenty-eight branches of the company in the New York metropolitan area. This rapid change of venue was not due to failure on his part, but more likely to the fact that Armour recognized executive material in him. For he was a very hard and intelligent worker.

The hours imposed by the marketing routine were arduous. Bucky went to work at three A.M. and finished, if he was lucky, at five P.M.— a fourteen-hour day, often at hard physical labor such as manhandling quarters of beef aboard refrigerator ships bound for Europe. His extraordinarily tough constitution enabled him to take it, and even to like it.

For Bucky, alert to profit by every experience, was learning a great deal. He studied at first hand the techniques and economics of slaughterhouses, refrigeration, by-product utilization, and preservatives. He also acquired more than a superficial knowledge of marketing, shipment of perishables, distribution, accounting, shrinkage, and, most important of all to him, human relations in a competitive and complex business.

For his diverse functions Armour paid him the magnificent sum of $15 a week. But, though he was often tired and had little if any recreation, Bucky had "a sense of deep enjoyment."

He was able to survive on his meager earnings only because he lived with his mother. Mrs. Fuller had sold her house in Milton when Bucky first went to Harvard, and her daughter, Leslie, who had grown up to be "a charmer," had married Edward P. Larned, a brother of William A. Larned who was eight times tennis champion of the United States. Neddy Larned was pleasantly affluent and almost as fine a tennis player as his brother. In fact, he twice played him in the finals at Newport— an all-Larned match for the championship of the United States.

Probably to look after her sparkling black sheep, Mrs. Fuller rented an apartment in a small apartment hotel at 22 East 31st Street in New

York. Bucky lived with her there. It was not an entirely happy arrangement—too close quarters for two such high-powered people, but Bucky
was so absorbed in his work that he was impervious to minor inconveniences.

Then he fell in love for the first and final time.

CHAPTER IV
LOVE AND WAR

THAT summer of 1915, Bucky's sister Leslie and her husband rented a house on Lover's Lane in Lawrence, on the south shore of Long Island. In July, Bucky went down to spend the weekend with them. His friend Tilden Hazard, whose father, William A. Hazard, had a big, ivy-covered house overlooking the polo field of the Rockaway Hunting Club where Mrs. Fuller frequently visited, arranged to take him to a young people's dance given by Mr. and Mrs. Anthony Perkins for their niece, Mary Esther White, in their charming brick colonial house on Ocean Avenue. It was a pleasantly informal, teen-age party—at twenty Bucky was one of the oldest people present. There were fifteen or twenty ex-traordinarily pretty girls dressed in demure, ankle-length chiffon or voile dresses and an equal number of tuxedoed boys, who were either at one or another of the famous prep schools or were freshmen in college.[1]

Bucky loved to dance, and that evening he particularly enjoyed dancing with one of the older girls—aged nineteen. She was an extremely pretty brunette, with a softly curving figure, dark brown hair, riant brown eyes, and cheeks exactly the color of the roses that were climbing the pergola outside the house. He learned that her name was Anne Hewlett, and he gathered that she was the best girl of his friend, Kenneth Phillips, who also lived in Lawrence.

The next day, Sunday, Kenneth suggested that he take Bucky over to the Hewletts for a double date with Anne and her younger sister, Anglesea. Anx, as she was called, was even prettier than Anne, an authentic beauty with the same exquisite skin, sea-blue eyes, and veri-table golden hair worn in long corkscrew curls of which she was so vain that she refused to put her hair up until she was eighteen, which was three years off.

[1] The author was present and there met Bucky for the first time.

Bucky liked Anx immediately. Though he had first been attracted to Anne, she seemed to belong to Phillips, and he was far too honorable to try to take a friend's best girl away from him. Besides, Anx was so beautiful it fairly stopped his heart.

After that Bucky, who was living at the YMCA on Fort Greene Place in Brooklyn while his mother was on Bear Island, spent many weekends at the Larneds, and had many double dates with Kenneth and Anne and Anx. They sailed over to Lawrence Beach in Kenneth's one-design sloop and had picnics among the dunes of that almost deserted sandspit, which is now famous as Atlantic Beach, but then had neither roads nor bridges to the mainland. They also went to the movies in Far Rockaway, and to small parties.

Just staying home at the Hewletts was great fun. There were five boys and five girls, who, with their father and mother, Mr. and Mrs. James Monroe Hewlett, lived in a long, brick and shingle house at the end of Martin's Lane in Lawrence, looking over the salt marshes to Reynold's Channel and beyond the white beach to the open sea. Nearby, past the duck pond and the red barn, Anne's grandmother, Mrs. James Augustus Hewlett, lived with her two bachelor sons, George and Arthur Hewlett, in Rock Hall, originally Rockaway Hall. It was unquestionably the most beautiful eighteenth-century house on Long Island. Built by Josiah Martin of Antigua in 1767, it was white-shingled with the grace of simplicity. There was the conventional broad hallway running across it so as you came in the front door, you could glimpse blue water through the garden door at the other end. Four big, square rooms on either side of the hall had fireplaces with finely wrought mantels, and there were exquisite moldings which are now regarded as classic examples of the period. As in warm climates, the kitchen was originally separate from the house, near the slave quarters, though later it became part of an east wing. Anne's great-great-grandfather, Thomas Hewlett, had bought the house and farmlands from the Martin heirs in 1824.

Rock Hall had never been profaned by electricity or central heating —Grandmother Hewlett only lived there in summer. The finely proportioned rooms were lit by the soft glow of candles and oil lamps, which, reminding Bucky of Bear Island, made him feel very much at home.

Compared to the rather stately measures of life at Rock Hall, Martin's Lane was a place of violent turmoil. Anne's mother, a beautiful woman who had thus endowed her daughters, was a semiinvalid who seldom left her upstairs bedroom. James Monroe Hewlett, a celebrated architect noted also for his superb mural paintings, was a gentle, quiet man who usually sat in a tweed jacket smoking a pipe and regarding his boisterous progeny with genial amazement. Ranging in age from nineteen (Anne) down to Roger, a toddling two-year-old, they were, with the exception of Jim, the oldest boy, all extroverts with high spirits, high tempers, and such quick wits as made life in their midst a constant gaiety. With their father frequently away on important commissions and their mother unable to cope, they were bringing themselves up, and doing a surprisingly good job of it.

Bucky came to love them all, and they him. In time he became more at home with them than with his own family—a sort of honorary Hewlett.

When autumn and schooldays came, the Hewletts retired to their house at 80 Columbia Heights on Brooklyn Heights overlooking New York Harbor. Bucky wondered, rather unhappily, if he would see much of them now. But by great good fortune he was then working at the Armour plant near the Long Island Rail Road in Brooklyn. As he says, "I don't think Anx was particularly interested in me,[2] but Anne seemed to think it would be nice for me to come to dinner. So I was invited there several times by her. I was very much honored. . . ."

Though Bucky was, by now, falling in love with Anne, who was far warmer and more loving than Anglesea, he dared not admit it to himself and made no move even to flirt with her because he thought she was engaged to Kenneth Phillips, and to do so would be dishonorable.

However, Anne soon set him right. In Bucky's words, "She made it perfectly clear to me that she was *not* engaged to Kenneth and she thought it was perfectly appropriate for me to call on her. Really, that would not have happened if she had not made that very clear."

So began Bucky's courtship of Anne, which was one of the more rugged ordeals of his life.

"It was a very extraordinary experience with a family like that," Bucky says, "to be the first outsider coming into that closed circle. Mr. Hewlett sat at the head of the table, and Anne at the foot, with the other nine children in between. When I was there that made twelve of us. You know the Hewletts; they did not go out of their way to spare your feelings, particularly an outsider."

That is an understatement. Roger Hewlett says, "Bucky came into the family when the full force of the opposition was there, with Jim

[2] Half the boys in Lawrence were madly in love with Anglesea, including the author.

leading it." The Hewlett children did everything possible to tease Bucky and Anne. Because he worked for Armour and Company they referred to him as "The Butcher Boy." They never gave the lovers a moment's privacy; one or another, or all of them were constantly popping into any room they sat in. Later, when Anne and Bucky became engaged, they would chant in unison:

> Listen! Listen! Listen!
>
> Anne and Bucky kissin'.
>
> Where? Where? Where?
>
> In the big, red chair.
>
> How? How? How?
>
> WOW!

The children used to have terrific family fights, first-class brawls with five or six of them taking part, punching, biting, and pulling one another's hair; boys and girls all mixed up, fighting like wolf cubs. Once Bucky incautiously stepped into the fray to try to separate them, whereat the whole pack turned on him and nearly tore his clothes off.

The twins, Hope and Hester, who were only four years old, did not take part in the teasing. They never said a word, but stood side by side silently staring at Bucky, which was, perhaps, more unnerving.

Many an evening Anne and Bucky would sit with Mrs. Hewlett in her big bedroom on the second floor. It was not privacy, but it *was* quiet.

Eventually the children took Bucky into their hearts. "It really developed into a wonderful friendship." But they never stopped teasing, not even today.

Bucky's affectionate response to friendship even included the Hewlett servants, especially Mammy Annie in the kitchen, an enormous black woman who held the household together. Then there was Roger's nurse, Mrs. Van, who was quite short and built like one of the wooden dolls of the period, with a small head and a bosom that jutted out horizontally. "Roger used to sit on this plateau she had up there."

A far more dangerous obstacle to Bucky's courtship than Anne's siblings was her maternal grandfather, Daniel Willetts. He was a magnificent old gentleman with fine, white hair and side-whiskers, a nose like the prow of a ship, and icy blue eyes; the very picture of a merchant prince, which he was. In fact, he owned the warehouse on the water-front street below Columbia Heights, the roof of which, covered with turf, formed the Hewletts' backyard. There was a trapdoor set in the grass through which he could descend to his office in the warehouse.

Mr. Hewlett and the twins (Hope and Hester).

Grandfather Willetts loved Anne more than anything in the world, and she "loved him to pieces." He sometimes took her to Europe with him on the slow but comfortable cattle boats named after Indian tribes —*Minnetonka, Minnewaska*—and he could deny her nothing except a serious beau. The thought of *any* man, let alone a chap with Bucky's poor record at Harvard and dubious prospects, marrying his darling granddaughter turned him hard as black ice. He lived at 77 Columbia Heights, right across the street from the Hewletts, and every time Bucky walked up their brownstone stoop he thought he felt Mr. Willetts' eyes boring into his back.

However, Bucky continued his courtship. He says, "The only way I could express my feelings for Anne—I was pretty inarticulate about my emotions—was to send bunches of red roses from Weir's, the florist on Fulton Street. It was quite an investment for me—five dollars a week for flowers, leaving me ten dollars for everything else. But I saw that she liked them."

Then Bucky asked Anne for her picture. Unlike most girls, she did not have a formal photograph; so she rummaged through some drawers and finally found one of her standing beside an old gentleman, with very white hair and black brows, on the deck of a liner. Bucky took it gratefully, and when he got home snipped the old gentleman out of it. Mark Twain went into the scrap basket. "Which," Bucky says, "shows my priorities at that time."

Finally things came to an impasse. Both Mr. and Mrs. Hewlett liked Bucky, as they proved later, but he believes that Grandfather Willetts put it straight to Anne and that she yielded—temporarily. In a sad and emotional scene Anne "sort of dismissed me." Bucky was undone; this rejection was more than he could bear. But it did not last long. Anne called him up and asked him to come back.

Mr. Willetts and his ally, Anne's great-aunt Kate Barnard, had one more card to play. Hoping that distance would make Anne's heart less fond, Aunt Kate asked—no, commanded—Anne to go with her on a long trip across the United States to California, and to British Columbia and Lake Louise.

The trip had the opposite effect from what had been intended. It precipitated Anne's feelings, and when she arrived back in Lawrence again she accepted Bucky's proposal of marriage.

Then, of course, he had to go and ask Mr. Hewlett for his daughter's hand in the approved manner of that vanished time. He must have been very worried since he had so little to offer a wife. However, Mr. Hewlett had penetrated beyond the superficial oddity of Bucky's manner and become very fond of him; Mrs. Hewlett was even more affectionate. Their consent was immediate.

Then Bucky received the most scarring blow ever dealt him. When he told his mother he was engaged to Anne, Mrs. Fuller became frantic with alarm. She said Bucky was unfit to marry a charming young girl like Anne; that he was too lacking in stability, ambition, and means to support a wife. Driven by anxiety and her Puritan conscience, as Bucky believes, she actually called on Mr. Hewlett and told him that Bucky was irresponsible, thoughtless, and selfish, and advised him that he was sure to make Anne unhappy and on no account to let his daughter marry her son. It was one of the bitterest moments of Bucky's life.

Mr. Hewlett, bless his generous and loving heart, replied that he liked Bucky very much and had confidence in him.

So Bucky and Anne became formally engaged. Mrs. Fuller made some amends by giving Bucky a beautiful ruby ring that his father had given her, for Anne's engagement ring.

The engagement was announced in the early summer of 1916 in Lawrence, and was followed by a round of parties including a dance in their honor in the Hazards' Victorian-Gothic mansion. Immediately afterward Bucky left for the camp at Plattsburg, New York, where former President Theodore Roosevelt and General Leonard Wood were unofficially training young men for the defense of their country in the event of the United States' entering the European war. Bucky was alive with patriotism and ardent in the belief that America should take her part in what he and many of his fellows believed was the defense of freedom and civilization against the German warlords.

The intensity of Bucky's emotion had been force-fed by a chance event. In the spring of 1915, he had been checking a cargo of Armour's beef into the hold of a freighter lying at a North River dock. Across the narrow strip of water between the piers, the Cunarder *Lusitania* was preparing for a voyage to England. To Bucky, who loved ships so much, she was the most beautiful man-made object in the world; the fastest and most graceful of liners. Enviously he had watched the passengers boarding her, and thrilled to the tremendous vibrations of her whistle, as with flags and pennants flying from her masts and the red ensign at her stern, she slowly backed into the stream and, shepherded by her attendant tugs, swung stately on the tide and headed out to sea.

Outing at Rockaway Beach 1916. Left to right: *Tilden Hazard, Anne Hewlett, Bucky, Anglesea Hewlett, unknown young man, Margery Beard, James M. Hewlett, Jr.*

Five days later he read the black headlines that told of her torpedoing by a German U-boat off the coast of Ireland, her sinking in twenty minutes, and of the drowning of 1,198 men, women, and children. He almost wept as he vividly pictured that beautiful ship in her final agony and the gay, innocent people he had seen crowding her rails struggling in the underset of her sinking. To him, innocent as we all were then of the terrible potential of human savagery, it seemed the most barbarous act ever done by man against his fellowman. He raged against its perpetrators.

Bucky enjoyed Plattsburg as he ever did camps and simple living. In addition, many of his former Harvard classmates were there. But it confirmed his former intention of joining the navy if there should be a war. Army ways were old-fashioned, even primitive, compared to the advanced technology of ships; besides, he felt at home on the sea. However, when President Woodrow Wilson was reelected on a peace platform in November, the immediate prospect of American involvement in the war receded somewhat.

During that autumn and early winter, Bucky continued to work very hard at different Armour and Company operations in the metropolitan area. This left him little time to be with Anne, mostly just at family dinner at the Hewlett's and a quiet hour in Mrs. Hewlett's room before he had to rush home to his mother's new apartment at the old Hotel Wentworth on 46th Street for three or four hours sleep before starting off to work at three A.M.

On weekends he and Anne sometimes had a gala evening when Mr. Hewlett would take them to one of the dances at the American Academy of Design on 57th Street where the New York Architectural League then had its headquarters. In those days the leading sculptors, painters, and architects of New York were closely associated, and Mr. Hewlett, who functioned in both spheres, knew them all. Bucky always remembered one fancy dress ball at the Academy called the *Fêtes des Foux* where "Anne and I had a lovely time." There he met many well-known artists, among them Ray Hood who, a very young man, had just won the Tribune Tower prize and thus achieved fame; sculptor Leo Lentelli and his wife, Mimi, and the Tony Salaemis, all of whom became his close friends. Bucky always felt more at ease with artists than with the members of any other profession, except, perhaps, men of the sea.

The false detente in American-German relations ended abruptly on January 31, 1917, when the imperial German government announced a policy of unrestricted submarine warfare—every ship that sailed in unilaterally delimited war zones would be sunk on sight. President Wilson sorrowfully broke off diplomatic relations with Germany. The American people, formerly badly divided on the issue of belligerence, united behind him. Everyone knew that this meant war.

Bucky was determined to become a naval officer. He knew that with his poor eyesight he had not the faintest chance of passing the navy physical examination, but he thought of an ingenious circumvention. He persuaded his mother to present the *Wego* to the navy, provided her son commanded her. The navy, desperate for ships to patrol the coastal waters against submarines, was taking anything that would move on the water. They gladly accepted the deal Bucky proposed to them, and gave him the rank of Chief Boatswain.

This was, as Bucky says, "a fantastic rank." At that time there were comparatively few chiefs in the navy, all old hands who had twenty to forty years of service. It was the highest rank to which an enlisted man, who had not been to the Naval Academy, could rise. They were commissioned warrant officers and their uniform was the same as that of an ensign except that the single gold stripe denoting their rank was broken by short blue bars. In those last days of naval snobbery they were considered officers but not necessarily gentlemen, and they messed apart from both the officers and crew. The young ensigns just out of the academy were supposed to learn about seafaring from them and obey their orders. When Bucky first walked into the Navy Yard in his new uniform with his dress sword slapping satisfactorily on his thigh, he was amazed to find the ensigns respectfully saluting him. "Considering my naval experience," says Bucky, "it was slightly ridiculous."

Bucky was to enlist his own crew, and his first choice for first mate was Link Pierce. Other members of the crew were Wolcott Fuller, who was ready to enter Harvard but keen to volunteer, and Richard Morse, as deckhands, William Hall as engineer, and Warren Tribou, cook—six in all, later augmented to seven. When they were finally all aboard, the little *Wego* was as crowded as Noah's Ark.

Bucky, Link, and Wolcott went up to Maine to get *Wego* ready for sea. Bear Island in winter, with mushy salt-water ice covering the harbor, winds blowing straight out of the Arctic Circle, and no heat except the fireplace in the Eating House and the iron wood-burning stove in its kitchen, was rugged. But Bucky was aflame with enthusiasm. He worked hard and fast, so fast that late in February *Wego* was officially commissioned as Navy SP (Scout Patrol) 1196.

Wego was only about forty feet long—too small to mount even a machine gun, but her valiant crew was armed to the teeth. Her top speed was 8 knots—a U-boat could have left her standing. She was an ugly little boat, anything but streamlined, with a square stern and sharp bow. Her entire length was crowded by living quarters, the forecastle rising abruptly to a wheelhouse barely big enough for two men squashed together. Just aft of it was the main cabin which looked like a little square house with round holes for windows. Behind it was no more than three feet of open deck. In naval service she had a disproportionally tall mast from which to fly her signal flags. In good weather Bucky, standing unprotected on the flat top of the main cabin, conned her at an auxiliary wheel.

Wego was probably the smallest regularly commissioned vessel in the entire United States Navy. Based on Bar Harbor and the only "warship" in that area, she was known for a time as the "State of Maine Navy."

Bucky says: "So we started off in that strange little boat without the slightest idea of what the navy really was. Of course, we had seen pictures of submarines, but I had no real conception of them; I thought they were far smaller than they turned out to be."

U.S.S. Wego.

But Bucky had read books about the navy and had a highly romantic notion of its traditions and usages. He took his responsibilities as captain intensely seriously. Even if his ship was the tiniest, he was determined that she should be as smart as the biggest battleship. He worked his crew very hard, polishing brass, painting everything, working on the poor old engine to bring it to peak efficiency. He says: "I wanted my boat to be in good shape and the rest of the crew did not care too much. As I continually kept trying to improve her, they thought the captain was much too fussy." Bucky did carry his naval punctilio rather far. Having read that the captain always ate alone, he insisted on having his meals in lonely state.

On April 6, 1917, the United States declared war on Germany. Now what had been practice became the Real Thing. Even in springtime the North Atlantic off the coast of Maine can be a furious ocean, gale winds howling over huge, white-capped seas that smash against rocky promontories and boil over half-submerged reefs. If there had been small craft warnings in those days, the big red SCW pennants would have been flying three-quarters of the time. But if Bucky was ordered to patrol, by Poseidon! he did so if it was humanly possible, pushing little *Wego* through thundering seas to the uttermost limits of prudence and beyond.

The moment war was declared many other yachtsmen gave their boats to the navy. They were quickly accepted and commissioned, usually under their professional captains and crews. A number of fine yachts turned up in Bar Harbor to join *Wego* in patrolling the coast. Since the navy had become chary of giving away rank, it had made their captains boatswains. As a chief boatswain, Bucky was the senior officer present and thus became commander of the Bar Harbor flotilla, consisting of such splendid yachts as the *Mist, Content, Cherokee,* the *Hobo,* and the mystery ship, *Eta M. Burns.* His only discontent was that his flagship was so small and slow that when his little fleet sailed on maneuvers the others soon left her hull down behind them.

Pure chance and Bucky's favor with the gods of the sea enabled *Wego* to perform the only significant war service of the entire flotilla. One day orders came for a full-speed emergency run to Jonesport in desolate eastern Maine near the Canadian border, where a submarine sighting had been reported. The flotilla tore out of Frenchman's Bay and headed east wide open, flags whipping, crews alight with the hope of combat. Naturally, *Wego* was soon left far astern. One can imagine Bucky's furious frustration as his fleet disappeared hell-bent over the horizon.

As if that were not enough, toward midnight in a heavy fog *Wego's* engine began to miss and slow. Bucky, who knew this coast as an engineer on the New York Central knows the run from Albany to New York, reckoned they were abreast of Cross Island. Reluctantly he ordered his helmsman to port his helm and head for the coast. Skillfully he navigated *Wego* through the fluffy fog into Machias Bay inside Cross Island, where they anchored at about one A.M.

Leaving Wolcott Fuller and Dick Morse on watch, Bucky, Link Pierce, and Bill Hall went furiously to work on the engine. At about two o'clock the fog lifted. Woolly and Dick, who were "sharp on Morse code," saw a rapidly flashing light at the end of the Machiasport pier, answered by similar flashes from Cross Island. In high excitement they called Bucky up on deck and told him the flashes were in Morse, but they could not read the message as it seemed to be in a secret code. As they watched, a big diesel-engined sardine fisherman came out of Machiasport and hustled across the bay toward Cross Island, without apparently seeing *Wego,* which lay without lights.

As soon as his engine was repaired, Bucky headed back for Bar Harbor, where he reported the incident to the naval authorities. Within twenty-four hours United States destroyers swooped down on Machiasport and navy intelligence agents swarmed along the coast.

Not until after the war did the *Wego*'s crew learn that she had inadvertently unearthed a refueling depot for German U-boats, the very spot where the German spies Boy Ed and Count Von Papen had landed to conduct a sabotage campaign in the United States.

The place was well chosen. The Maine coast in that vicinity had been colonized by German immigrants, some of whom remained loyal to the Fatherland. Two years before the war, in 1915, a German-American businessman from Chicago came to Machiasport and offered to buy the big sardine factory and its fleet of fishing boats. Its two New England owners, expecting to be bargained with, asked double its value. The Chicagoan snapped up the offer. The astounded partners, feeling they had sold too cheap, conferred and decided to double the ante by announcing that they had meant the asking price for only one partner's share. Unfazed, the Chicagoan met the raise, only insisting that the transaction be kept secret.

This became the perfect setup for a U-boat base. Maine natives were accustomed to seeing tank cars full of diesel oil for the sardiners and cottonseed oil for packing their catch arrive at the installation; a few extralarge shipments went unnoticed. The lonely, fog-bound coast was far east of the big resorts, and with its many deep-water coves, would have been ideal for secretly transhipping fuel and supplies from the big sardiners to submarines had it not been for *Wego*'s faltering engine.

The only thing that marred Bucky's delight in the activity of serving his country on his favorite element was his separation from Anne. He missed her more than he could have thought possible, and she missed him more than that. It was not an insoluble problem.

At Armour and Company Bucky had been making $15 a week; as a

Chief Boatswain his salary was $1,800 a year, more than twice as much. He felt affluent for the first time in his life—"absolutely high order." The obvious answer was to marry the girl. Anne was willing.

In June she wrote Bucky to be sure to get leave to marry her on Saturday, July 12, his birthday. He immediately asked Link Pierce to be his best man. They both obtained leave, which pretty well put *Wego* out of action for the weekend, but all hands felt that the United States was not endangered.

The ushers were Tommy Whitehall, Tilden Hazard, Mack Lloyd, and Anne's brother, Jim Hewlett, who was also in the navy. Her next brother, Willetts Hewlett, who had joined the marines, was also to have been an usher, but he came down with measles and had to watch the proceedings from the quarantine of a car.

Anne asked Anglesea to be her maid of honor, and among the bridesmaids were Helen Babbet, Josephine de Selding, Catherine Bunnell, and Anne's younger sister, Laurence Hewlett, all strikingly pretty girls.

At this point the author must step into the mainstream of his narrative.

On the morning before the wedding I went down to Martin's Lane to call on Anglesea, as I did nearly every day. It was a scene of even more happy chaos than usual, with bridesmaids and ushers arriving by every train. Bucky was there, of course, looking very trim in a brand new uniform on which the gold braid fairly glittered. Most of his ushers were in the uniform of their respective services. Everyone was in high spirits. I pictured them planning a gala party, and in the hope that they would ask me along, I hinted broadly, "What are you all doing this evening?"

"Nothing," they said. "We have not planned anything."

"You can't do nothing the night before your wedding," I exploded. "Let's see if I can fix something."

I called my mother, who at that time had a large house in Woodmere, some three miles away, manned by six or seven servants. "Muzzi," I said, "we're having fourteen for dinner tonight."

"Really!" Mother answered. "Who are they?"

"Anne's wedding party," I said. "They've got nothing to do tonight and I thought they should have a party. Can you do it?"

"Of course," Mother replied. "Tell them we dine at seven thirty."

That evening I sat happily at the head of the long, candlelit table with Anne on my right and my beloved Anglesea on my left. During the meal Anne said never a word, her eyes looking into an unknown future. Finally I said to her, "My, you're silent, Anne," and quickly added, "but I can understand your feelings. It must be quite something to think about—going off with a strange man in the morning."

Anne snapped out of it, stared hard at Bucky, his big head close-cropped navy style, his eyes lambent with love behind his gogglelike glasses, and said briskly, "You know, he isn't as strange as he looks."

Over half a century later, when Anne and Bucky, at the peak of his worldwide fame as the prophet of a benign and unimaginable universe, came to visit me in Florida, I said to her, "Anne, you know you were wrong. He was even stranger than he looked."

East façade of Rock Hall where Anne and Bucky were married.

The wedding was on the south lawn of Rock Hall on a perfect summer day. The old house, with roses climbing up the trellis of its porch and the dark green turf running down to meet the lighter green of the salt marshes, had a graceful air of permanence in a world in the flux of war.

Anne had wisely dressed her bridesmaids, not in the current tube-skirted fashion, but in white, low-cut organdy dresses with belled skirts and bright sashes. Anne's wedding dress was the same except that her lovely face sparkled under a veil of ancestral·lace. She had chosen the dresses "to go with the house" and the scene was straight out of the eighteenth century when Rock Hall was new.

Anne and Bucky took their vows before the Episcopal minister, then formed the receiving line. The families of both sides were almost all there; Hewletts of all generations, Fullers and Kings and Wolcotts; and most of the people we knew from the Five Towns. As Bucky stood in the line, his little sister Rosey kept running around his knees offering him food and drink, taking care of her big brother.

It was very charming and happy, with a kind of pre-twentieth century, innocent gaiety. But beneath that was an edge of anxiety—the war, pushed temporarily to the back of our minds, but raising the question if we would ever again see those laughing boys in their bright uniforms. When the time came for them to leave, Bucky and Anne ran under an arch of flashing swords toward a future that in its tragedies and accomplishments was beyond anyone's dreaming—least of all theirs.

Anne and Bucky drove straight to Brooklyn to spend a few hours with Mrs. Hewlett and Grandma Willetts, who had left the wedding early.[3] Then they took the midnight train to Boston and the old *J. T. Morse* to Bar Harbor. At the dock the captains of Bucky's flotilla met them, and presented them with a beautiful silver basket with all their names engraved on it. Bucky, so sensitive to any gesture of friendship, was very deeply touched.

The Fullers rented a little cottage on Snow Street in Bar Harbor for their honeymoon, which was, of course, very episodic because Bucky was continually at sea with his little fleet. In any event, a Hewlett honeymoon was not the conventional aloneness, but rather a family affair. Link Pierce inevitably had fallen in love with Anglesea, and she found his masculine good looks and sunny disposition very attractive. So Anx came up to stay with the Fullers, and Link also stayed with them. Jim Hewlett was in love with Margery Beard, whom he afterward married. "So," says Anne, "she stayed with us, too." They were pretty crowded. Bucky did not mind.

[3] Mr. Willetts had died a few weeks previously.

A few weeks later, the navy decided that *Wego* was no longer useful and retired her. The crew was broken up. Link Pierce and Wolcott Fuller went to the naval training school at Harvard. Woolly afterward served in the transport *Mount Vernon,* which had formerly been the *Kronprinzessin Cecilie.* Link Pierce served in the battleship *Louisiana.* Bucky was ordered to command the much abler *Whistler,* patrolling the outer approaches to Boston Harbor.

As for the *Wego,* she was eventually returned to Mrs. Fuller. For forty years she served as Bear Island's family boat, general freighter, and ferry until she was retired in 1957.

CHAPTER V

THE HAPPIEST YEARS

BUCKMINSTER Fuller's happiest years were those he spent in the navy. He had no need to drive himself. He was doing what he liked best of all to do; and he was learning a great deal. Above all, he was learning to think in the terms that eventually made him the most original philosopher of our era. In addition, he was a damn fine naval officer; for what he lacked in experience he made up for by that ability for inspired improvisation.

Bucky commanded the *Whisper* very briefly. Then he was ordered to take command of the *Inca* (SP 1212), a superb, seventy-two-foot express cruiser, capable of the phenomenal speed for that time of 28 knots. Compared to *Wego*, she looked like a real warship, with a three-inch gun mounted on her forward deck, a tall mast to carry the wireless aerial, and a luxurious owner's cabin for her captain. She was one of a fleet of six sister ships given to the navy by members of the Eastern Yacht Club. Bucky was made flotilla commander of three of these ships—*Inca, Ellen,* and *Snark* and ordered to take them to the Naval Air Station at Newport News, Virginia, to act as crash boats for the new navy flying school.

In World War I navy planes were the only American-made aircraft to make a significant contribution to aerial warfare. All the American aces in France flew French or British planes. The few land planes we sent over were redesigned British De Havilland biplanes, with Liberty motors. They were so bad that their unhappy pilots called them "flaming coffins"—hardly a triumph for American know-how. However, the navy eventually had hundreds of Curtiss flying boats and seaplanes patrolling the coastal waters of England and France.

In the sheltered waters of Hampton Roads the fledgling pilots were being trained in Curtiss biplanes mounted on a single float, Curtiss boats, and seaplanes with twin floats. They were a gay and daring lot, who equated recklessness with courage. As a result the mortality rate was appalling.

One of the most common types of accidents was caused by the novice pilot coming in to land at too steep an angle, which caused the plane to trip on the water and flip upside down; the stunned pilot, hanging head down from his safety belt, would be submerged as the plane sank to float level. Bucky's boats were very fast and the planes' landing pattern quite tight, so he could usually reach the scene of a crash in a minute or two. The entire crew of the *Inca,* except the man at the wheel, would spontaneously dive overboard and try to get the pilot out before he drowned. Frequently they were too late. Though there was always a doctor on board to try to resuscitate them, many a young man, not otherwise seriously injured, died on the *Inca* and the other boats of the flotilla.

Bucky was terribly shaken by these losses, unaccustomed as he was to violent death. He and Anne were living at the Norfolk Country Club where many of the young flyers and their wives were billeted. "There were some wonderful young people there," Bucky says, "the young men who were learning to fly, many of them my friends from Harvard and from Massachusetts." There would be much laughter and gaiety in the evening and tragedy in the morning, as some young man Bucky knew died on his boat. In some ways it was worse than war, where casualties are inevitable, to have these boys die uselessly in the pleasant, peaceful autumn sunlight.

Bucky says, "It became a terrific challenge to me, with all that life involved, to try to find some way to get those men out quicker." He spent long sleepless nights flogging his brain to devise a method of quick rescue, jumping out of bed to make innumerable sketches of possible solutions. With these sketches in hand he had long discussions with Commander Patrick Bellinger, who was in charge of the Naval Air Station. Finally he produced a working drawing of a device, which Bellinger approved for trial and authorized Bucky to install in the *Inca.*

It consisted of an auxiliary mast set in the stern of the crash boat with a strongly reinforced boom from which hung a grappling hook attached by a steel cable to a winch. With this Bucky hoped to be able to snatch the whole plane out of the water and quickly free its pilot.

After several practice runs with already-wrecked planes, Bucky tried it for real. A plane came in and flipped in the usual sickening way.

Bucky got the *Inca* to it in ninety seconds, swung her in her length, and expertly backed her to the plane. The grappling hook was dropped and engaged the wreckage, lifting it dripping from the water with the unconscious pilot hanging from his belt. A dozen hands ripped him loose and laid him face down on the deck, where the doctor went to work pumping the water out of him and giving artificial respiration. He worked for five eternal minutes before the young man's eyes opened, and he threw up. It was one of the happiest moments of Bucky's life.

Rescue masts were installed on the other boats of the flotilla. Some pilots still died, but many were saved.

Oddly enough for such a stubborn individualist, Bucky usually got along beautifully with his commanding officers; perhaps he was lucky in getting good ones. The first commander he served under at the Naval Air Station was Lieutenant Commander Edward MacDonald, who became his longtime friend. A little later MacDonald went overseas to be replaced by Commander Patrick Bellinger—one of the best. Pat Bellinger was Naval Aviator Number 4, a delightful and dashing character who had no use for naval puntilio. Later, in 1919, he commanded the NC 3 on the famous transatlantic flight of the giant four-engined Curtiss flying boats. Seeing that Bucky was doing a fine job, Bellinger gave him great leeway, and it was he who arranged for Bucky to live at the Norfolk Country Club with Anne, instead of aboard ship.

However, Bucky did get himself tangled up in navy red tape. One of those silly interservice rivalries was in full spate at Hampton Roads between Naval Aviation, so feckless and free, and the admiral commanding the Fifth Naval District at the Norfolk Naval Base, who thought planes were silly toys. Though Bucky worked with Naval Aviation, he was officially under the admiral's command. Thus he occupied the classic position of the man in the middle.

Quite frequently Bucky had to take the *Inca* to the Norfolk Navy Yard to get supplies and take on water. It was quite a long trip round the point and across the mouth of the James River, from which the *Merrimack* had sortied for her famous battle with the *Monitor*. He grudged every second away from the base lest there be an accident while he was gone.

Another chore that took him away was being sent over to Old Point Comfort to ferry VIPs across the Roads. The regular ferry service had been discontinued, so Bucky would land at the ferry slip, which was equipped with water pipes. Right there he saw a way to avoid at least some of his trips to the Navy Yard by filling his water tanks from those pipes.

The admiral found out about it and there was a tremendous row. Bucky was ordered to report to him, and found himself on a hot carpet. Sitting at his desk, stout and wrathful, with his chest covered with ribbons and his dignity at full staff, the admiral laid Bucky out for his unauthorized pilfering of somebody else's water. "It was an act of out-and-out piracy," the admiral concluded. "We're going to have to court-martial you—for piracy!"

Bucky was thoroughly disgusted and a little frightened. Fortunately, Naval Aviation had high priorities, and Pat Bellinger was able to avert the worst and save Bucky from being hanged from his own yardarm.

If Bucky had a gift for getting into trouble, he also had the luck of being at the right place at the right time. Doctor Lee De Forest, who in 1907 had invented the triode tube which made possible voice transmission by wireless, came to Hampton Roads to conduct an experiment for the navy in ship-to-plane voice transmission. The *Inca* was given the assignment in addition to her other duties.

It is easy to imagine Bucky's intense excitement as the heavy electronic equipment was loaded onto his boat and Doctor De Forest himself came aboard to oversee its installation. Bucky was with him every possible second, examining every circuit, switch, tube, and meter; asking innumerable questions; learning about the shape of the future.

On a bright, cold autumn day, he took the *Inca* out into the Roads, with De Forest standing beside him on the bridge. One of the largest Curtiss flying boats staggered into the air laden with radio equipment and circled above the *Inca*. After much twirling of dials and adjusting of switches Doctor De Forest spoke into the clumsy microphone. Through crackling static, blurred by distortion but intelligible, a voice answered him. It was the first time a man on a ship had talked to a man in a plane.

The winter of 1917–18 came on fast and cold. Ice formed in the water around the air base and though Bucky used his flotilla as ice-breakers to keep things going for a while, they were hardly designed for the job. The navy sensibly decided to transfer the whole operation to Pensacola, Florida, and Bucky's Hampton Roads tour of duty was over.

World War I brought a huge expansion of the United States Navy. The authorities realized that to man it they would need far more officers than the Naval Academy could provide in its regular program, even though shortened from four years to three for the duration. Officers' training schools, like the one at Harvard, had been set up, but these only gave once-over-lightly instruction to cadets who were then commissioned as reserve officers. The navy decided to inaugurate a three-month crash course at the Naval Academy, whose graduates would be commissioned ensigns in the regular navy. Naturally, the three-year men sneered at what they called "ninety-day wonders," but some fine officers came out of it. Pat Bellinger had one appointment and he made Bucky his nominee.

The requirements were stiff. A cadet had to have been overseas; he had to be sponsored by a senior officer, and he had to have the equivalent of a college education. Bucky met only one of these conditions. However, he had a fine record commanding patrol boats and he had been to Harvard, if somewhat ingloriously. In addition, Pat Bellinger's backing was very powerful, and Bucky's invention of the rescue apparatus counted heavily. He was accepted, though how he passed the physical examination with his poor eyesight is just one more mystery in his career. Of course, he could see perfectly well with his glasses on.

The only damper on Bucky's delight was that he expected to be separated from Anne. However, the Larneds, who owned the two leading hotels at Annapolis, Carvel Hall and Arundel House, arranged for Anne to stay very inexpensively at the Hall. Bucky lived in the cadet barracks, but often after evening parade he could get away for two hours more or less. Anne would be at the parade and they would walk back to the hotel together. "It was very beautiful having Anne there."

The Naval Academy was one of the major landmarks in Bucky's life; the source of much of his technical knowledge and the inspiration for his major preoccupation with ephemeralization. For in wartime a patriotic Congress was shoveling dollars into the navy by the billions and the entire effort was never based on what a thing cost, but whether it was the best obtainable. All the latest technological developments were being adapted and refined; experimentation, which is now called Research and Development, was proceeding "full ahead." And because a warship requires the most intricate machinery occupying the least possible space and weighing as little as possible, efficiency was the goal.

A 10,000-ton "heavy" cruiser carried eight 8-inch guns, a large secondary battery, torpedo tubes, and armor plate. In addition, its hull had to be designed to withstand the tremendous stress of moving through huge waves, and to contain the essential life-support features such as water, fuel, electric generating capacity, and provisions for several hundred men. Most important of all, it had to contain enormously powerful engines capable of driving it through the water at thirty knots or more. Bucky was struck by the thought that, though a building required none of these things, a building structure of the same length and cubic capacity as a cruiser would weigh twenty or more times as much.[1]

Bucky thus realized that naval architecture was a triumph of the efficient use of materials. He began to see the infinite possibilities of design science if applied as enthusiastically to improving the living conditions of men as to killing them. The first glimmer of his vision of a world in which, by the efficient use of technology, natural resources could be stretched to provide ample living for all mankind, lighted his brain.

Since the cadets were supposed already to have a classical education, the three-month course at Annapolis dispensed with such irrelevancies and concentrated on engineering, navigation, ballistics, and the whole intricate technology of handling warships at sea.

It was highly concentrated and very tough. Bucky says, "I never worked so hard in my life." In fact he ate it up.

The higher mathematics involved revivified his former interest in them and set his brain working in the true direction on which so much of his philosophy is based. In his own complicated phraseology, "Such a pattern-experience continually excited conceptioning in the potential accruable to new complex design integration . . . with forwardly conceived and theoretically designable entities."[2] It also made him more dissatisfied than ever with conventional geometry and restarted the trains of mathematical thought that he was to pursue to completely unorthodox, though brilliantly logical, conclusions.

Another important enlightenment that came to Bucky at the Naval Academy was that, whereas at most universities the most brilliant students were encouraged to specialize, at Annapolis the brightest were

---

[1] Bucky could not ascertain exactly what such a building weighed because nobody bothered to calculate it, but this is a very conservative estimate.

[2] *Ideas and Integrities,* Buckminster Fuller, Prentice-Hall, Englewood Cliffs, N.J., 1963.

given generalized courses to enable them to understand science as a whole. He said, "In 1917 I assumed that Nature did not have separate compartments for chemistry, physics, mathematics, etc., but only one department and only one arithmetical angle-and-frequency-modulating and coordinating system."

At Annapolis Bucky was competing against several Harvard graduates of his class of 1917. Due to his enormous capacity for hard work and his affinity for the subjects of his studies, he was graduated well toward the top of his class. The other Harvard men were "washed out." This gave Bucky much-needed self-confidence. "For my own comfort I realized that my getting fired from Harvard had nothing to do with my capability to master my work when I really wanted to."

The Annapolis experience also renewed Bucky's interest in what he called his "Chronofile." Most children like to collect things. At the age of four or five, Bucky had begun collecting odd items of news, letters, and ideas concerning world patterns of developing technology. At first this was just a little boy's interest in the wonderful things that were being invented—automobiles, wireless telegraphy, X rays, etc. Somewhat later he began noting his reactions to these things and their effect on his own development. At various times this extraordinary record showed some lacunae as he became too busy or uninterested to maintain it.

Beginning late in 1917, intuitively knowing that someday it would be of enormous value to him and possibly to the world, Bucky kept it meticulously. It became a record of a boyhood at the turn of the century and maturing during mankind's epochal movement from "the inert, materialistic nineteenth century, into the dynamic, abstract twentieth century." For he became convinced that a greater technological transformation was taking place in his own lifetime than in that of all the previous generations of humanity. The "science-quaking fact" of his boyhood seemed to him to be the discovery that light has speed. The fact that it was invariable had been proved by the experiments of Morely and Michaelson on the very sea wall of the Naval Academy.

Bucky was graduated with the rank of ensign (temporary). A little later he passed the required examination to become a regular line officer of the United States Navy—Ensign R. Buckminster Fuller, USN—*not* USNR. That was a powerful difference.

On graduation, Bucky was given a week's leave after which he was to report to the transport *Finland*. He took Anne straight to Bear Island. It seemed cold and somewhat cheerless to her. Bathing in icy water, using outhouses, making a wood fire in the old iron stove to cook by was not exactly to her taste. But she had Bucky to herself at last—their first real honeymoon. He, of course, was greatly refreshed.

When they returned to New York, he found that the *Finland* had been torpedoed on her return voyage and was in drydock. He was ordered to the staff of Rear Admiral Albert Gleaves, commanding the cruiser and transport operations, as a communications officer. As usual—in the navy—he was very lucky.

The headquarters were in Hoboken. The officers in the communications section were a fine lot. Among them De Coursey Failes, Henry Glieb, Oliver Jennings, and William Long became close personal friends of Bucky's. Admiral Gleaves took a great liking to him, and made him his personal aide for secret information: "a very exciting position."

There were 130 ships in the transport operation, which had to be coordinated into convoys with appropriate destroyer and cruiser escorts. Nearly two million men were transported to Europe. With immense pride Bucky says, "We did not lose a single army man to enemy action on the sea. On the return trips, which were unescorted, we did lose some ships. That was the price the navy had to pay."

All the ships reported their positions daily to Gleaves's headquarters. Bucky was the only one who knew where every American ship was at all times. He kept the records in a supersecret black book, but with his excellent memory, he kept them in his head as well. Every day he sent a report to the office of the Chief of Naval Operations in Washington. He was also in charge of communicating with all the ships at sea. This was another important part of his education. He says: "At this time I developed a thought that has been very powerful in my theory of communication ever since. I said: 'I don't care if I am not understood as long as I am not *misunderstood*. For if I am misunderstood the captain of a ship may do the wrong thing with fatal consequences, but if he does not understand me, he queries the message and you give it to him again until he gets it right.' This principle became absolutely fundamental in my life from then on."

The messages had to be sent in code in as few words as possible. Thus Bucky learned to convey enormous amounts of information with minimum wordage in such a way that he could not be misunderstood.

In October, 1918, Bucky was ordered to the transport *Great Northern* and sailed in a convoy to France. On the return voyage, on November 11, word came by wireless of the signing of the Armistice. This, of course, brought the transport service to a temporary halt, prior to reversing its direction to bring the troops home.

In December, Bucky was ordered as a communications officer to the *George Washington,* which was being elaborately reconditioned and refurbished to take President and Mrs. Wilson to the Peace Conference in Paris. Among the most modern communication equipment that Bucky helped to install in her was a long-distance wireless-arc telephone. The De Forest tube and spark-set squawk, which had been used at Hampton Roads, had a maximum range of only about seventy miles; the new equipment was designed to make possible transoceanic voice transmission.

Bucky sailed on both the presidential trips of the *George Washington,* spending much of his time with technicians tinkering with the new radio equipment, which was far from perfected. On the second trip Bucky was present at another technological leap forward. As the ship lay in the harbor at Brest, the voice of a man speaking from her was heard and understood at the great government wireless installation at Arlington, Virginia.

For many of the reserve officers the signing of the Armistice meant that their service was drawing to a close. But Bucky's status as a regular line officer gave him the option of remaining in the navy if he so desired, which he did. For to him the service meant the opportunity to continue a way of life in which making money was a tertiary consideration. He had neither any desire to amass a fortune nor interest in a world dominated by the profit motive, and based on what he already considered a false system of reckoning real wealth. Rather he wanted to continue exploring the realms of scientific knowledge which were expanding with the incredible acceleration imparted to them by the necessities of war. His theory then, and ever since, was that the great technological advances were always made under the impetus of war. Later, when they were superseded by still more advanced technology, the masters of industry adapted them to civilian purposes in order to be able to use profitably the machinery for producing them. His ambition was to cut out the preliminary steps and apply the most advanced technology immediately to what he later came to call "livingry" as opposed to weaponry. Meanwhile, the navy seemed to him the best place to learn.

CHAPTER VI
ALEXANDRA

ON December 12, 1918, shortly after Bucky had returned from France on the *Great Northern,* Anne gave birth to a daughter whom they named Alexandra. From the moment Bucky first saw her he loved her with an intensity that was part of his deeply emotional character. He marveled at the perfection of her tiny body, her miniature hands and feet, her long-lashed blue eyes. To him she was unique, the ultimate accomplishment of the Great Designer.

Anne was living with her family at 80 Columbia Heights and continued to live there and at Martin's Lane while Bucky was attached to the *George Washington.* When the ship was decommissioned, Admiral Gleaves asked Bucky, who was now a lieutenant, jg, to rejoin his staff aboard his flagship, the USS *Seattle,* stationed in New York.

What might have been an especially happy time for the young Fullers was shadowed by sickness and sorrow. The great influenza epidemic was raging throughout the world. Alexandra caught it and almost died. In succession she came down with spinal meningitis and finally with polio. How she survived those terrible illnesses, about which so little was then known, was almost a miracle, aided by love and arduous nursing. At times three trained nurses gave her round-the-clock care. There was little money available to pay for them, but both the older Hewletts and Mrs. Fuller helped out. Anne and Bucky were ridden by anxiety for months at a time.

Then Admiral Gleaves was ordered to take command of the Asiatic Squadron, and asked Bucky to go with him. Thus he was confronted with a difficult decision. He had intended to remain in the navy for the foreseeable future. He says: "I loved the navy. Having been brought up with boats on Bear Island, my feeling about ships was different from that of most of my shipmates who had been raised inland and regarded them as machines you got on board—just big buildings. But I'd had all those little boats that were fine in calm weather but didn't work in storms. And suddenly I was in great ships that really worked under all conditions. I was very excited about the whole evolution of the design of ships. And I had been mixed up with the new voice radio, so I was experiencing very advanced technology long before it came to the rest of society. The places I had been in the navy were really the frontier point."

But Bucky realized that Alexandra could not possibly go to Manila, where the Asiatic Squadron was based, and therefore Anne could not go either. He thought, "If I do go I will never see Alexandra again." Furthermore, he could not remain in the navy because of the peripatetic life of a naval officer; if he were not sent to the Far East, it would be Europe or South America or the Canal Zone. It would not be fair to the two people he loved so much to subject them to that sort of existence. If Alexandra had been strong and healthy, he would not have hesitated. But under the circumstances it was impossible.

So, very unhappily, he requested transfer to inactive status, almost tantamount to resigning his commission, and asked Armour and Company for a job. Impressed by his previous work with the company, and his excellent naval record, Armour made him assistant export manager. It was a very responsible position. Bucky was in charge of sales to any corporation engaged in foreign operations with headquarters in New York, and of supplying many big companies with their meat products. The pay was $50 a week, just about what Bucky had been getting as a lieutenant jg without the perquisites that belong to a naval officer.

"The years of little Alexandra were a terrific struggle," Bucky recalls. "We really didn't have any money."

The Fullers rented a dilapidated little house on Pearsal Place in Lawrence, not far from Martin's Lane. Bucky did all the physical work of repairs and repainting the house. Anne decorated it beautifully, and Mr. Hewlett, being so sympathetic, gave them some nice pieces of furniture and other household necessities. Still Bucky says: "Those were very painful days and sad. Our expenses with the nurses and medicines were very high. My mother helped us, but it was terribly difficult. It was so typical of the mess that poor young kids sometimes get into even now. Expenses: always more expenses than they are able to produce money to meet."

Of course, it was not all sadness. At times, Alexandra seemed to be getting better. Then Anne and Bucky would go out with some of their old friends. Mr. Hewlett "liked to cheer them up" and occasionally took them on the Bohemian circuit. One night Betty and Toni Salaemi, who had an apartment on Washington Square South next to the Judson Hotel, took them to a tiny restaurant in one of the crooked little streets just south of the Square. It belonged to a gypsylike woman known as Romany Marie, who already was becoming known to the Greenwich Village people.

When Bucky's party came in there were only two people in that small room in which a few tables were crowded together—Romany Marie and a white-faced, burning-eyed young man, who was introduced as Eugene O'Neill. They spent the whole evening together talking of many things and forgetting their troubles. Though Bucky did not realize at the time, Romany Marie was to become far more important in his career than Eugene O'Neill, who appeared only that once.

No matter how bad things were, it was always fun to go over to the Hewletts for a merry evening. They were forever putting on shows to celebrate some birthday or other occasion; with such a large family and innumerable friends they were sure of an audience. Bucky loved to dress up in ridiculous costumes and spout his own verses written for the occasion. He had a genuine gift for light, witty verse that set them all roaring with laughter. That was another paradox—he hated ferociously to be laughed at; but delighted in playing the fool to be laughed *with*. Of those evenings Roger Hewlett says: "Bucky was always a wellspring of creative things. He would sit and write songs and dialogue and we'd all howl with laughter.

"None of this side of Bucky, or the wild things he did, ever gets into the books about him. They make him out to be this great, quiet, sober intelligence who wasn't appreciated at Harvard because his ideas were so great. Why, he didn't have an idea when he was in Harvard.

"It's a great pity that the biographies leave all the light, wild things out, because they miss a great deal of what Bucky is. Those things don't make him any less a remarkable person. His special genius is without question, but it had its foundations in very human fallibilities."

The Fullers only lived at Pearsal Place for about a year. It was, in fact, a miserable little house, very hard to heat in winter. So for Alexandra's sake, and for Bucky's, who hated commuting, they rented a tiny apartment in Montague Street, Brooklyn, for the following winter, and came back to Martin's Lane in the summer of 1921.

Alexandra, at two and a half, was still partly paralyzed, but her developing mind was a wonder and a delight to Bucky. He says: "Alexandra was not able to get around like other children, but she had the same curiosity they had about their environment. There was no damage to her beautiful head and so with her lovely little mind she demonstrated the extraordinary compensations that life has.

"Today, if we are designing an airplane or going to the moon, we provide alternate circuits for the important electronic functions, so that if the primary one fails there is another to take its place—we call it fail safe. Nature has many of those alternate circuits. If there is something the matter with a person's eyes, they use their ears or get the information in other ways.

"Alexandra acquired her understanding of her environment through people. She was fantastically sensitive to the people around her. Often Anne and I would be about to say something to each other or to the nurse, and before we could get it out of our mouths Alexandra would say the very words we were about to speak. This demonstrated quite clearly to me that there is this thing called telepathy, and that all people really have it, but they don't use it as Alexandra did because it is a fail safe. I think that everybody has these experiences that can only be explained as telepathy. Alexandra really told me that there was something beyond our ordinary senses going on; something metaphysical. Young people are particularly able to tune in on it."

As winter approached, Bucky and Anne decided that it would be good for Alexandra to get away from the dampness and cold that always seemed to set her back. Through his many foreign connections as Armour's export manager, Bucky was able to get an inexpensive house in Bermuda for Anne and Alexandra.

Like all Hewlett enterprises it became quite a family affair. Anglesea went to Bermuda with them, and Laurence Hewlett, who had recently married Robert Burr, came briefly with her young husband. Later Anglesea's great friend Gladys Bedford also joined the household.

That was a happy winter for Anne. She says, "We had lots of fun. We collected a count—Count Gaedon d'Ivry or something like that. First he rushed Anx; then he switched to Gladdie, and finally gave me quite a bit of attention. We had a fine time."

Best of all, it did Alexandra a great deal of good. She regained the use of her legs and could run around quite normally. When Anne brought her back, Bucky was amazed and delighted by her progress.

Meanwhile he had made a business decision that seemed logical, but turned out to be incredibly unlucky. The previous summer, Eddie MacDonald, Bucky's first commanding officer at Newport News, had rented a house in Hewlett. He was devoted to Bucky and relied on him for advice about his future career in civilian life. During the war he had saved Trubee Davison's life. Young Davison's father, Henry P. Davison, a partner in J. P. Morgan and Company, was utterly grateful to MacDonald. He persuaded him to leave the navy, promising him a splendid career in business.

Very coincidentally, Mr. Davison made MacDonald president of the Canada Connecticut Cotton Mills, for which Bucky had worked in the winter of 1914. This became a further bond between them, for Bucky was able to give MacDonald a great deal of technical information about the Sherbrooke Mills, which was enormously helpful to the young executive who naturally did not know very much about the textile business.

Then, in the spring of 1922, Mr. Davison made MacDonald president of the Kelly-Springfield Truck Company, a subsidiary of Kelly-Springfield Tires. MacDonald offered Bucky the job of National Account Sales Manager of Kelly-Springfield Trucks at a considerable increase in salary. Mrs. Fuller, with acute intuition, tried to persuade Bucky not to change jobs; but to him it looked like a twenty-karat-gold opportunity. What neither he nor MacDonald knew was that Morgan and Company proposed to phase out Kelly Trucks, which had been a principal supplier of trucks to the Canadian Army, but was now suffering from the competition of such industrial giants as Mack Trucks, White, and Pierce-Arrow.

For three months Bucky worked demoniacally at his new job, using all his foreign connections as well as his American contacts to get orders. He rolled in an impressive amount of new business, but the decision had already been made in that low, white marble building at 14 Wall Street from which the power lines extended to so much of American industry.

In the very flush of success, Bucky learned incredulously that Kelly Trucks was shutting down. He was out of a job, with no chance to have saved any money.

This shattering, unmerited blow indubitably had much to do with forming Bucky's low opinion of the masters of industry—later he was to call them "the great pirates." It also shook his confidence in himself, and sent him into a cycle of depression about his future. During his work for Armour and Company and Kelly-Springfield Trucks he had not been drinking at all. Now he began to drink rather heavily. He was quite literally penniless.

Fortunately, his many friends in the navy temporarily rescued him by having him restored to active duty in command of Eagle Boat Number 15, which was to be used as a training ship for the naval reserve during the summer.

When Anne and Alexandra had come home from Bermuda, the Fullers had rented a house on the East Rockaway Road in Hewlett with the Bobby Burrs. The joint Burr-Fuller household was a dismal failure. Bucky says: "Everything seemed to go wrong. First Kelly Trucks was liquidated; I was broke. Now Bobby Burr seemed to share the opinion of a lot of other people that I was a ne'er-do-well. I was not paying my share. It was a mess. The only good thing was that Alexandra seemed to be prospering."

But if Bucky was miserable ashore, he was, as usual, very happy at sea. His Eagle Boat was the biggest ship he had commanded—a sort of hybrid between a destroyer escort and a PT Boat. Mass-produced by Henry Ford during the war for antisubmarine service, the Eagles were flat-bottomed, slab-sided, with square sterns and sharp bows which made them cranky in a seaway. But they were fast, and the quarters were comfortable. Not much use in war, they were ideal for summer training work. Though Bucky was completely aware of the Eagle Boats' shortcomings, the fact that Henry Ford had been able to build them by assembly-line methods excited him. In fact, Ford became one of the very few industrialists Bucky admired for his imaginative solutions of production problems and his excellent labor relations.

On Eagle Boat 15 Bucky had a skeleton crew of regular navy ratings, and a shipload of reservists. He also had a delightful companion. Young Vincent Astor, who had inherited approximately $70,000,000 on his twenty-first birthday, was as ardent a sailorman as Bucky. After serving in the navy during the war, Astor had joined the naval reserve in order to maintain his naval affiliations. Because of his reserve rank Astor was given command of the Eagle Boat squadron in the metropolitan area. He chose Eagle Boat 15 as his flagship.

Thrown into such close quarters with his commanding officer, Bucky was sure to either hate him or love him. Astor was an enthusiastic officer, knowledgeable in the ways of the sea with none of the board-stiff formality of the old-school types. He was a year younger than

Bucky—twenty-six—tall and thin and keen. He took his duties seriously, but he was ready for a frolic any time it did not interfere with them. In that the two young men were very much alike. Furthermore, Astor took an immediate liking to Bucky. As always, Bucky responded with eager affection and loyalty.

They had great fun with the flotilla. At one point they made the New York Police Commissioner an honorary officer in the naval reserve, in return for which he made all the captains honorary police officers. Bucky became an honorary captain in the aviation division of the New York City Police with a big gold badge. His duties consisted of serving one day a year. During the World Series Bucky put on a uniform and stood in the nonsmoking section of the stadium making people put out their cigarettes.

Since Bucky liked to drive very fast, the gold badge came in very handy. He would be boiling down a thirty-mile highway at sixty, when a motorcycle cop would haul him in. The cop would come up in a state of justified outrage. Bucky would simply show him the badge; the cop would salute, and go away in furious frustration. Bucky kept the badge until the whole Tammany Hall–Jimmy Walker era ended in an odoriferous burst of scandal and Fiorello La Guardia took all the honorary badges away.

In Bucky's Chronofile, there is a good deal of publicity dating from that summer. The newspapers were interested in the naval training program; and with two such colorful characters as Astor and Fuller involved in it there was plenty to write about. Astor managed to get orders for a training cruise to Newport, Rhode Island. His little fleet dropped anchor in the harbor at the height of the season. Newport was Astor's home territory; his grandmother had been the regal ruler of Society, with a capital S. In a city of millionaires, he was the golden boy; as rich or richer than any of them. And young! The chatelaines of the turreted mansions, Italian palazzos, and gargantuan Grecian villas along Belleview Avenue invited—no, entreated—him and his senior captain to come to their elaborate dinners and balls. The newspapers played it up in headlines. Bucky loved it all.

In return, Bucky took Astor to *his* home territory. Anne's uncle, James Crosby Brown, owned an island in Buzzard's Bay. Young Roger Hewlett, who was staying there, vividly recalls the day that what looked to him like the whole United States Navy suddenly sailed into the little harbor. Anchors splashed into blue water, bo'suns' pipes shrilled, and launches put off from the ships. Laughing young officers in dress whites strolled down the dock, and Roger ran breathlessly to greet his dashing brother-in-law.

Uncle Crosby laid on a fine clambake New England style with barrels of steamers, and lobsters baked in seaweed. It was memorable.

On another occasion Bucky proposed that he and Astor visit his friends the Saltonstalls in West Chop. Astor sent for his private plane, and they flew over for another series of informal parties which delighted the golden boy.

In September the flotilla was disbanded and Bucky was on the beach again. But the friendship continued. Astor took the Fullers to a number of elaborate parties. To repay him Bucky took him to Romany Marie's where he met many of the emerging young artists. Bucky also persuaded the Salaemis to stage a Greenwich Village party for Astor. The Bohemians rallied around. There was Chianti in straw-covered flasks—Prohibition never bothered the Village. The splendid pianist was a girl called Pitot, who later went on to work with Gershwin and Richard Rodgers and other famous popular musicians.

It was after this party that Astor said to Bucky: "I have to go to Paris on family business for a few weeks. My plane will just be sitting in Port Washington doing nothing. It's all paid for through the month of October; pilot, insurance, everything. It costs me a packet. I would like very much if you would just take the plane and use it. The more you fly it the better."

Bucky accepted, his eyes gleaming with anticipation.

Astor's plane was one of two * designed and built by Grover Loening, who later became famous for designing the first really successful amphibian. It was a monoplane flying boat capable of carrying four passengers and a pilot, powered by a 400 hp Victory engine with six in-line cylinders, water-cooled. The engine was mounted above and behind the cockpit with a four-bladed pusher propellor. If you planned to fly above 10,000 feet you had to put lags in the radiator to prevent it from freezing up. The plane was the first designed for private use which embodied all the new technology discovered during the war. Capable of 120 mph, it was the most modern private vehicle in the air.

Anne and Bucky had a marvelous time in it. Since Alexandra seemed very well, they had no hesitation about leaving her with her nurse and

* The other was owned by William K. Vanderbilt.

her devoted slaves, Hope and Hester, at Martin's Lane. So they flew off, with Astor's pilot Clifford Webster at the controls, to weddings on Long Island and Newport and Boston. Many of Bucky's friends happened to be getting married that autumn; he was best man here, an usher there. Everywhere they arrived with enormous éclat. The New York *Times* and the *Tribune* followed them almost breathlessly, to Bucky's great delight; he has always loved publicity, favorable if possible.

Then Anne and Bucky took off for Maine, stopping briefly in Newport and in Boston to refuel; thence to Bar Harbor. Bucky's delight in speed, his *belief* in speed as part of the solution of mankind's problems, made him ecstatic. He carefully noted the distances and elapsed times—4¾ hours flying time from Port Washington to Bar Harbor—a record. Inevitably, they went to Bear Island—they had taken Alexandra there earlier in the summer. The plane landed in the lee of the island and taxied through the narrow harbor entrance, to be moored under the enclosing cliffs, which sheltered her fragile wings. It made an ideal base.

Even Anne enjoyed Bear Island that time. In October Maine is fantastically beautiful, the air cold and crystalline, sky and sea and earth sharply seen to the farthest horizon. Bucky made short flights every day—to Camden, Wiscasset, Bar Harbor, getting new perspectives on the channels and shoals so familiar to him from water level. He exultantly noted the flying times—Rockland ten minutes, Wiscasset twenty-five minutes, Eagle Island, to which he had so laboriously rowed, three minutes. He often took the local lobstermen up with him to show them their fishing grounds and spot new reefs on which to anchor their pots.

His was the first plane ever to base on Penobscot Bay. Everywhere they landed, crowds turned out to see the wonder of modern transportation that they had heretofore only read about. The local papers ran headlines and pictures; the *Times* and the *Tribune* followed their progress there also.

Then October was over and Bucky returned to earth with a thud. As he said: "It had been a preposterous sort of thing. There we were without a cent to our names, deeply in debt; living like supermillionaires."

But what fun it had been! And, though he did not know it, the last splendor of carefree youth.

Back in Lawrence, Bucky sank into deep despondency. He could not seem to find a job and considered working for his father-in-law, who had invented a new kind of building block. The whole prospect seemed so dismal that in a recrudescence of his old irresponsibility he decided to go to the Yale-Harvard football game to try to shake himself out of it.

On a fine autumn day Anne and Alexandra walked down to the Lawrence station with him. The measure of her recovery was the fact that it was a good two miles there and back to Martin's Lane. Bucky was using a snappy cane, partly because of his wonky knee, and partly because canes were the thing that year. He chatted gaily with Alexandra, telling her all about the picturesque spectacle of a Harvard-Yale game— the football heroes who became famous in an afternoon, the clash of the teams in sweat and mud, the chanted cheers and the songs the fans sang to encourage their teams in that traditional rivalry; the great stadium filled to its topmost ring by frantic rooters waving the crimson or blue pennants attached to little canes which the hawkers sold at the gates.

Alexandra looked up at him and said, "Daddy, will you bring me a cane?"

Bucky promised that he would.

There was a Harvard victory. Bucky celebrated through the night with his college friends, suddenly become more dear than they had ever been, drinking and laughing, singing and cheering and toasting the heroes of the day, drinking and forgetting his troubles, drinking and forgetting everything.

He took the one o'clock to New York the next day and telephoned Anne from the Pennsylvania Station. Her voice was strained and full of tears as she said: "Alexandra is very sick. She has pneumonia. She is in a coma."

"I'm coming on the next train," said Bucky.

When he reached Martin's Lane Alexandra was still unconscious, lying very small and forlorn, her face flushed with fever, her breathing harsh, eyes closed. Bucky and Anne stood beside her bed, helpless and desperate, for he never knew how long, while the doctor and nurses bustled about doing what they could. Sometime in the night Alexandra opened her eyes and looked at Bucky, knowing him, smiling a little. "Daddy," she said, "Did you bring me my cane?"

No physical pang could ever equal the agony that pierced Bucky's soul; the shame that forced him to turn his eyes away. He had forgotten.

A few hours later Alexandra died in his arms.

Alexandra's death literally devastated Bucky's life. He blamed himself, crazily, beyond all reason; blamed himself for not being able to provide her with better living conditions, more luxuries, more *things* that in his distraught mind might have made the difference. All the money he had spent on foolish extravagances and self-gratification haunted him; and the fact that he had failed to make money as other men had, exacerbated his sense of personal inadequacy, of failure. Later, he was able to rationalize some of this self-blame away. He came to believe that part of the onus lay with the builders of housing who, through stupidly or willfully ignoring the modern techniques available to them, had failed to provide adequately healthful living conditions. To some extent this alleviated his sense of guilt while it became the powerful motivating force in his lifelong crusade to improve the shelter of all mankind by forcing the whole world to accept his imaginative use of a new technology, much of which he invented himself.

But the thing he could not forgive himself, the thing that irrationally haunted his thoughts for more than forty years and was a scar upon his soul, was that forgotten cane. Even now, when at last he has gained absolution, he weeps when he tells of it.

The manner of his absolving is a strange story. To understand it one must always remember that Bucky is not only at the spearhead of scientific design planning, and believes in technology as the salvation of the human race; but he is one of the great mystics of our world. His Universe consists of the physical and metaphysical and to him the latter is infinitely more important. The man who could describe himself as "A self-balancing, twenty-eight joined, adapter base biped; an electro-chemical reduction plant, integrated with segregated stowages and thousands of hydraulic and pneumatic pumps with motors attached, 62,000 miles of capillaries, millions of warning signals . . . guided with exquisite precision from a turret in which are located telescopic and microscopic self-registering and recording range-finders . . . ," also has written that a human being is "basically a pattern in integrity" that is indestructible . . . "you and I are essential functions of the universe. . . . I'll be seeing you. Forever!" [1]

[1] "Challenges and Choices," *Saturday Review,* Sept. 26, 1965.

In 1967, on his way around the world, Bucky stopped on the island of Bali. "These were really quite beautiful circumstances," he said, "being there with all these Balinese who do everything as a single family. They go out, the whole colony, in single file to the rice fields, then they come back bringing things in. They all go into painting; they all do music; they do dancing. The whole community does all these things beautifully together."

Thus Bucky immediately felt great empathy with the Balinese. One day he was asked to go with some fine Balinese artists up into the hills to look at an unusual house and meet the artist who lived in it. They climbed a high volcanic mountain. Torrential rains had scored deep ravines in the volcanic ash that became raging rivers when the clouds opened, as they did almost daily. It was very difficult going for Bucky with his weak knee, crossing the ravines, climbing up steep slopes.

His Balinese guide was "a beautiful man," sympathetic and helpful. Even while struggling over the rough terrain Bucky was questioning him about the language, as he does wherever he goes, finding common origins of words in all the tongues men speak, and trying to get at the fundamental similarity of languages and through that the common heritage of peoples. The guide was very good at thinking of words that were almost the same in English and Balinese.

Inevitably they were caught in a sudden violent downpour and took refuge in a little hut made of split bamboo. Bucky was extremely interested in its construction. "I've studied a great deal about bamboo splitting," he says. "How you do it to make either thatching for a roof or supports for a big structure, fractionate it for whatever purpose. These men had fantastic expertise with their machetes. After the rain, one narrow gorge had become a torrent, so they went to work with those heavy, swordlike tools and built a bridge across it."

Bucky asked them to slice some more bamboo in a certain way, and with some string he built a small tensegrity sphere for them. They were fascinated by the fact that the compression members did not touch each other and there was just tension between them. So he actually delivered an impromptu scientific lecture which "they understood beautifully."

Coming down the hills was even more difficult for Bucky than going up. One of the Balinese cut a fine, long bamboo staff for him which he could put down in front of him and lower himself a step at a time down the declivities. He used it all the way home.

When they reached the car Bucky's guide put the staff in back and rode into town with him. At the hotel the guide said, "I would like very much to have your staff." Of course Bucky gave it to him.

The following morning the guide came to him and said: "All of us, we Balinese, are saying that you are not a stranger. You were here long, long ago and you have just come back to us." And Bucky felt that this was true.

Then the guide continued, "So I have set aside a room in my house and put your staff in it." And he said, "Nobody will ever go into that room again because your cane is in there."

Suddenly Bucky felt an enormous sense of relief. "I said to myself, 'This is a very mysterious thing. All those years and all those things that have happened since little Alexandra died. Now somehow I feel intuitively that this is a kind of message. That she has her cane at last.'"

CHAPTER VII

STOCKADE

THE winter of 1923 was, in Bucky's words, "a winter of horror." Tragedies seemed to pursue the Hewlett family. The year before, Anne's brother, Willetts, had been killed in an automobile smash. In 1923, Mrs. Hewlett died suddenly, leaving Monroe Hewlett desolate. Anne took over the management of the household and the care of the younger children. A little later Bobby Burr died of scarlet fever which he caught from his two-year-old son, Page Burr.

Bucky was deep in debt and jobless. However, Mr. Hewlett had invented and patented a new type of building construction, specially formed blocks which gave the structure unusual solidity and strength. Bucky says: "I thought it extremely good, but nobody would do anything with it. So I said to Mr. Hewlett, 'I think I'll just go ahead and produce it for you.'"

Bucky's factory was the red Rock Hall barn. The first problem was what material to use for the blocks which were the basis of Mr. Hewlett's invention, so that they would be both strong and light and would insulate. Bucky experimented with marsh grass and peat moss; then he tried chopped-up cornstalks. Finally he hit upon excelsior bonded with a binder of magnesium-oxy-chloride cement and formed in a mold under heavy pressure. The finished blocks were shaped like dominoes and looked a little like shredded wheat. In fact, one night Bucky had Scott Perky, the son of the man who had invented shredded wheat, to dinner at Martin's Lane to describe the technology of making it.

Though they looked like a breakfast food the blocks were excellent for supporting walls for a house or curtain walls for a larger structure. They were 16 inches long by 8 inches wide by four inches high with a hole 4 inches in diameter at either end. When the blocks were piled on top of each other and concrete was progressively poured through these holes it formed interior columns four inches in diameter. At every floor and at all doors and windows these columns were tied together horizontally with concrete lintels, thus forming a continuous, integral concrete framing.

These big building blocks weighed only two pounds each—doing more with less. They provided insulation equal to 4 inches of cork, were fireproof and waterproof. The system was a genuinely new development in building construction. Bucky felt that he and his father-in-law had made a real advance toward his ultimate goal of better housing for people everywhere.

The relations between those two were extremely warm and affectionate. Bucky had great respect for Mr. Hewlett, and the older man understood him and recognized his extraordinarily imaginative mentality. Mr. Hewlett's confidence and wisdom and loyal support kept Bucky going during a very difficult period of his life. Many years later, when people throughout the world were acclaiming Buckminster Fuller's daring ideas and profound philosophy, he said, "Mr. Hewlett was the first man ever to tell me that my own ideas were valid."

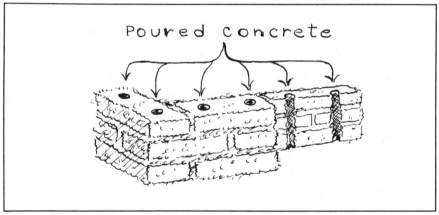

From patent drawing of Stockade Building System.

Seeing that he was really on the track of something big, Bucky moved his "factory" to Mr. Hewlett's studio in Brooklyn. It was a former roller-skating rink, a huge place where Mr. Hewlett had painted his murals and the scenery for various Broadway productions including the fantastic sets for Edmond Rostand's *Chantecler* in which Maud Adams had been a smash hit.

There Bucky set to work to invent the machinery for the mass production of what was now aptly named the Stockade Building System, because the concrete pillars were like the supporting poles of a stockade. After very hard work, in a surprisingly short time he designed the machinery and built a working model on which he was granted the first of the twenty-odd patents he holds—Stockade (Building Structure) No. 1,633,702 and Stockade (Mold and Process) No. 1,634,900.

President R. Buckminster Fuller of the Stockade Building System was now ready for business. Stock was sold in the company to people who wanted to start organizing for manufacturing the blocks and erecting houses by the Stockade Building System; and subsidiary companies were organized, under the parent company. Many of the investors were kinfolk of Bucky's. The first factory was in New Jersey. Then Neddy Larned started one in Baltimore called the Blue Ridge Company. There was one in Massachusetts in which Anglesea's husband, George Abbott, had an interest—five in all, including one in Joliet, Illinois, just outside of Chicago, run by Bucky's cousin, Andrew King. The houses could be built much more cheaply than by conventional methods and were better than those costing far more. With the postwar boom in building rising to a climax the investors foresaw a fabulous opportunity to make money.

Bucky was very busy, rushing from one location to another, overseeing the construction of the houses, giving advice, improvising brilliantly to meet unexpected problems. In his home office he was concerned with financing the expanding business, marketing new issues of stock, organizing new companies, keeping the materials flowing, and the work up to his high standards.

But he was very unhappy. The work-filled days were fine; the nights were hideous. For Alexandra's death had thrown him into profound melancholia. The moment the day's work was done he began to drink. He often drank all night and went to work the next day with undiminished vigor. Somehow his ironclad constitution withstood it.

Bucky says: "I was never what you would call an alcoholic. The drinking side in those first years was really for companionship; I craved friendship and understanding. People would take me on as a comrade when we were drinking together; they would not take me on sober. The unfriendly ones became friendly, and I don't like anybody to be unfriendly to me. Drinking did not make me testy as it does some people, but rather very warm and optimistic; overoptimistic. This was a false kind of manner, which I did not like, for it made me undertake to do more than I could carry through, and would often get me into trouble.

"It was really a very peculiar part of my life. I do whatever I do very thoroughly. I would drink very copiously, but my behavioral reflexes were tremendously under control, so I was able to handle it to such an extent that people did not talk about me, or think about me, as a drunk."

Bucky in a genial mood was a most delightful person, the gayest of companions. That talent for light verse, warm and witty, was put to frequent use. An example was when Mr. Hewlett was scolding the now teen-age twins for some peccadillo. Bucky wrote:

> They were young with young ideas
> And their eyes would fill with tears . . .
> "You say we can be a pain
> And will never do what you ask us to
> We're young and foolish twins."

But quite little things would put Bucky in a foul mood. Anne was still a very young and pretty woman who loved to flirt in a perfectly harmless way. Bucky would get the idea she was being disloyal or did not love him anymore. One evening in the Hewlett house when Anne was flirting with Alaric Mann, Bucky sat silently, his face getting blacker and blacker. Suddenly he stood up and stormed out of the house. He walked all the way to New York; twenty miles over country roads and boulevards with no sidewalks, while the night traffic roared by. Across the Queensborough Bridge he went, into the city, which by the time he reached it was gray and weary in the dawn. Anne did not hear from him for two days. He had very little money. Where he slept, how he ate, no one knows; perhaps in speakeasies or empty warehouses, perhaps in some girl's room. Then he came back cheerfully nonchalant as though nothing had happened. Anne was serene.

After a while Bucky moved to Chicago to oversee the starting-up of the Stockade Company in Joliet. Anne remained behind to hold the Hewlett family together. Bucky was even lonelier in that alien city. The days were still all right, the nights disastrous. He soon found his way to the speakeasies. A favorite was a gangster's hangout on the way in from Joliet, where the new factory was building. He stopped by almost every evening on his way home. There he met Al Capone, then rising to the height of his underworld career as the chief of the rackets and head of the immensely profitable bootlegging industry. By his ruthless organizational ability, he had changed it from a haphazard individual enterprise into just that—an industry. Bucky did not like Capone. "He was not a very attractive man," he said.

Bucky, still in search of company, also frequented brothels. With customary exaggeration he says: "I'm sure I went to over a thousand of them. They seemed to be the only place where people really talked straight to me; those girls. Many of them had babies. I wanted to see them as human beings, to know how they got there. They were terribly interesting as people. I enjoyed talking to them."

When Anne came to Chicago to join her husband in 1926, things were better. As president of one Stockade Company, general manager of another, an officer of a third, Bucky was getting a rather good salary. The Fullers took a very pretty apartment overlooking Belmont Harbor and Lake Michigan. It was quite close to where Birchwood Farm had been when Bucky's mother was a little girl. Bucky loved to watch the coming and going of the yachts in Belmont Harbor. It was good to have Anne with him.

To his delight she became pregnant again. He was happier than he had been for a long time.

The stockholders of Stockade were not happy in 1927. The golden tide they had envisioned ebbed instead of flowed. Some of them blamed Bucky. In some respects they were right; in others it was not his fault.

The construction industry was the most backward in the United States. Architects and builders were intensely conservative. The former looked backward to the beautiful models of antiquity; they copied Greek temples, Gothic cathedrals, Renaissance palazzos, Wren churches. They carried it so far as to adorn the Woolworth Building, the tallest in the world, with Gothic spires and gargoyles. The builders were equally backward. They opted for the time-tried ways that assured them a fancy profit with as little risk as possible.

The strong building trade unions—carpenters, bricklayers, steelworkers, plumbers, electricians, and so forth—with their hard-won perquisites, like work rules, apprentice systems, closed shops, and white supremacy policies that made it impossible for Negroes to join a craft union, were equally calcified. They viewed with distaste any innovation that might increase efficiency and thereby cut down the number of jobs a given piece of construction required. So the entire building industry establishment—architects, contractors, and unions—however much they might fight among themselves, were solidly united against progress. Since, under the Stockade System, a house could be built far more cheaply with less labor and much more quickly than by conventional methods, they were against it.

Nor was this all Bucky had to contend with. There were also the government-enforced building codes and zoning restrictions. Originally conceived to protect the citizenry against dangerous building practices, inferior materials, and shoddy workmanship, they had become the sacrosanct means of perpetuating antediluvian techniques, backed as they were by the enormous political power of the construction establishment.

Baffled by deliberate inertia and voluminous red tape, morally outraged by the stupidity and greed he encountered, and furious with frustration, Bucky became totally disgusted with the whole building industry and all its members. More than ever he conceived Alexandra's death as due to its roadblocks to progress. Though his bitterness against this establishment was justifiable on technological and humanitarian grounds, it was less than logical in regard to Alexandra.

In defense of his position, Bucky points out that the diseases she contracted have now been brought pretty much under control. But the finest housing conceivable could not impede the entrance of poliomyelitis viruses, or pneumococci; and at the time of Alexandra's death she was living in the Hewlett's house, an extremely comfortable residence in which ten children grew to adulthood in abounding health. Rather, it was due to the fact that medical science, through no fault of its practitioners, was a few years late in discovering the serums and antibiotics that stopped those epidemics.

Though the Stockade Companies were badly handicapped by the obstructions thrown in their way, Bucky was not entirely blameless for their lack of profitability. He is, in fact, one of the world's worst businessmen. To succeed in any financial enterprise, a man must have a strong affinity and great respect for money. Bucky had none whatever. He regarded it as a false quantity, a fallacious way of computing wealth, which at least as early as his Annapolis days he believed to have been foisted upon the human race by the greed and cunning of their rulers— his "great pirates." To him the only sensible way of reckoning real wealth was by "the addition of value (or wealth) by manufacture ef-

fected between raw materials and gained by the rich synergetic mixture
of technology and energy . . . [both of which] were fundamental assets
that defied exhaustion in apparent universe."

At the time, what he wanted to do was to build better housing for
human beings. The money involved was to him nothing but counters in
a game whose rules he distrusted to the point of abhorrence. Increasingly
he came to regard the natural desire of those who invested in his companies to make money as an obscene example of greed. From Bucky's
point of view, this was perfectly logical, but it was rough on his associates
with more conventional views of the object of enterprise. At least he
succeeded in building quite a few houses—234 of them to be exact.

As long as Mr. Hewlett held a controlling interest in the Stockade
Building System, Bucky was safe, for Hewlett's loyalty and faith were
unshakable. However, financial difficulties forced him to sell his stock
in 1927. Eventually it came into possession of the Celotex Corporation,
which thereby gained ownership of Bucky's patents. Improved and modified almost beyond recognition, they are today embodied in some of the
company's insulating and sound-proofing systems.

Bucky was now in the situation of being merely an employee; a position that never suited his temperament. He continued to work as hard
as ever, and do his best according to his principles. But, perhaps with
some justification, the new regime did not appreciate his methods. As to
what fired the train that eliminated Bucky, there is a story, possibly
apocryphal, that an official of the holding company called up Stockade's
main Chicago office late one afternoon. Whoever answered the phone
incautiously left the line open, so while he waited for Bucky to come
on the official was treated to a Rabelaisian chorus sung in not very
close harmony by Bucky and his brother-in-law, Carmen Hewlett. There
was also a bitter fight with his cousin Andy King about policy at the
Joliet plant.

Whatever the cause, Bucky was fired without benefit of severance
pay. "I got pushed right out," he says, "and the people who pushed me
out were eager to be vindicated for doing so. They tried to make me
out a bad man."

Since he had saved no money, he was again almost penniless. Furthermore, Anne had just given birth to a daughter whom she named Allegra.
"Allegra was a good name," said Bucky. "Anne had been reading the
letters which Lord Byron's bastard daughter, Allegra, wrote him from
the convent; so our Allegra was named after her. I think she has been
a happy child."

CHAPTER VIII

DIALECTIC BY LAKE MICHIGAN

To Bucky, Allegra's coming had seemed like a miracle, a second chance to prove himself. "It was a mysterious matter that we suddenly had this child again," he said. "She was the inspiration for all the great resolves."

Thus it had appeared as though Allegra's birth would mark the end of the five-year-long nightmare that had warped Bucky's soul and driven him to almost psychotic melancholia ever since the death of Alexandra. But just as he was regaining sanity the disastrous termination of his job with Stockade plunged him into a yet deeper pit. In order to understand his exaggerated despair one must remember that he was intensely mercurial, soaring to the heights on the frail wings of fantasy; plunging hellward when they shriveled in the icy blast of reality. There was also that inordinate strain of guilt, which had been ever-present in his mind since Alexandra's death—sometimes pushed down below the surface, but always rising again to destroy whatever anodyne he found in alcohol.

Now his reviving self-confidence was totally shattered. Even Allegra seemed doomed; for he felt that he had brought nothing but tragedy to those whose lives he touched. Indeed, he came close to believing that the people who were blackening his character were right, that he really was a "bad man."

"All these things happening when there was a new child and we were stranded almost penniless in Chicago . . . I said to myself, 'I've done the best I know how and it hasn't worked. I guess I'm just no good, people seem to think so; even my mother has always been afraid that I was worthless. I guess she was right.' I really thought I was some kind of freak."

At this stage, the very nadir of his life, which he once called "the critical detonation point," Bucky walked out of their pretty apartment one night and down to the shore of Lake Michigan with the intention of throwing himself in and relieving those he loved of the burden of his presence. In that cold, windy place, he stood for many hours asking himself searching questions and answering them with implacable logic.

This apocalyptic debate between Buckminster Fuller and Buckminster Fuller—and Buckminster Fuller and the God of Things as They Are, revolved around what was best for Allegra's future. That ineluctable sense of guilt sharpened it unbearably. If he came to the conclusion that he, in truth, was no good and a fatal influence on those he cared for most, then logic commanded that he eliminate himself before he ruined their lives. Though neither his family nor Anne's were wealthy, they were fairly comfortably off. If he died, they would somehow manage to provide for Anne and Allegra better than he seemed likely to do, if he were truly unworthy. On one thing he was adamant: he would not himself go back east to beg the charity of his relations.

Thus the negative proposition was clear in his mind, but before he acted upon it Bucky set himself to explore the alternatives. The locale he had chosen was hardly conducive to accurate rationalization. The north wind swooping straight out of Canada, the sharp waves snapping at his feet, the tumbling wilderness of water beyond, and the sullen darkness of an overcast night were all inducive of despair rather than optimism. However, Bucky's tremendous power of concentration, the irresistible force of his mind once set in motion, enabled him to ignore totally the external circumstances; he reasoned as lucidly as though in his own study. One can see him standing there, stocky and solid, unswayed by wind, unhearing the waves, totally oblivious to the elemental forces of his Universe in his total absorption in the invisible and metaphysical as he began the dialogue with his soul and its Creator.

"The absolute first big question I asked myself concerned God," Bucky said. "I put it this way to myself; 'You have been taught a great deal about God and Jesus Christ by people who love you very much—your grandmothers, your mother and father—and by the church. But now you must think for yourself. You have gotten into this mess by taking other people's word for things—your family and your father's friends who told you that your ideals were impracticable, that this was a tough hard world with not enough goods to go around, therefore you must get yours first and then perhaps you can afford the luxury of ideals. But, if I am to believe in myself and the validity of my own ideas, I must stop thinking as other people told me to and rely on my own experience.

" 'Now,' I asked myself, 'is there anything in your own experience that forces you to admit that there is a greater intellect operative in our Universe than man?'

"And I answered, 'I am overwhelmed by the certainty that there is, because the principles of Universe, the exquisite design of everything from the invisible microcosm of atoms to the macromagnitudes of the galaxies, and all of them interaccommodating with absolute integrity, are intellectual conceptions whose principles can only be discovered intellectually.' "

Bucky therefore assumed a priori the existence of the Greater Intelligence, which in truth he had done for a long time. That being accepted, he now asked himself the next question: "Do I know best or does God know best whether I may be of any value to the integrity of Universe?"

The answer was that neither he nor any man knew; but "the faith you have just established imposes recognition of the a priori wisdom of the fact of your being."

And he thought back on his life and the remarkably varied experiences he had had which were considerably beyond those of most human beings, due partly to chance and partly to the very "instability" which had led him into so many different occupations and areas of activity. He thought of his boyhood on Bear Island and the things he had learned about ships and the sea; of Harvard and what he had learned there, even though negatively; of the mill at Sherbrooke, and Armour and Company, and the Naval Academy; of the chance that had brought him to the frontiers of knowledge about aerodynamics and electronics; of his association with Mr. Hewlett and his artist and architect friends. Finally he thought of the last five years of involvement in the construction industry, which, with all its frustrations and anxieties and final catastrophe, had taught him so much about "the very stormy big patterns of industry in the way of corporations, lawyers, building codes, and unions" even if what he had learned was mainly how things should not be done. He thought of the people he had known, ranging from Admiral Gleaves to the mechanics in Sherbrooke, from J. P. Morgan's partners to Al Capone, not for what they had told him but in terms of experience with human beings. He said to himself, "I am making the assumption that there is a greater wisdom which has arranged that I have this extraordinary number of experiences; and I am making the further assumption that my experiences are on inventory and of value to others."

Then he said to himself: "You do not have the right to eliminate yourself; you do not belong to you. You belong to the universe. Your significance will remain forever obscure to you, but you may assume that you are fulfilling your role if you apply yourself to converting your experience to the highest advantage of others."

And he thought: "That is the thing I should turn to account, and if I should do this, I might be able to eliminate the possibility of other people going through the pains I have had. Perhaps I am part of the great design of things."

In order to do this Bucky realized that he would have to devote himself completely to that supreme purpose. But there was the question of how Anne and Allegra were going to live. He was absolutely convinced that the necessity of earning a living had confused all his earlier endeavors. He denied the basic assumption that you have got to make money for living. He said to himself, "I don't think that is necessarily so; I don't think there is money between Mars and the sun. Furthermore, I think we are in an entirely new phase of man on our planet. This new technology and industrialism is something not understood by man, who is exploiting it and trying to make money. Rather, I think evolution is trying to do something very much else with these tools and this knowledge than what man is trying to do. I think that if industrialization were understood as an organic affair and part of Universe, it would be managed very differently, and I'll try to understand it that way. I'll try to employ its capabilities to produce as much of the new technical advantages of man as to make him the success that Universe intends him to be."

That was when Bucky got the insight that became basic to his philosophy of action. All previous ideologies had been attempts to reform human nature; and experience made it obvious you can't reform people. So Bucky proposed to reform the *environment,* not man.

But that still left him on the lakeshore with virtually no money and no prospects at all. What of Anne and Allegra? "I thought that if my daughter becomes as wonderful as I feel she is going to be—I see children don't do things to make money; they don't operate that way—so if Allegra grows up and finds that I have used my best endeavors just to look out for her in a world where people are really suffering, she would be sorrowful. She will only be really happy if I have been effective in trying to get things done for the total well-being of people everywhere. If she grows up in a world where all humanity is a little better off than they are now she will probably be happier. And I said, 'If the intelligence directing Universe really has a use for me, it will not allow us to starve; it will see to it that I am able to carry out my resolve.' "

One is reminded of the Puritan saying, "The Lord will provide." Strangely enough, He did.

So Bucky went back to Anne and told her of his resolve to dedicate himself to serving humanity without regard to making a living. And she accepted it.

The first thing was to get out of their beautiful, expensive apartment. Bucky combed the city until he found the very cheapest apartment hotel, which was also fireproof—for Allegra's sake. It was dismal and rather dirty in a slum section of the city. The Fullers' apartment consisted of one fair-sized room, with a sort of cubicle off it to store baggage in. There was a small window in this storage space, so they fixed it up for Allegra. There was also an alcove with a stove and sink where Anne did the cooking. "It was very tiny, but it was really all right," she said.

Bucky said, "Of course Anne bore the brunt of it."

The hotel appears to have been an underworld hangout. That was some time before the terrible St. Valentine's Day murders. Anne said: "The place was swarming with gangsters, but they were really very helpful. One in particular, who lived in the next room, would come and haul the garbage out. I don't think he took part in the St. Valentine's Day thing; he was really very nice. But, of course, he wore all his equipment—two guns in shoulder holsters."

In that apartment the Fullers lived penuriously. There was no more drinking—no money for that or need of companionship—and very little to eat. Much later Bucky made a rhyme about it:

> Lady Anne went to the store
> To buy food for a week or more
> She bought an egg and half a roll
> And a nice red apple that she stole.

It was never as bad as that, but it is true that Anne frequently only had money enough to buy one slim meal a day. Still, Bucky's faith in Universe was kept. With absolutely no means of support, visible or invisible, they managed. One or two people died and left them tiny legacies. A few old friends stopped by to pay forgotten debts—Bucky had loaned money to anyone who asked for it when he had it. You might say the ravens fed them.

Bucky realized that if he were to follow his resolution to believe only those things that he could verify from his own experience, he must clear his mind of everything he had been told. Many of these things had been contradictory, so that in trying to follow them he had arrived at what he called "a pinch point of pain." Now he must unlearn all the things he had been taught. Eventually he called himself "The most unlearned man in the world."

It seemed to him that all his troubles had begun with words—the most extraordinary tools evolved by man. But tools can be used in the wrong way, and he felt that he had acquired all the fallacious ideas and conflicting thoughts through words that had been spoken to him; and words that he had thoughtlessly spoken—"I became very suspicious of words."

Very logically then, Bucky decided to take a sort of Trappist vow, to declare a moratorium on words. He would not speak to anyone nor allow anyone to speak to him until he was sure what words he wanted to use. He would force himself to really understand what he was thinking, not just parrot words someone else had said to him. Then he would be sure that, "When I made a sound, I really wanted to make that sound."

Anne says, "Of course he did not seal up his mouth as his students now seem to think." And Bucky agrees. "It was tough on Anne," he says. "I did speak to her a little, but to no one else except Allegra. Anne made all my oral contacts with the outside world."

Bucky's silence lasted for almost two years. Part of what he was trying to do was to restore a child's ability to tune in on the metaphysical aspects of Universe. "There is such potential in children. I wanted to see if I could regain the sensitivities I was born with, which all this good advice that had been given me had blunted, for I knew I was going to need them very badly."

Bucky says that through many years, "I find that very gradually I have regained these precious childish sensitivities to such an extent that I really see and feel life very much as I did when I was a little kid."

Without realizing it, Bucky was emulating the retreats from the world which, whether deliberate or enforced, have molded the spiritual crises and enlarged the wisdom of so many men who have made enormous contributions to mankind. Prince Siddatthu under the bo tree, Jesus in the wilderness, Cervantes and Gandhi in their prison cells, Franklin Roosevelt, a prisoner of polio, all had time for contemplation which Bucky took willy-nilly.

Think not that Bucky's decision to meditate was received with acclamation by his family. They regarded it as another example of irresponsibility; a cop-out in the striking phrase of today. Woolly, now an engineer with the General Electric Company, wrote asking him to explain what he was doing. Bucky answered at great length, trying to describe his slowly forming philosophy of the relationship of man to Universe and his reasons for his seemingly unreasonable decision. The answer apparently only confused Woolly, who wrote saying in effect, "Won't you please write me something definite, not all these complicated words and this esoteric philosophy?" Woolly was not interested in philosophy; he was, in Bucky's words, "a very good engineer and absolutely precise."

So Bucky wrote again, this time using very explicit engineering terms, "a nice, clear piece," though far beyond the conventional scientific thinking of the time. It seemingly infuriated Woolly, who replied sharply that this stuff was absolutely no good, "I don't understand you. It's nonsense."

Bucky says: "It was very sad to have my brother say that my ideas were nonsense and imply that I was crazy or no good. There had always been absolute love and devotion between us. . . ."

Bucky was so deeply distressed and so badly shaken that Anne felt she must do something. *"I'm* going to write to Woolly," she said.

Bucky did not see how that could do any good. Anne's devotion to him was absolute, but though she listened attentively to what he said when he was trying to clear his mind and formulate his thoughts by speaking them, he was convinced that she did not understand a word he was saying. She lived in her own world, a world of books and poetry and music, quite apart from his. He thought that she believed in him not from understanding, but in loyalty and blind faith.

When Anne finished the letter she showed it to Bucky. "To my amazement," he said, "the letter she had written was a most extraordinary one explaining what I was doing so clearly that Woolly understood it perfectly, and our differences were resolved. That was the only time I had seen her show that she understood what I'd been thinking. And all the time it was buried quite deeply in there."

While so many people thought that Bucky was just frittering away his time, he was, in fact, working harder than most men ever do. The compulsion, which drives him still, was there in full force. One thing that bothered him was the time lost in the mechanics of existence, eating, getting places, sleeping—especially sleeping. He devised a regimen for himself to reduce those five or six lost hours of sleep. Each time he felt his concentration slipping because of weariness he stopped abruptly and took a half-hour nap.* He would wake to find himself fully restored. In this way he found he could do with only two or three hours sleep out of twenty-four.

Out of this intense period of silent thought emerged in embryo most of the great philosophical and mathematical innovations that have made his fame and moved the world forward a little.

Bucky's determination not to accept anything but his own experiences as a basis for his philosophy did not apply to books, provided they were about facts—facts of history, facts of mathematics, facts of physics—but he reserved the right to reevaluate them in the light of his own experience, and mostly he did so drastically. He did a great deal of research in the public libraries—presumably he had to speak to the librarians—very briefly. This disposes of the canard which one of his relations put out that "The only books Bucky ever reads are his own." However, one could definitely say from that time forward that the only thoughts Bucky has thought have been his own.

The first thing he had to do was to learn how to think. He decided that experiences are finite, they begin and end; so he tried to catch himself thinking in terms that did not have to do with experience. When he could not, he was satisfied that he was thinking only in terms of his own experience.

Central to his developing philosophy was the fact that everything in the universe was constantly in motion, atomically if not visibly. A boulder, seemingly immovable and dead on a mountainside, is in fact a seething mass of energy. That is the triumphant difference between Newton's static universe and the new revelation of Albert Einstein's intuitive Theory of Relativity, which was even then just being confirmed by pragmatic experimentation. All the opposing forces throughout this kinetic picture are always in neat balance, and everything invariably moves in the direction of least resistance. Therefore, Bucky decided,

* Thomas Edison did the same thing when in the midst of an experiment.

the history of man's creative endeavor is the story of his effort to control direction by eliminating resistance. To the degree it is controlled the course of society can be better charted.

Then Bucky considered the dramatic acceleration of Universe alterations brought about on earth by the very swift progress of the industrial equation in his own lifetime, from the first American automobile in his birth year, 1895, to Lindbergh's flight across the ocean in 1927, and all the enormous forward progress in every phase of man's inventiveness in between. To make these advances clearer for study he worked out some mathematical figures. He imagined a globe twenty feet in diameter and representing earth and considered how long a man on foot would take to circumnavigate it if there were a dry path around it. Then he gave the man a horse and that reduced the size of his sphere to a six-foot diameter. Providing man with a clipper ship—a large industrial tool—brought it down to the size of a basketball, trains and steamships reduced it to a baseball. Later, when jet planes were invented, the comparative size of man's negotiable earth on Bucky's scale was slightly larger than a pea. All these steps except the horse were due to tools created by industrialization.

Therefore, Bucky concentrated on the great advantage man had, gained by the employment of tools created by industry. And he realized that if they were used properly and further developed at an ever-accelerating rate, the glimpse which he first had at the Naval Academy in 1917, of the possibility of all the human race enjoying a high standard of living, with plenty of everything to go around for a hugely increased population of the world, was already within grasp or would be shortly. He became certain that with their environment changed by the elimination of the fear of scarcity, the struggle to "get yours first" would also be eliminated. To quote a favorite Kipling verse of his:

> No one shall work for money, and no one shall work for fame,
> But each for the joy of the working . . .

That was his first great intuition.

It was obvious that such a dramatic environmental revolution would only be accomplished by doing ever more with less. So Bucky set his mind to work, starting with the general principle and moving to a practical application as to how this could best be accomplished. Inevitably, he first thought of housing because it was a basic human need and the most backward of all industries, and also because he had the most experience in it. But he remembered his proposition that in order to avoid opposition from the entrenched vested interests connected with it, he must think and design fifty years ahead of his time. This he did.

In his engineering experience Bucky had learned that the strength of various materials was amazingly greater in tension than in compression. It varied from two to one in certain materials like bricks to as great as twenty to one in steel alloys. In other words, if a steel column of a certain diameter could support a load of so many tons in compression, it could support twenty times that weight hanging from it in tension. Houses had always been built by piling things on top of each other so everything was in compression. Obviously, the way to do more with less was to design a house that was suspended in tension which would then require twenty times less supportive material, and still less if the house were built of the lightweight materials then becoming available instead of the conventional bricks and mortar or concrete or wood.

Bucky began to plan along these lines, and to read about the latest developments in architecture. The most advances seemed to be taking place in Germany. Inspired by such purely functional American buildings as silos, factories, and warehouses whose clean lines had a pure functional beauty unencumbered by decorative frills, a group of German architects led by Walter Gropius had developed what appeared to be a severe, purely functional style of building, which became known as the Bauhaus International Style.

After studying it, Bucky totally rejected it because it only *looked* modern and was really a fake. All the old steel skeletons supporting the buildings in compression were still there, hidden by "suspended curtain walls." The modern look was no more than a prestidigitator's trick resulting in "faddish nonsense." This attitude was the reason for Bucky's later heated exchanges with Frank Lloyd Wright, the leading American practitioner of "modern architecture."

As a basis for his own construction plans, Bucky became fascinated with the engineering of lighter-than-air dirigibles. They consisted of rigid frameworks of the lightest available metal alloys tied together by cables in tension. This framework was covered by a thin waterproof envelope within which were individual bags of hydrogen—or, preferably, nonflammable helium—to provide lift. The latest dirigibles were nearly a thousand feet long and capable of carrying fifty passengers and all their life-supporting necessities across the Atlantic. As designed by the

Zeppelin works in Germany they were the strongest structures in the world for their weight.

Bucky began drawing designs for a building ten or twelve stories high suspended by cables from a strong central mast. The different floors were hexagon-shaped, in conformity with his discovery of the principle that the tetrahedron—a pyramid with four triangular sides—was the basic building block of the Universe because it had the greatest strength with the least surface of any geometric figure. Six tetrahedrons combined to form a hexagon. The life-support machinery was contained in the central mast.

One of Bucky's strongest beliefs was that progress meant mobility. "Trees have roots; men have legs." Therefore, men should not be rooted in one spot, but free to move all over the earth. So, he reasoned, should their shelters. For that reason his multiple housing unit was designed to be so light that it could be delivered anywhere in the world by dirigible. A foundation hole would be blasted out by a bomb; the central mast dropped into place and anchored firmly in concrete.

But, since tying up to sewers and gas mains or electric cables meant putting down roots, Bucky's dwelling must contain within itself all these necessities. He knew perfectly well that the means of accomplishing this would not be invented for twenty to forty years, but he was deliberately following his principle of being fifty years ahead of his time. However, he did sketch in the systems and general principles by which it would all become possible. He named his invention the 4D—fourth-dimension—house.

One of Bucky's inventive ideas was to be able to open doors and windows or activate other mechanisms by interrupting a beam of light with a gesture of the hand. He went so far as to write to Woolly to ask if General Electric was working on any device that would translate light into power. Woolly wrote back rather irritably that no such thing was in prospect, and why couldn't Bucky stop fantasizing. Some time later Woolly handsomely sent Bucky an apologetic telegram saying: "YOU CAN NOW OPEN YOUR DOOR BY WAVING YOUR HAND AFTER ALL STOP WE HAVE DEVELOPED PHOTOELECTRIC CELL AND RELAY STOP SEVENTY TWO DOLLARS FOR THE SET. WOOLLY."

Bucky intended that his dwelling should make it possible for men to live in formerly uninhabitable parts of the earth, in great cold or devastating heat. He discovered that much of the variation in temperature within a house was caused by its wind resistance, which creates a vacuum on the lee side. This effect has since been recognized and is now recorded in a wind-chill index that measures temperature plus wind velocity. To obviate this and conserve heating energy, Bucky designed a streamlined plastic shield to surround his dwelling in rigorous climates. Since neither plastics nor air conditioning had yet been perfected, he was still far ahead of practicability.

As Bucky had intended, his plans were so wild that they aroused no anxiety or opposition from the vested interests, who regarded them genially as particularly outrageous science fiction. However, they did arouse a certain interest among devotees of futurism. In 1928, the Chicago *Evening Post* published an article and drawings by Bucky of one version of his 4D living machine. This was the first breakthrough, the concrete expression of his year of intensive thought.

However, like the metaphysical universe, the most important results of his thinking were still invisible. Conceived or gestating in his mind during the great silence were such revolutionary ideas as his energetic-synergetic geometry; his theory of the origin of homo sapiens in the western Pacific, thereafter spreading around the globe by the sea routes following favorable winds and currents, which proved that there were no different races of men, but only *one* human race; his principle of the tetrahedron as the basic unit of Universe; the dictum that "nature never fails; it always complies with its own laws. Nature is infallible"; apparent failure is due to man's knowledge being inadequate; life as a pattern in integrity; man as an essential function of Universe and the probability of the ultimate success of man as such; the concept of real wealth as the application of intellect to energy, which can never diminish but must always and forever increase; and the necessity for design science planning on a cosmic scale—that is not through specialization, because nature is never compartmented, but is one indivisible, exquisitely coordinated system.

This, of course, is a far from complete list of Bucky's discoveries and intuitions during this period, many of which were embryonic and subject to development in later years. The point is that he emerged from it measurably closer to his ideal of the cosmogonal man, though still with a remarkable plenitude of human frailties.

Portrait of Bucky, 1928, by Anne Fuller.

CHAPTER IX

THE HOUSE ON A POLE

ONE person Bucky did talk about—and to—was Allegra. He was determined not to blunt her sensitivities and not to instill fear into her; for he considered fear responsible for most of the evils of the world. This meant that he would not say to her, "Don't do this or that, you'll hurt yourself." But how to keep her from injury without those prohibitions? Anne argued with him as any normally protective mother would, but seeing him so passionately concerned about this, she went along with him as much as she could. Bucky says: "Anne did something that I was unable to do. She was fantastically inventive and ingenious about introducing a subject that diverted Allegra and so was able to steer her out of dangerous actions, thus giving her a chance to see later on whether she really wanted to do them or not. Anne was brilliant at it."

One of Bucky's few relaxations at this time was to take Allegra out in her baby carriage for long walks in Lincoln Park and down by the lakeshore. Later on, when she was about two, he would point out all the different types of yachts and tell her their names. "From the earliest time," he says, "I made up my mind never to talk to Allegra as if she were a baby. I felt that she knows more than I do; she's less spoiled, and I'm really going to honor her absolutely impeccable intellect. She always responded because she had grown up that way with me.

"I think it is interesting that when she was about fourteen at the Dalton School in New York, she came to me and asked me to explain about sex; she didn't go to her mother. I think she felt that I would be able to talk frankly about those things and her mother would not. Intuition made her do that."

When Allegra was three years old, and they were back on Bear Island, Bucky began to tell her fairy stories like the story of Goldilocks and the Three Bears, winding suitably simplified scientific information into the story so that after Goldy and the Three Bears had procured ice cream sodas and were comfortably seated in their three famous chairs with Goldy in a new portable armchair, they started talking about this or that, which would always lead to the most challenging scientific subject. But the bears and Goldy never quoted mathematics or science as such.

In *The Bear Island Story* Bucky wrote, "That was the beginning of my spontaneous-thinking—out-loud discourses that I now give publicly. I became convinced that through the expansion of the fundamental experiences of the child, it would be possible to tell her about the most complex and profound phenomena.

"I also found that the best way to study the thoughts of whatever scientist I was reading was to test myself by disclosing what I understood to the child."

There followed a six-year series of these discourses. Then one day in 1937, Allegra "realized that she no longer needed this fictitious device to initiate exploratory thought. She suddenly looked at me and said, 'Daddy, just one more Goldilocks story!' . . . we both knew that a wonderful chapter in life's book had been completed."

But much, much later, there was one more Goldilocks story, when father and daughter stood together looking at the constellations in a night sky over Penobscot Bay. Bucky pointed out the Big Bear (Ursa Major) and the Little Bear (Ursa Minor), and then brought in a third. This was Bear Island, named for the littlest bear. "Allegra was, of course, and forever will be, Goldilocks, and that night she described Spaceship Earth to the other two bears, Ursa Major and Ursa Minor." [1]

The article in the Chicago *Evening Post* in 1928 started Bucky toward local recognition. He decided to concentrate on something slightly more practical than his multistory dwelling, and began designing the 4D House, later nicknamed "The House on a Pole." It was basically a one-story version of his multiple-unit design, hexagonal in shape, hung from a strong central column, and braced by cables in tension with exterior, islanded compression struts. The mast contained the power unit and served as a distributing tube for air, light, heat, etc. The exterior of the house was made of double triangular plates of nonshatterable glass with vacuum between them (not yet invented) covered by electrically operated roll-down shutters. On top was a fifty-foot playdeck shielded by a Duralumin hood designed to stream wind over the house.

[1] *The Bear Island Story* by Buckminster Fuller (unpublished).

Rain drained down the central mast, and the masthead contained lenses for utilizing the light and heat of the sun for power.

The interior was divided into four triangular rooms—two bedrooms, a utility room, and a library—and one large 40′ × 20′ double triangle or rhomboid-shaped living room, into which the electric grill for cooking opened. All the utilities were hung in the rooms, which in turn were separate units hung from the mast, any one of which could be removed and replaced by a newer model if desired. The two bathrooms were cast metal units hung in the bedrooms. Since, like the multiple-unit dwelling, the house was intended to be transportable, it was completely self-contained. Used water was filtered and reused, solid waste was compressed into packages and sent off to be recycled or used as fertilizer. Power was derived from solar energy. The whole "living machine," a phrase of Le Corbusier, was designed to be mass-produced like an automobile. It would weigh only 6,000 pounds and sell for $1,500.

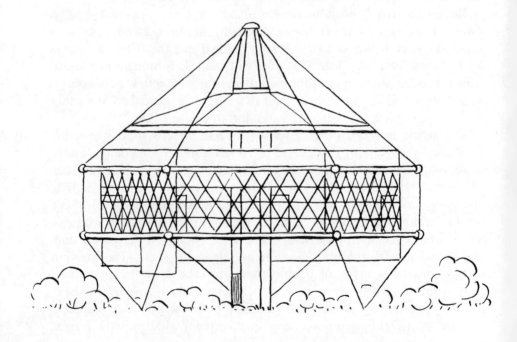

First Dymaxion House, Chicago, 1927 (taken from original 1927 patent drawings).

Bucky imagined some fine science-fiction conveniences for his house. There was a "fog gun" by which you could take a shower using only a quart of water, a washing machine that dried and pressed clothes; a dishwasher that cleaned and dried the dishes and *put them away*. He had revolving closets and shelves; all dusting and cleaning was done mechanically by centrally located compressed air and vacuum systems.

The dining-room table was hung from the ceiling. The library or "go-ahead-with-life room" was designed so children could develop self-education on a selective basis, with radio, television (not then invented), maps, globes, revolving bookshelves, drawing boards, and typewriters. Beds were filled with compressed air to any desired degree of hardness. Underneath the hanging house was space to garage a car and a jet-propelled, wingless aircraft (not invented even now!).

The publicity Bucky received from the *Evening Post* interested some financiers in his project, among them Russell Walcott. With their financial backing he formed the 4D Company with offices in a post office box and R. Buckminster Fuller as president; and secured patents on various features of his house. During the winter he had written 2,000 pages of a book which was in effect thinking out loud. In it appeared many of the far-ahead-of-his-time ideas concerning the future of man and his function in Universe. Since his main preoccupation at this time was shelter and the advantages of mass production of truly modern houses making use of the new technology, which the building industry had never done and has not done yet, he concentrated on this field.

Cut down to less than fifty pages it was presented in St. Louis to eighteen members of the American Institute of Architects, who were picked out as being broad and unselfish thinkers, with more than satisfactory results. "They praised it with astonishing remarks as to scholarly ability." [2]

This paper, entitled *4D Time Lock,* was then privately printed as a brochure. Bucky sent it to an extraordinary list of prominent people including Vincent Astor, historian Gamaliel Bradford, President Lawrence Lowell of Harvard, John T. McCutcheon of the Chicago *Tribune,* Roger Babson, Bertrand Russell, John Galsworthy, Richard Washburn Child, Bruce Barton, Dr. Max Mason, president of the University of Chicago, Henry Ford, Arthur C. Holden, and a dozen more who were in positions to influence public opinion.

[2] From *4D Chronofile* by R. Buckminster Fuller, privately printed, 1928.

In return Bucky received some extremely enthusiastic replies. Babson wrote, "It is great." [3] Child "read it with great interest," Holden wished "it could be published and published right away." [4] On the other hand he got some severe rebuffs. President Lowell, according to his secretary, was too busy to read it, and Bruce Barton wrote, "Possibly there is something in Mr. Fuller's idea, but if so, it is so well concealed in his language that I have not discovered it." [5]

Through Mr. Hewlett, Bucky generously offered his patents on the 4D House as a gift to the American Institute of Architects. The board of directors, not qualifying as "broad and unselfish thinkers," turned it down with wrinkled noses, and promptly passed a resolution that stated: "The American Institute of Architects is opposed to any kind of house designs that are manufactured like-as-peas-in-a-pod." Though Bucky had rather expected it, he was hurt as usual.

Meanwhile, financed by the 4D Company, Bucky had built a complete scale model of the 4D House with the help of some architectural students and was ready to show it to the world.

As can be imagined, Bucky had not been able to keep his Trappist vows during all these exciting developments; but he had talked as little and thought as much as circumstances permitted. His main communications had been by letter. In 1929, he really began to talk again. He has not stopped since, going at the rate of 7,000 words per hour for at least sixteen hours a day. He addressed the City Club of Chicago and then, with his model on exhibition, talked at the Chicago Home Owners Exhibition. This brought a representative of Marshall Field's Department Store around to see him.

It appeared that Marshall Field had bought a large stock of ultra-modern French furniture and wanted to put it on exhibition with Bucky's model as a crowd-attracter. Bucky was delighted.

Marshall Field's public relations manager, Waldo Warren, then came to discuss publicity with Bucky. It was a pleasant conversation up to a point, for Bucky has always loved publicity. However, Mr. Warren did not think highly of 4D as a name for the product and, in truth, it sounded more like a failing grade in school than a bright new world. "It doesn't mean anything to people," said Mr. Warren.

Bucky explained that it referred to Einstein's fourth dimension—time.

---

[3] Letter from Roger Babson to R. B. F., August 13, 1928.

[4] Arthur C. Holden to R. B. F., August 12, 1928.

[5] Bruce Barton to L. J. Stoddard, June 8, 1928.

"Who knows that?" asked Warren. "We'll have to think of something."

Bucky was very eager for the exhibition and therefore, willing, though dubious. Later in life, he would not have permitted anyone to tamper with his phraseology. Warren suggested that Bucky just talk to him about the house while he thought, which Bucky did—at 7,000 words an hour—possibly more. Then Warren went home to think it over.

The next day he returned with some ideas. "I noticed that you frequently use certain words that have great thrust and sound scientific," said Waldo Warren. "They are dynamic, maximum, and ion. I have combined them into a word that seems to me to express the essence of your imaginative thinking and has, I believe, dramatic appeal." Then he said the word—"Dymaxion."

Bucky thought it was great—he always had a flair for words even if they were not his own. Warren generously presented the word to him—later had it copyrighted in Bucky's name—and Bucky adopted it as his trademark. Wherever in the world men see that word it means to them Buckminster Fuller.

Anne had inherited another small legacy, so the Fullers had rented a better apartment at 426 Belmont Avenue and were living more comfortably. However, Bucky felt that now that he had gained a certain amount of recognition, it was time to return east. In the summer of 1929, they packed up and headed for Bear Island.

As the *J.T. Morse* passed Owl's Head Light and headed for Rockland, Bucky was on deck, breathing the strong salt air of his boyhood, so delightfully different from the flat, sour smell of Lake Michigan. When they went down to breakfast Bucky stood Allegra on the table so she could look out the window at the yachts in the harbor. In high delight the little girl shouted in her clear treble voice, "Oh, my God, Daddy, there's a ketch! Oh, my God, Daddy, that's a sloop! Oh, my God, Daddy, there's a *schooner!*"

She was perfectly right about the different rigs, but embarrassed Bucky decided that his conversations with Allegra had been a bit too adult.

Bear Island was just as it had always been, the Big House filled with family and their offspring, the Eating House manned by a sturdy local cook; the family sailboats and the *Wego* anchored in the harbor. The only changes were that the trees had grown up around the Big House sheltering it in a pleasant grove; and Jim Hardie had taken over as Captain of the Island and lived in the Boy's House, which had been done over for his convenience.

Hardie, who was about Bucky's age, had grown up with him on Bear Island. As boys they had competed for Mrs. Fuller's attention and praise. Jim had helped Bucky build Birch Lodge; also the road across the swamp from the harbor to the Big House, which required tons of rocks hauled by oxen; and the clay tennis court where the Larned brothers had practiced their championship tennis and often played doubles with Bucky and Wolcott. Later, with the kindest intentions in the world, Jim ruined the court by putting in a concrete surface, which he thought would be superior to clay.

Jim was married now to a big, buxom Maine girl and was raising a family. His son, Pearl, was almost the same age Bucky had been when he first came to the island.

Woolly, too, was married—to Persis Sears Wellington, who would never come to Bear Island. She either was, or pretended to be, deathly afraid of crossing the bay, but there is reason to believe that she just did not like the primitive conditions and communal family life. But Woolly loved the island so much that he bought a house at Sunset on Little Deer Island, which was connected by a causeway to the mainland. Leaving Persis there, he would come over to Bear Island in his boat, the *Giddy Gaddy,* and his children learned to love it as much as he did.

The year 1929 was the summer of the *Lady Anne.* She was an old-timer originally called the *Loreena,* which had been used as a cargo boat and tug among the islands of Penobscot Bay. Bucky bought this antique for a small sum of money, but considering the condition of his finances she may well have been the inspiration for Roger Hewlett's much-quoted line, "Bucky's found a sixpence and he's off to buy a yacht."

After two years of intensive thinking in Chicago, Bucky instinctively knew that he needed the relaxation of hard manual labor—and some fun. The *Lady Anne* was the answer. Roger Hewlett, ready to matriculate at Harvard in the fall, was staying on Bear Island, and together they set to work to make the *Lady Anne* into a spruce yacht worthy of her new name. She needed new masts, so they felled two tall straight trees on the island, debarked and delimbed them; smoothed them with planes and sandpaper; varnished them, stepped them in the hull, and rigged lugsails on booms made from smaller trees.

She needed paint and fittings of all sorts. Somehow they scrounged the money to buy these things—seventy-five cents here, two dollars there. Her decks were a shambles, but that could be fixed with elbow grease—gallons of elbow grease.

Most of all she needed a new engine. Originally steam-driven, she had a tall, thin, pipelike smokestack, which served no purpose since at some point an ancient gasoline engine had replaced steam. But this was coughing its lungs out in its final stages.

Now it so happened that at Lamb's Shipyard at Camden, Maine, where Bucky and Roger bought most of their marine supplies, there was a magnificent Lathrop engine, just standing in the boathouse. Roger said: "Every time we went to the shipyard, which was owned by Mr. Lamb—his first name was Charles, believe it or not—Bucky would say, 'Gee, wouldn't it be marvelous if we could set it right in.' I'd say, 'Yeah, it would be marvelous.'"

"The *Lady Anne*'s old rheumatic engine didn't fit Bucky's idea of what his sleek yacht should have. And there was that long, lean, powerful, sixteen-cylinder Lathrop that would drive his old barge along like Vincent Astor's *Nourmahal*. I'd say it was at the back of Bucky's mind to beat Astor at his own game.

"Well, one day I was alone on the *Lady Anne* at Camden, just scrubbing decks and polishing brass, when a battalion of workmen came down from Mr. Lamb's shop and said, 'We have to put this new engine in.' When Bucky came bouncing down I said, 'What's happening?'

"Bucky said, 'It's all set. It's all set.' He was smiling."

It was a long time before Roger figured out what the deal was. It seems that Bucky persuaded Mr. Lamb to have the engine installed in the *Lady Anne* in return for which Bucky gave him a half interest in the boat and Lamb still owned the engine. Only instead of having the engine sit in the shop doing nothing, it would be in *Lady Anne,* which would make her a more salable property. Roger said: "Bucky pointed out to Mr. Lamb that his engine would be doing some good in the whole wide world; and Mr. Lamb would be the richer for it, since he would still own it and a half share in the *Lady Anne* as well. A real con job! And Bucky was a master at that. He could convince a silkworm that nylon was better.

"Well, after a full half day's work by a crew of expert mechanics, there were Bucky and I, with this sleek purring monster in the engine room, sailing out of Camden harbor waving to a bewildered Mr. Lamb."

Roger has never been sure of what eventually happened. He thinks that perhaps Mr. Lamb got thinking it over in the quiet of a Maine winter and eventually sent Mrs. Fuller a bill for the engine. In any event, for three summers Bucky had much pleasure in the *Lady Anne,* a wonderful old craft, 45 feet long and broad of beam that looked a little like a North Sea trawler with her tall smokestack still in place, and her lateen-shaped lugsails filled by the nor'east wind steadying her as she dashed along propelled by sixteen splendid cylinders.

The auxiliary lugger Lady Anne *lying at Wiscasset, Maine.*

In September the Fullers left Bear Island. Anne and Allegra went to live in a very nice little house on the East Rockaway Road in Hewlett, Long Island, and Bucky to begin a vagabond life in Greenwich Village and traveling around the country with his model of the 4D Dymaxion House, which he carried disassembled in a huge suitcase.

He was getting a good deal of recognition. Mr. Hewlett arranged a one-man show for him at the Architectural League of New York. Antonio Salaemi had him lecture at his studio in the Village, where he also allowed Bucky to park his model house. Bucky gave a one-man show at the Princeton University School of Architecture and a series of lectures at Romany Marie's tavern in Greenwich Village. The following year, 1930, he gave fifteen lecture-shows at such places as the Wadsworth atheneum in Hartford, Connecticut, the Fortnightly Club in Chicago, Carnegie Institute of Technology, Yale University Architectural School, the Columbia University Club, the Chicago Arts Club, etc. People everywhere were fascinated by "The House on a Pole," while intellectuals were excited by the brilliant originality of Bucky's emerging philosophy of utilizing the new technology to improve the environmental condition of the human race. He called it "New Form versus Reform." His audiences did not believe it was possible, but they were swept along on that torrent of thought.

When he was not on the road Bucky lived mostly in Greenwich Village, spending weekends with Anne and Allegra on Long Island. It was during his lectures at Romany Marie's that he met the Japanese sculptor, Isamu Noguchi, soon to be world famous, who became his close friend and constant companion. Noguchi asked Bucky to pose for a bust. Cast in brilliantly polished chrome nickel steel, it is regarded as one of his masterworks.

Neither he nor Bucky had any money. Bucky says: "All the money I had went into being sure Allegra and Anne were safe at home. I really lived very much on a pauper basis. My mother would ask me to come to her apartment and hope that I would have dinner with her from time to time, but I did not. I was trying to be very, very independent, much like the kids today. And to parry the challenges I had to my design revolution."

Fortunately, other people helped to keep Bucky and Noguchi from starving, tactfully so it did not injure their pride. There was K Halle, a big, blond beautiful young career woman from Cleveland whose family owned a department store. K—just K she was called—had an apartment on the third floor of the Elysee Hotel with a big terrace off it. She was interested in artists and was one of the first connoisseurs to recognize Noguchi's genius. She was fascinated by Bucky's mind. She worried about them both.

"Sometimes when I had a rich beau coming for dinner," she says,

Bucky lecturing.

"I would ask Bucky and Isamu to drop in beforehand. Then, when my beau came, I would take him aside and say, 'I've done the most awful thing. I forgot I promised to have dinner with these young fellows. They are very poor so we'll have to eat at some dreadful place, but I can't turn them down.'

"Usually the beau would say, 'Let's all have dinner together on me.' We would go to a swell restaurant and they would get a good feed."

It was K who ingeniously gave Noguchi his big break. He had sculpted a delicately beautiful little deer which she greatly admired. "Leave it with me; I'll try to sell it for you," she said.

A few days later George Gershwin dropped in to see her and was transfixed by the deer. He asked who did it and she told him. "I've got to have it," Gershwin said.

"You can't afford it, George," K said. "It's fabulous and Isamu knows it."

"I *will* have it," Gershwin said. "Call him and ask him how much."

K privately called Noguchi and told him what had happened. "Ask an awful lot for it," she said. "No, more than that. Still more!"

Of course, Gershwin bought the deer and made a big thing of it when people came to his home. Later, when the Museum of Modern Art wanted a bust of Gershwin, the composer chose Noguchi to execute the commission. Noguchi sculpted a magnificent head in black marble and became famous almost overnight. He said to K Halle, "You saved me from joining the Communist party. Now that I have money I don't have to."

Bucky's main source of food became Romany Marie. The year 1929 was the year of the Wall Street crash and the beginning of the Great Depression, which, of course, only confirmed Bucky's low opinion of the captains of industry. "Everything was in a mess," he says.

Just at that point Romany Marie was forced to move from her place on Washington Square South to Eighth Street, just west of the old Whitney Museum. Marie asked Bucky to decorate her new restaurant. He was eager to try out his ideas on modern interior decoration, and accepted. He lighted the place with huge aluminum cones with very powerful bulbs in them so that it was illuminated by bright indirect light, which brought out the strong colors of the decor. In addition, Bucky designed and *made himself,* all the tables, chairs, and other furnishings. The result was striking.

Romany Marie said to Bucky: "I can't afford to pay you anything, or at least not what you're worth, but as long as I am alive and in the restaurant business I will give you a meal every day. You can always count on a free meal."

Bucky says: "I did not take full advantage of that; I did not want to bust her. But I used to go for a meal *every other* day, and that's all I was eating in those days."

But even when he did not eat there Bucky often went to Romany Marie's. She wanted him there as a "table sitter," to dress up the place and enliven it with his coruscation of ideas. He drank nothing but coffee or tea, so it cost her very little.

Romany Marie's was, in fact, a marvelous meeting ground for the intelligentsia—artistic, literary, theatrical, and politically radical. Celebrated European painters came there when they were in America; the aging artists who had startled the world by their "modern" paintings at the first Armory Show and after that the Ashcan school artists, and the young men who were the wave-of-the-future, nonobjective painters, and the equivalent people in architecture, and the rising generation of writers. "It was really a great Bohemian headquarters," says Bucky. "There has never been a large public meeting place of the artist-pioneer-explorer types since that time, to my knowledge, in America."

In that strange twilight era of the early thirties when the whole economic system of the United States seemed to be breaking up and the Revolution, unlike prosperity, seemed to be just around the corner, the talk was extremely radical at Romany Marie's. The Communist John Reed Club was just a few blocks up Sixth Avenue, and many of its members were habitués. To the strong intellectual thinkers—the self-thinkers—and to many others as they passed the seedy apple sellers on the corners and the shambling lines of beat-down men before the soup kitchens, communism seemed the only answer to the breakdown of the free enterprise system. Many of them joined the Communist party.

Radical though his thinking was, antiestablishment though his emotions, Bucky was never tempted to join the party. His originality of thought could not tolerate the regimentation it demanded of its members. "What I immediately observed," he said, "was that when any of my friends who had been very good conversationalists, good thinkers, artists, joined up they stopped doing their own thinking. They had only the party line and it absolutely killed their initiative in thinking.

"I had very powerful arguments for my proposal for a design revolution in relation to a political revolution, and I was backed by many very bright people. They did not yet see how it could happen, but they respected me and liked me. And the kind of arguing I had with these friends helped me tremendously to know all the questions I was going to have to face up to."

CHAPTER X

THE GURU OF
ROMANY MARIE'S

IN 1930, Bucky lived in the most original housing he ever occupied, at least until he invented and lived in a geodesic dome. He had been "sleeping on people's floors, in artists' studios, in Noguchi's place or Tony Salaemi's; anywhere he could throw down a mattress and curl up. Then one day he went to look at the new Lehigh-Starrett Warehouse Building on 26th Street.

Until that time warehouses in New York were even more backward than the rest of the construction industry. For the most part they were old brick lofts, often located on the narrow streets of old New York, which made transporting goods to or from them in the ever-larger motor trucks a traffic horror. Their elevators were inadequate, their space badly cut up. They were as inconvenient as possible.

The Lehigh Building was the first really modern warehouse in Manhattan. Located on West 26th Street over the Lehigh Railroad freight yards, it occupied two whole city blocks and was twenty stories high. The elevators were designed to take the largest trucks then used so that people who rented space in it could have cargoes delivered directly to their floor without being manhandled in and out of elevators. Finished just at the time of the crash, it was still largely unrented.

Bucky explored it with approval he seldom gave to any conventional structure; it was a step in the right direction. When he reached the roof he found in that vast expanse only the fat water tanks and the housing for the enormous elevator machinery with a storeroom alongside. Looking at the superb view of lower Manhattan and New York Harbor to the south; the Hudson on the west with great liners snugged down in their piers, and all New Jersey beyond; and to the east the midtown towers with the still-unfinished skeleton of the Empire State Building rising above them, he decided that he wanted to live right there.

In a burst of real supersalesmanship, he talked the rental agent into having a window cut in the storeroom and renting it to him for thirty dollars a month. In a few days he moved in.

Certainly it had its inconveniences. Bucky says, "There was a lot of noise from the elevator motors grinding away right next to me. The elevators stopped running at five o'clock, which meant that I had to walk up twenty-one stories, sometimes carrying my big suitcase with the house model. But it was a fantastic place. I had the whole roof: a concrete lawn the size of two football fields, and that superb view."

The people from Romany Marie's liked to go there—what was a twenty-story walk to reach such remarkable scenery! Bucky recalls the night Diego Rivera came: "He was quite large and corpulent, so we had to stop at every floor to rest. Each floor we came to was a forest of steel columns extending two city blocks, completely deserted at night."

Bucky gave some marvelous parties there. Many of the guests, including Noguchi, climbed the vertical steel ladders up the forty-foot water tanks to get a better view. Once they brought over some African drummers who were performing at the Natural History Museum. The uproar was magnificent. But as Bucky says, "When you got up to my roof you could run shrieking through New York without anyone hearing you."

Bucky still loved parties of all sorts, the wilder the better. Some of his favorites were the artists' and models' balls given by the Kit Kat Club, which he often helped to organize. His compulsion to be always going full ahead prevented him from relaxing for more than an hour or two at a time. Sometimes at twelve or one o'clock of a Saturday night at the Hewletts' in Lawrence, he would suddenly say, "Let's go into town and round up some girls for the Kit Kat dance." They were just as restless as he was, and they would all tear into New York to spend the rest of the night roaring around Greenwich Village.

One Kit Kat dance he did not get to was when he took one of his quick naps beforehand and Woolly tiptoed in, stole his clothes, and went instead.

The Beaux Arts Balls were a favorite romp of Bucky's. They were run by the established artists he knew and were attended by all his Bohemian friends as well as the rich society people who liked to mingle in that world once a year. They were fancy dress with an announced theme such as the Court of Louis XIV or a Night at an Indian Maharaja's Palace. The Bohemians contrived their own costumes, but the grand prize was usually won by a social leader like Mrs. S. Stanwood Menken, who once paid $30,000 to be dressed up as the Sacred White Peacock.

The Depression Beaux Arts Ball in January, 1931, was different. No one felt like encouraging wild extravagances so the theme of the ball was the World of the Future; red and silver were the colors. You were supposed to use your imagination. This was Bucky's dish. He was determined to win.

He selected Mrs. Evelyn Baird, who later married Vilhjalmur Stefansson, to go with him and designed her costume—Anne was much too ladylike for the clothes of the future as Bucky conceived them. Mrs. Baird was a dashing blonde. Bucky dressed her as a twenty-first-century Amazon, with great silver breastplates over her luxuriant bosom; a Martian's helmet with antennae on her pale golden curls; Mercury's winged sandals bound with silver lacings up her slender legs, and a very short silver skirt made like a Roman soldier's armor. The rest was her own lovely snow-and-roses skin.

As always for the Beaux Arts, the ballroom of the Astor was jammed to its capacity with a heterogeneous crowd imaginatively dressed in everything from all-enveloping raccoon togas to practically nothing. A jury of twelve famous artists each selected the girl whose costume he liked best. Then the chosen twelve paraded on the stage for demos— the audience—to judge.

Here, once more, the author descends from Olympus. I had imported a young lady from Philadelphia, who had made her own costume, which was a long princess-cut gown of American beauty velvet with a high cone-shaped medieval hat. What it had to do with the future I do not know. In fact, so little did we think of her chances of winning anything that we did nothing about it until John Held, Jr., suddenly chose my girl to be his finalist—he was tired of his own kilted flappers.

The twelve chosen beauties lined up on the stage to a grand flourish from the band. Then dead silence fell as the master of ceremonies announced their names and the rules. He then stood in back of the line and held a wand over each girl's head in turn, while the audience signified their sentiments by applause.

It was a pretty even thing until the wand was held over Bucky's girl. That produced a major ovation, with Bucky's Bohemian friends leading the cheers. However, when he reached my girl the sound was even louder—I hoped.

The other girls were sent off and Bucky's girl and mine stood alone on the stage. As the wand waved over the Amazon there was a goodly response; as it came to my medieval lady, the sound was like a typhoon. There was not a shadow of a doubt who had won.

Thinking back on it, the verdict was unfair. Unquestionably, Bucky's costume was far more imaginative and much more in the spirit of the World of the Future than that of the winner. What had happened was that Bucky, as usual, was too far ahead of his time. Demos were wary and frightened of the strange new world that confronted them with specters of revolution and the crumbling of tradition. They opted for old-fashioned beauty and elegance.

Unfair or not, it was the only time I ever came out ahead of Bucky.

Bucky and Anne and Allegra survived financially during this period on his meager earnings from lecture fees and one good temporary job. Articles had been appearing in national magazines about the Dymaxion House, some good, some crazy, like those that said it revolved to face the sun like a sunflower, which it did not. There was one in *House Beautiful* and one in the Chicago *Tribune* by the art critic, Inez Cunningham, who wrote a very sensitive piece about Bucky's philosophy and what he was trying to do, in which she said: "Here is Buckminster Fuller, a young man with an idea so sane it seems insane to most of us . . . the problem he elected to attack is not . . . merely an architectural problem, not an economic problem, not even an esthetic one. It becomes all these things incidentally, but first of all it is a feminine problem . . . while women are hardened by drudgery and children endangered by accident in the places called home. . . .

"Mr. Fuller had a dream of freeing women and children from the housing problem but . . . the dream had to filter through the mind and so become a philosophy . . . Fuller felt that we had come to that state in our progress where mind must use matter instead of matter controlling mind . . . the problem was cosmic. . . ."

Later, *Fortune* had a series of five articles about housing in the United States, and devoted one entire piece to the Dymaxion House as the ultimate answer to the problem of cheap, modern housing. It was very beautifully written by Archibald MacLeish, the poet who became Librarian of Congress.

Officials of the American Radiator–Standard Sanitary Manufacturing Company had read some of the articles and noted that the bathrooms in the Dymaxion House were supposed to be mass-produced and cast all in one piece. In 1930, they hired Bucky to design such a bathroom. He spent six months off and on in Buffalo doing so. Technically it was highly successful; practically it was a failure. The Plumber's Union got wind of it. Horrified at the idea of a bathroom that could be hooked up to the mains by four simple connections instead of all the lovely make-work of intricate separate connections for bathtubs, sinks, toilets and, hopefully, bidets, they blasted it in their trade paper. This so terrified Standard Sanitary that they hid Bucky's bathroom in the sub-cellar of a warehouse and never mentioned it again.

This was a disappointment, but a worse blow followed. The head of the research department had come to Bucky's apartment and admired it enviously. One month, in 1931, Bucky forgot to pay the rent while he was away on a trip. The research man offered the rental agent a big raise in rent, so when Bucky returned he found himself out on the street again. "That was the end of my having a place that I lived in regularly," says Bucky.

At this time, as business sank to new lows, the hotels in New York had hundreds of empty rooms. As a way of attracting people they would ask Bucky to show his model house in a hotel and give him a parlor in which to exhibit it. He was not supposed to sleep there, but he did. The parlor would not have any bed linen or towels, but he and Noguchi would suborn the night clerk, buy paper towels, and sleep on air mattresses under the model.

Late in 1930, Bucky went into the publishing business. George Howe of Howe in the Skies, Architects, who was one of the few members of that profession whom Bucky admired, was financing the publication of an architectural magazine called *T Square,* sponsored by the Philadelphia Sketch Club. It was a very advanced, sophisticated little paper run by two young Philadelphians named Levenson who did the publishing, wrote many of the articles, and did all the legwork.

In 1930, Charles Scribner's Sons, who owned the copyrighted name of another *T Square,* a reprint magazine for their important publication *Architecture,* called upon them to cease and desist using the name. Howe decided he would no longer back it. The Levensons came to Bucky to see if he could help them. In a flash flood of optimism and a surge of idealism he decided to take it on himself as a medium for publicizing his ideas and nudging the architectural world into the twentieth century.

To raise the necessary capital Bucky cashed in all his insurance policies, including his navy life insurance, which had somehow survived his financial crises. He changed the name of the magazine to *Shelter* and prepared to make it over in his own image.

The first thing he did seemed completely insane—he cancelled all the advertising. When he notified the advertisers of this, in the midst of the depression, they were dumfounded. Typical of Bucky is his explanation for the apparently suicidal move: "I felt compromised because your advertising contracts required that you come out on a certain fixed date and I said, 'Anybody publishing on a deadline is obviously being forced; he is doing it to make money, and he is not coming out only when he needs to. I put my magazine on a spontaneous basis. It would come out when we had something to say, and when we were ready to say it and say it right.

"And I said, 'The magazine is going to pay for itself.' So I charged two dollars a copy, and the subscription rate was for so many copies in whatever amount of time it would take for me to publish them."

The extraordinary thing was that Bucky succeeded with his very unorthodox, *laissez-aller* system of publishing. By November, 1932, *Shelter* had an average circulation of 2,500 copies, which at two dollars each represented a very comfortable gross return. It equalled the circulation of the well-established *Architectural Forum.*

As Bucky intended, it was paying its way, "though it did not pay me anything for editing it, and I edited all of it." In fact, it was a drain on his minuscule resources, because, aside from the time and energy he put into it, publishing and printing the book in Philadelphia required him to make numerous trips there.

The reason it succeeded was that it was very skillfully edited, and represented very advanced thinking in the architectural field. With his enthusiastic persuasiveness Bucky induced very good people to write articles for it—paying them peanuts, naturally. In addition, he discovered brilliant young men who were eager to have a forum for their ideas. In his very first issue the "guest editor" was a young architect named Philip Johnson.

Each issue was built around a particular theme and, true to Bucky's principles, was not published until he felt that it was a complete entity, expressing the best and latest thinking on that particular subject. Often the theme was beyond the mentation of its time. For example, his second really big issue was on environmental controls, with pictures of black smoke pouring out of the factory chimneys of New York to show the pollution going on. Its emphasis was on ecology! This was in 1931, when even most intellectuals had never heard of the word.

Bucky did not use his own name or even his Dymaxion trademark on the publication. "I called myself 4D," he says, "because I had learned that the jealousies of designers and artists, particularly artists, are just terrific; and they don't like to concede that the other guy is right. I decided I was not going to buck that; I just would not take a position."

During all this time Bucky continued to roost at Romany Marie's. "I did all my editorial thinking sitting at tables there. It was such an extraordinary place, testing me, educating me." He was becoming more and more a fugleman of that unique establishment.

True to her gypsy forebears, Romany Marie had a strong streak of mysticism, and mystics gathered around her. Chief among them was Gorchiev, the Russian guru of a strange cult that mixed oriental theologies with Western philosophy and some of his own ideas in a brew that appealed strongly to many people in search of a faith in a world in flux. Bucky had many conversations with Gorchiev, who added to his enlightenment without converting him or diverting his basic train of thought—an impossibility.

To his embarrassment, Bucky himself was becoming a bit of a guru to many of the truth-seekers there. His mechanistic-metaphysical universe with its Supreme Intelligence, his modern transcendentalism, drew them powerfully.

"I found myself being followed by an increasing number of human beings, particularly women, who were beginning to make me into some kind of messiah," he says. "I became a cult, and that was exactly what I did not want to be. In other words, I did not want to get into social movements or special ideologies. I had become so absolutely powerful in guarding my personal disciplines—the organic me—that I could control my behavior under almost any circumstances, so what I now did was deliberate.

"I shall never forget my New Year's resolution of January 1, 1933. I decided to shake off the cult, and the only way I could do it was to be very unpleasant to my "disciples." I premeditatedly began to drink, and having known the patterns of the brothel, I made myself extremely offensive, doing things that I ordinarily would never do, drunk or sober. As a result they soon began to avoid me.

"Between 1933 and 1941 I drank deliberately; I drank copiously. Then I saw that it was harmful to my design revolution, so I stopped immediately. Forever!"

Prior to that, in September, 1932, Bucky came to another decision that completely changed the pattern of his life. It became evident to him that Franklin Roosevelt was going to be elected President of the United States and with him a great liberal majority in Congress. Bucky believed, rightly, that the New Deal would mean an entirely new world in which the liberals would get a great chance to put their ideals in concrete form—"to get things done." So he decided "to stop kibitzing around," and get into the mainstream of action.

The first thing he did was to wind up *Shelter* magazine. He informed all his subscribers that he was going to dump everything he had into one great final issue and close up the magazine.

Once again he dumfounded everyone, because his magazine was on the point of becoming really successful. But Bucky said, "I am not doing things to make money. The success lies in what already has been done; and I've gotten credit for the new ideas I have put forward. That is enough."

This is Bucky's late, ex post facto explanation of his action, but it is only partly true. There were other motivations. His restless mind, teeming with ideas, seeking ever-new experiences and knowledge for its grist, never could be satisfied with a routine, however stimulating and creative. In addition, *Shelter* was about to begin making money, and Bucky at this stage had a moral repugnance for any enterprise of his that did. It was almost as though he felt it might corrupt him in spite of himself, as though it were, in the Orthodox Jewish phrase, *tref*—unclean.

He escaped that easily. *Shelter* closed with no outstanding debts, but all the money Bucky had put into it—the equity of all his insurance policies which was his only capital—had disappeared.

Bucky had one other reason for moving on. In numerous engineering sketches drawn on odd scraps of paper, on tablecloths, later on carefully prepared scale drawings in *Shelter,* and finally on the drawing board of his brain, a new form was taking shape that he fervently believed would move the design science revolution a significant step forward.

CHAPTER XI

THE DYMAXION CAR

As early as 1917, when he was at Hampton Roads, Bucky had begun to think about an aerial vehicle driven and maintained in flight by jet propulsion; he had never forgotten those white jellyfish in Penobscot Bay, which moved so smoothly and effortlessly through the water. Many evenings were spent with Pat Bellinger discussing the idea. Bellinger's venturesome mind, far from rejecting it, had encouraged it. There was no question that it would be far more efficient than propellers, which wasted a large percentage of power through slippage. No one had even thought of a jet engine at that point. Bucky's engine was to be fueled by liquid oxygen which when heated would expand with enormous thrust.

Then, in 1929, after Bucky had designed the Dymaxion house, he realized that, if its owners were to be able to live the self-contained existence in uninhabited regions which he envisioned, they would need an equally unique form of transport. So he developed his idea of the omnimedium jet-propelled streamlined transport with inflatable-collapsible wings to permit it to travel by road, sea, or air. Explaining it to two-year-old Allegra he called it a "zoommobile." He placed a porpoise-shaped object in the parking space under the model of the Dymaxion house to represent it.

In 1932 Bucky's mind returned to the zoommobile. Since alloys that could withstand the intense heat of expanding gases in a jet motor had not yet been developed, Bucky decided to experiment with a land vehicle powered by a conventional motor.

Because the greatest stresses to which any aircraft is subjected occur when it makes contact with ground, his experimental model would enable him to make preliminary investigations of its ground taxiing capabilities such as its behavior in crosswinds, its stability, the effectiveness of its streamlining, and such. He made engineering drawings of this vehicle, and published them in the final issue of *Shelter* into which he "dumped everything."

Philip Pearson of Philadelphia apparently read that copy of *Shelter* and was fascinated by the idea. Pearson has been described as "a very interesting, very square sort of guy who made his living sitting in a boardroom buying and selling stocks; and every day coming home a little bit richer." Unlike most of his fellow plungers, he had judged the stock market correctly and made a fortune selling short. Sensing the precarious situation of the banks in late 1932, he converted a large sum of money into cash and stashed it in various safe-deposit boxes. There it sat, safe but neither earning interest nor growing.

In January, 1933, Pearson and his tweedy wife, Temple Pearson, who was a niece of Isadora Duncan, came to Bucky to discuss financing the building of a prototype Dymaxion car.

Like everyone else on whom Bucky turns the full force of his intellect and enthusiasm, Pearson was completely enthralled. An especially telling point Bucky made concerned the wind resistance of the conventional automobile of the era. At thirty miles an hour wind resistance made little difference, but since this effect increased at the rate of the second power progression, at sixty miles an hour the resistance to the square-shaped automobile body then in vogue was four times as great as at thirty, and continued to multiply by the square of each unit of increase in speed. As a result, at speeds over sixty, the engine was using most of its power simply to overcome the tremendous resistance and drag created by its horse-and-buggy contours. Bucky believed that his streamlining of the Dymaxion car would greatly decrease this effect with huge savings in energy and fuel—more with less.

Pearson was completely convinced by Bucky's brilliant exposition of the advantages of the Dymaxion design. He immediately offered to finance the building of a prototype. However, Bucky remembered his painful experiences with the stockholders of Stockade and he was even then having trouble with the people who had helped to finance the Dymaxion house, who, despite all the publicity, had received no return on their money. He explained to Pearson that he must be completely free to work out his own ideas. "I won't take your money," he said, "unless there is a clause in the contract stating that if I want to spend it all buying ice cream sodas, that will be that, and there will be no questions asked."

Pearson, that hard-headed businessman, was so bedazzled by Bucky that he even agreed to this strange proposition. Perhaps he thought: "This is just an inventor's eccentricity. He doesn't really mean it, or if he does I will find a way to exert the power of money."

The seeds of later trouble lay in their different conceptions of the purpose of the prototype. Pearson thought of it as a new type of automobile, which might make him a fortune. Bucky envisioned it as the tadpole from which his omnimedium, jet-propelled 4D transport would develop.

Immediately the deal was concluded, Pearson gave Bucky the entire amount he figured he needed *in cash*. Bucky promptly formed the Dymaxion Corporation with R. Buckminster Fuller as director and chief engineer, and set out to find a place to build the prototype. In the very nadir of industrial activity that was not difficult. For a modest amount he was able to rent the big Dynometer Building of the Locomobile Company (which had recently expired), in Bridgeport, Connecticut. For his consulting engineer he persuaded Starling Burgess to join him at a comparatively small salary—"though it was pretty big for those days," Bucky says. "He took the job because he had nothing to do at that time, and found it very exciting."

Burgess bore a famous name as an aeronautical engineer and naval architect. He was an authentic genius. At the time of World War I he had designed the Burgess-Dunn airplane, which, though not used in the war, had many unusual features including the delta wing. Like Bucky, he was ahead of his time, for the delta wing did not come into its own until supersonic speeds made it necessary. Burgess's genius was finally recognized by the presentation of the Collier Trophy, the most prestigious award in aviation.

In 1933, he was far better known for his superb sailing yachts. He designed the *Rainbow,* which defended the America's Cup in 1930, and later designed the cup defenders *Enterprise* and *Ranger.* The latter was the last of the huge J boats to defend the cup, and without question was the fastest sloop ever built. He also designed the beautiful schooner yacht *Iralita,* and the popular Atlantic class yachts. He also conceived the layout of the twelve-, ten-, and eight-meter yachts.

The relationship that developed between these two geniuses of the Dymaxion Company was exceedingly strange. They were so much alike and so unalike. Burgess, a slight, wiry man with an unfashionably long, wax-tipped moustache, knew every millionaire yachtsman on the East

Coast. He understood and profited by that deluxe racket where the ship-yards were in league with the captains of the great yachts for kickbacks. It was assumed that anyone who could afford a yacht was fair game, but the owners themselves were tough characters, who knew they were being cheated, but took their revenge in arrogance. Burgess was out to make money. But, as Bucky says: "He was such a capable designer; he had an extraordinary relationship with the yachtsmen. He loved to tell fantastic stories about them, people like the Du Ponts and Vander-bilts and Astors, a few of which may have been true."

Burgess loved high society and extravagant parties. He was as ec-centric as Bucky but without his depth and inner stability. He was married five times, perhaps because he never found his Anne.

Cynical though he was, Burgess had a vision of the future. He and Bucky had great empathy, tempered by a powerful mutual distrust. Bucky learned a great deal from Starling Burgess.

However, the principles of the omnimedium transport, Bucky says, were entirely his own. At first Burgess told Bucky that his idea for a jet engine powerful enough to fly an aircraft without wings could not pos-sibly work. He said, "It might work for a little over water, but you're going to want to go over land, and it won't work over land." Later he changed his mind.

But Burgess did contribute a great deal to the technical engineering of the Dymaxion car. Bucky says: "I had a great deal of experience be-fore meeting Starling in building prototypes, getting things going, but I had not tackled anything on quite such a high level, or going out on the highway with something dynamic that meant taking people's lives in our hands. I had to be very sure it was safe. So I found Starling's expe-rience to be very, very important.

"Philosophically we talked a great deal about the intuitive dynamic sense. Starling was one of the first in the engineering world, I think he *was* the first, to go along with me on the terribly important part intui-tion plays in design. Everything in me, my subconscious experience, said that if you got a revelation of that sort you just grabbed it. The intuitive dynamic sense has to do with things like pole vaulting or the way a man throws a baseball. When you design something you co-ordinate instinctively as an athlete does. You get a personal feeling as to how, if it's a boat, it will behave in the water."

Starling agreed with Bucky about this. He told about John Hereshof, the blind brother of Nathaniel Hereshof, the great yacht designer. John

Hereshof went around a hull with his fingers, feeling it all the time, and he would move his own hand through the water and thereby get an absolute sense of how this hull was going to move through the water. In this way John was able to design half-models and testing models which, when proved in the tank, were within 5 percent of perfect.

Burgess was also better trained as a mathematician, at that time, than Bucky; he was very good at calculus. "He would figure exactly what we would have to have in the way of forging this part or the tensile strength of that piece so that these things were not going to fail. And he would give me alternatives," Bucky said. "We went through a great many testing models, tracking models, testing behaviors of all sorts, wind drag, crosswind effect, stability on turns, braking, and so forth, before we built the first full-sized prototype. Sometimes he would propose things I thought were extravagant, but he could persuade me they were not.

"In other words Starling understood what I was trying to do with my principles, and always just by his disciplines, he carried them on. That was exactly the way I wanted it."

Bucky actually started building the Dymaxion car on Saturday, March 4, 1933, the day the United States went broke. That morning President Franklin D. Roosevelt ordered all the banks in the country closed and a moratorium on the payment of all obligations. Had he not, the banks would have been forced to close anyhow because of the money panic sweeping the country.

Bucky says: "Nobody in the country had any money, and I, having gone from the poorest guy in the world, had all this cash given me to do anything I liked with—the ice cream soda deal. And I could have anything I wanted."

What Bucky wanted was the best mechanics in the world and he got them. Rolls-Royce had started an American factory in Hartford, which they had just closed down because of the depression. They had sent over their best mechanics to man it, and these men were out of a job. Bucky's advertisement for skilled mechanics produced over a thousand applicants for twenty-seven jobs. He tried to select those most in need. If two applicants were equally good, he chose the one with a wife and children to support. Later he decided this had been a mistake. The heads of his body shop were two men Rolls-Royce had sent over to make certain the American bodies were up to their high standards. Bucky also was able to purchase secondhand machinery at bottom prices.

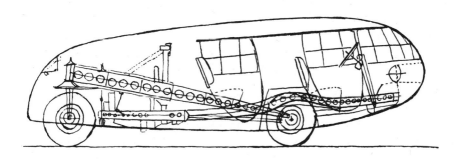

Buckminster Fuller scale drawing of first Dymaxion car, 1933.

The car was built in a secret room they made in the factory, boarded off and guarded. One of the things Burgess taught Bucky, which became a guiding principle with him, was, in Burgess's words: "Never show people botch work. Don't ever demonstrate a principle in inadequate materials. If you get up an old beer can that has your principle embodied in it but is hammered out of tin, people will call it a jalopy."

Burgess was so insistent on this principle that every day as a piece of work was completed it was polished or painted so that it would look like the finished product, and the room was kept as immaculate as a showroom of General Motors. Bucky says: "Those Rolls-Royce bodymakers were wonderful. I don't think anybody ever turned out more elegant work.

"In this way Starling made people really respect his work, the people who were building it, and the owners and everyone who was allowed to see it. This procedure in the plant was very expensive, but it made it so exciting for everybody that they felt everything must be done in the best way man knew how to do it. You were working in the championship beat and on the championship device. Starling said, 'If you don't do it right, you have no right to do it at all.' "

Not everything went as smoothly between the geniuses as this may sound. There were many flare-ups of temperament and clashes of ego. One thing that irritated Bucky was that on the sign in front of the plant Starling had his name painted beside Bucky's in equally large letters as though they were equal partners. "He was really my employee," Bucky says. "It shows his very great ego, but I did not make an issue of it."

To some extent this statement shows Bucky's sensitive ego. Though in future years his name will be remembered when Burgess's is a small-type footnote, at that time Burgess was far better known than he.

Rapidly the Dymaxion car took shape. As it finally emerged it was, indeed, a notable advance in automotive engineering. Mounted on triangular chrome-molybdenum frames hinged to each other, the aluminum, teardrop body was aerodynamically sound even to its fish-form belly which enclosed all the running gear, usually exposed, except the lower half of the three wheels. By this means mudguards were eliminated and the entire road width of the body was useful space. It had front-wheel drive with a single wheel in back by which it steered. There were "air nostrils" in front by which the car was air-cooled by the current of air flowing over dry ice. Headlights were recessed. Its multihinged multisprung frame made it ride smoothly even over a rough field.

Powered by a Ford V-8 90 hp engine mounted in the rear, driving the differentially-coupled front wheels, it attained a speed of 120 miles per hour, which in the conventional 1933 sedan would have required a 300 hp engine. Some of these innovations were not introduced in American automobiles for twenty years. Many of them never have been.

If there was a criticism of the car, it could be directed at the rear-wheel steering. Bucky was enthusiastic about it, because boats and airplanes are steered by a rear rudder; but rudders work against pressure whereas the single wheel had only contact with the road, which was less effective. But it had great advantages. In parking you had only to put the nose of the car against the curb, turn the wheel hard left and reverse, and the tail came right in. The Dymaxion car could park in a space four feet shorter than that required by a conventional car of the same length. It could also make a 360-degree turn in its own length. To this day Bucky valiantly defends rear steering. However, in a car he designed much later for Henry Kaiser, he combined the advantages of both systems. The Kaiser car steered with the front wheels. The rear wheel was locked, but could be unlocked and used for parking and other maneuvers.

When the Dymaxion car was shown to the public on July 12, 1933, it created a tremendous sensation. Bucky's name was in all the headlines. Crowds gathered wherever it went, causing such horrible traffic jams that Bucky was politely, even tearfully, requested not to use it at rush hours. Riding in it was a delightful sensation. No matter how rough the road it seemed to float effortlessly over the ground at tremendous speed. Seated in the rounded front with shatterproof glass all around, one had unimpeded vision. There were periscopes for excellent rear vision.

Bucky had enormous fun with the Dymaxion. Once, when he was showing it off to a group of *New Yorker* and *Fortune* editors, a traffic officer at 57th Street and Fifth Avenue stopped all traffic and said, "What the hell is that?"

While Bucky explained it through an open window, he rotated the car in a tight circle around the bemused cop. The officer at 56th Street saw the show and, when Bucky reached him, he insisted on a repeat performance. This happened all the way down Fifth Avenue to 34th Street. It took an hour to go that long mile. All of which may have been the inspiration for the *New Yorker* cartoon of two men in a very stream-lined car stuck in traffic with the caption, "Anyhow, we've got wind resistance licked."

Bucky at the wheel of the first Dymaxion car, 1934.

Bucky was invited to exhibit the Dymaxion car at the 1934 Automobile Show in the Grand Central Palace. Then the Chrysler Corporation, which was about to come out with a half-breed, extremely ugly car called the "air flow" model, forced the officials to withdraw the invitation, fearing a really streamlined car would make theirs look silly. Bucky, not to be rejected lightly, drove his car slowly around and around and around that block, while crowds watched him. Finally, sympathetic Police Commissioner General Ryan gave Bucky permission to park in front of the Grand Central Palace. So, in spite of Chrysler, he stole the show.

Bucky had intended to build only one prototype. However, pressures built up on him. Neither Burgess nor the Pearsons were happy about stopping production. But the strongest pressure came from the skilled mechanics. They came to Bucky, some of them actually weeping, and begged him not to close down and throw them out of work. They also instituted a slowdown. "So in order to get my first car finished," Bucky says, "I had to start a second one. And in order to get that one done, I started a third."

The truth is that Bucky was too softhearted to close down. Secure in the "ice cream clause," he would have defied Burgess and the Pearsons, and later did; but he could not stand against the pleas of those men who depended on him for a livelihood.

While the second car was being built, another enterprise took shape in the Dymaxion plant. Burgess had drawn up the plans for a small, ocean-racing sloop about forty feet long, which he hoped might become the prototype of a "Bermuda Class." He was desperately anxious to build her. There was plenty of spare room in the big Dymaxion factory, but no money. Bucky talked Pearson into financing it, and work was begun.

When completed she was a beautiful little boat with sleek, racing lines, a towering mast, and superbly cut sails; the craftsmanship of her hull was "exquisite." Though she belonged to Pearson and was designed by Burgess, she temporarily became Bucky's boat by the same process of osmosis by which he had acquired the Lathrop engine from Mr. Lamb of Camden. He named her the *Little Dipper*. At precisely the same time his sister Rosey on Bear Island was calling a new boat Jim Hardie had built for her the *Little Dipper*. Bucky's system of telepathy was communicating with remarkable precision.

Bucky loved the *Little Dipper* more than any boat he ever had until he acquired the Morgan-built sloop *Intuition* in 1967. He proposed to race her in the first long race of the season, the Overnight Race in Long Island Sound. Typically, he manned her with an almost all-Hewlett crew consisting of Carmen Hewlett, Arthur Hewlett, Roger Hewlett, and their close friend, Gilbert Stearns. The Hewlett boys were all good small boat sailors, but had no experience in larger craft. Gee Stearns was a first-class sailor in any size boat; but none of them, including Bucky, had had a chance to learn the special characteristics of this brand-new boat.

The race was sailed in a twenty-knot wind. As Bucky has often said, anything he does he does thoroughly. In this case, thoroughly meant taking the *Little Dipper* over the starting line flying every stitch of canvas she owned. Since she was, if anything, oversparred, it was a slightly terrifying experience for his crew. When the sun went down, the wind, instead of dropping, increased. *Little Dipper* labored through the darkness continually knocked down, "scuppers under," by the half gale. Not from fear, but from common sense, the crew protested that she would make more speed if Bucky shortened sail. But that was not his all-or-nothing way of sailing a race. Let the mast go if it must, the new sails be torn to ribbons, Bucky would drive her like a China clipper running her easting down.

Finally, Carmen Hewlett protested in language Bucky felt no skipper should permit. In the authentic tones of Captain Bligh, he said to his brother-in-law, "Carmen, go below and consider yourself in irons for the rest of the voyage."

All the yachting world was watching the performance of Starling Burgess's new boat. Unfortunately, it was not distinguished. A brand-new boat and an unfamiliar crew weighted the odds too heavily even for a hard-driving old salt like Bucky. *Little Dipper* finished back in the ruck. This did nothing to endear Bucky to Pearson and Burgess, who had hoped to profit financially by a brilliant coup.

However, Bucky had other finer voyages on *Little Dipper*. In 1936, she was sold to Elihu Root.

The first Dymaxion car was purchased by Captain Alford F. (Al) Williams, holder of the world speed record for planes. An English syndicate was interested in buying Dymaxion Number 2, which was still being built. In 1933, they sent Colonel William Forbes-Sempill, an English aeronautical authority, over to report on the performance of the Dymaxion car.

The dashing colonel arrived on the *Graf Zeppelin,* which on that voyage went to the Chicago World's Fair. Al Williams put his Dymaxion at Forbes-Sempill's disposal and Turner, a race driver, drove it from Detroit to Chicago. Later Bucky drove Dymaxion 3 over the same route, breaking the record between those two cities.

Then came one of the strokes of incredibly bad luck which Bucky seemed to attract in those early years. Forbes-Sempill was being driven to the airport in the Dymaxion by Turner, when a car belonging to a South Chicago parks commissioner came alongside and apparently challenged it to race. Off they went at seventy miles an hour, dodging traffic through the crowded streets. The inevitable happened. The commissioner's car hit the tail of the Dymaxion, sending it rolling over. The driver was killed and Forbes-Sempill badly injured.

This was bad enough from a public relations point of view, but worse followed. By the time reporters and police arrived on the scene the commissioner's car had been spirited away. The reporters saw only the bloodied hulk of the Dymaxion. As a result the headlines read: "DYMAXION CAR KILLS DRIVER".

The *New York Times* report stated: "The machine skidded, turned turtle and rolled over several times. Police say it apparently struck a 'wave' in the road."

The coroner's inquest, held thirty days later when Forbes-Sempill was sufficiently recovered to testify, brought out the truth, but by that time nobody was interested; it was back-page news. The public continued to believe that the Dymaxion car was dangerous.

Bucky and Al Williams conducted their own careful investigation which confirmed their opinion that there were no design or mechanical failures involved. The car was rebuilt and Williams continued to drive it until he sold it to the director of the Automotive Division of the United States Bureau of Standards.

The English syndicate wanted no more to do with Dymaxion cars, so Bucky eventually sold Dymaxion Number 2, which was finished in January, 1934, to a group of his mechanics. Dymaxion Number 3 was purchased by Johnson and Johnson heiress Evangeline Johnson Stokowski, wife of conductor Leopold Stokowski. It was exhibited at the Chicago World's Fair in 1934, and after passing through many hands turned up in Wichita, Kansas, in 1946, when Bucky was there building his second Dymaxion house for Beech Aircraft.

Despite the temporary burst of bad publicity, Bucky could have gone on producing Dymaxion cars and selling them indefinitely. But as usual, when he had proved a principle, he had no interest in making money. For years people infuriated him by saying, "Too bad the Dymaxion car was a failure," to which he irately replied, "It was *not* a failure. It was a resounding success in proving my principles and teaching me what I wanted to learn from it." He had no interest in becoming a minor Henry Ford.

When Bucky tried to close down the factory he ran into difficulties. Some of his workers took it hard, and windows in the factory were smashed at night. In addition, money was slow in coming in. Pearson's original stake had been used up, and Bucky had been financing it himself. His mother died in 1934. At least she had lived to see the Dymaxion car and to hear her son acclaimed a genius. Bucky was using his inheritance from her to finance car Number 3. But he had difficulty getting the trustees, Woolly and the bank, to sell shares of stock and turn the money over to him. He blamed them, thinking they were slow for their own convenience or that the bank wanted "to manipulate the market." In all probability they were trying to protect him from himself.

In any event, though Bucky was solvent, some bills were overdue. One day the sheriff came to his office to see him about a bill from a lumber company. Bucky explained the whole situation to him, and his anxiety to close down.

The sheriff was most understanding. He said: "I see what's going on. You'll never be able to close up while you are here. The only way you can get it done is if you would be willing to go away and leave it in my hands. I'll sell your machinery, pay your bills, and close it up for you, and this way you will not go bust."

Bucky accepted his offer and left. He says: "I made up my mind that never again would I be responsible for the lives of men who were working on prototypes, because I saw their fear of losing their jobs. When this fear entered the equation it wrecked your capabilities. That sheriff saved me."

But there was an awful row with Burgess and the Pearsons. They believed in the car, believed that it could be a moneymaking thing, and blamed Bucky bitterly for closing down. It was the same sort of bitterness that had been engendered by Bucky's idealistic indifference to making money in his other companies; and would happen again. He never understood it, never will; for he did things solely for the sake of the doing and even naïvely expected his backers to share his point of view. He would tell them his position frankly, but they would not believe him; they were incapable of believing that a man could turn his back on a fortune and walk away.

Eventually, when Bucky got his full inheritance from Mrs. Fuller, he used it to pay back all the investors in his company. But even that did little to assuage their bitterness. They thought angrily of the profits that might have been.

As for Bucky, he was back just where he had always been. Virtually his entire inheritance had been used up. He was, as usual, flat broke.

CHAPTER XII

NINE CHAINS

WHILE the cars were building in Bridgeport, Bucky lived a more normal life than he had in many years. The Pearsons had a summer place in Fairfield, a pleasant house overlooking an estuary of Long Island Sound, less than ten miles from the Dymaxion plant. There was a garage with a flat roof and an equally fine view. Learning that Anne was looking for a place to live, the Pearsons made her a kindly proposition. "If you will design an apartment on the roof of our garage," they said, "we will build it and you can live in it as long as you want to. Our boys are growing up and when you leave, it will be just the thing for them."

Pearson's confidence in Anne's architectural planning was not misplaced. Through osmosis or heredity she had innate skill and taste which, like many of her other qualities, had lain dormant until called upon. The garage backed against a hillside, so Anne planned a front door there at ground level. There was a double bedroom for the Fullers, a room for Allegra, a guest room, and, of course, a bath and kitchen. All one end of the apartment was a living room with long windows that opened on a wide porch, with a view of the bright blue estuary flecked with white sails. Bucky loved to sit there watching them.

With Anne's already-practiced flair for interior decoration, the apartment was so unusually pretty that the *Architectural Forum* ran pictures of it to show what could be done with a garage apartment.

The Fullers lived there very happily for about a year. Allegra, who was six, started school in Fairfield, but in the fall of 1934, when she was seven, Bucky convinced Anne that their daughter should have a more sophisticated kind of schooling. The modern transcendentalist's ideas on education were strikingly similar to those Ralph Waldo Emerson had expressed nearly a hundred years before: *There is a certain wisdom of humanity which is common to the greatest men with the lowest, and which our ordinary education often labors to silence and obstruct.*[1]

Bucky had always been fanatically determined to preserve Allegra's innate intellect from being silenced and obstructed. To this end he chose for her the most intelligently progressive school in New York—The Dalton School. The Fullers rented an apartment on East 87th Street, just around the corner from Dalton so that Allegra could walk to school without crossing the street.

When Bucky returned to New York, he found that the scene had changed dramatically; indeed, the whole country had been changed by Franklin Roosevelt and the New Deal. Instead of a Communist revolution, which the liberals had been predicting because of depression desperation, Roosevelt had instituted revolutionary reforms which, while they did not cure all the economic ills of the nation, did abate the worst abuses and gave people hope.

The best of the liberals were working with the government, leaving the radical fringe, who had joined the Communist party and hoped for revolution, in limbo. As a result there was an increasing polarization between the people who were trying to make the democratic system of government work and those who hoped it would not, between the true liberals and the radicals.

The whole world was changing, too, moving, as Bucky saw, toward another war. Hitler had assumed power in Germany shortly before Franklin Roosevelt's inauguration and was clearly heading toward a great confrontation with the democracies. Mussolini's New Roman Empire was becoming increasingly militaristic. Japan had begun her aggression against China; and Communist Russia under Stalin's iron dictatorship appeared ever more dangerous, because no one knew which side she would take.

In these perilous circumstances the United States Government began tightening security, assuming that there might be another general war. Bucky says: "The people who had joined the Communist Party down at Romany Marie's were coming under suspicion; and the people like myself who had not joined, did not want to be questioned about our friends. We did not feel that they had done anything even mildly wrong, but we felt that if we were questioned about them we might get them into

[1] "The Over-Soul," in *Essays* by Ralph Waldo Emerson, Literary Classics, Inc., New York.

trouble. So it became almost illogical to go to Marie's—you would almost precipitate trouble. But she was such a friend of mine. . . .

"That was really the end of the Greenwich Village we had known, and of Romany Marie's as a great Bohemian headquarters. From that time the Bohemians began to move uptown, but never again was there such a meeting place for them."

At about this time Bucky made one of his greatest and most lasting friendships. Felix Morley invited him to lunch at the Three Hours for Lunch Club, where he introduced him to his brother, Christopher Morley. At lunch Bucky recalled a poem of Christopher Morley's which he had read in *The Bowling Green,* Morley's column in the old *Evening Post,* about a month before Alexandra's death. It had so affected him that he memorized it and, after explaining the circumstances, Bucky recited it to its author, who had forgotten it:

To A Child

. . . The poetry innate I am told
Of being only four years old,
Still young enough to be a part
Of nature's great impulsive art
Born comrade of bird, beast and tree
And unselfconscious as a bee,
And yet with lovely reason skilled
Each day new paradise to build.

Elate explorer of each sense
Without dismay, without pretense
In your unstained transparent eyes
There is no conscience, no surprise.
Life's prayer can only you accept
Your strange divinity still kept . . .

Life that puts all things in rhyme
May make you poet, too, in time
But there were days, oh tender elf,
When you were poetry itself . . .

When Bucky finished, tears were flowing down his face, dimming his round glasses. Morley was deeply moved. Bucky says, "That was the beginning of our having a very, very extraordinary friendship."

At that time Morley had a charming little house at Roslyn, Long Island, which he called The Knothole. Bucky often went there with him, and he as often came to Martin's Lane where he and the Hewletts immediately took to each other. Bucky was asked to join the Three Hours for Lunch Club. He says, "I made this transition because the event of Greenwich Village was over, and suddenly there was the Three Hours for Lunch Club and a group of extraordinarily interesting writers and poets, people like Don Marquis and F.P.A., and many others, with whom I drank copiously." It was very good for Bucky, the more so as he was working on his first real book in which he put in permanent form many of the philosophical and technological ideas that were to make him famous. It was called *Nine Chains to the Moon,* meaning all of human-kind, because he reckoned that if all the people then living stood upon each other's shoulders they would make nine complete chains between the earth and the moon. Bucky wrote, "If it is not so far to the moon, then it is not so far to the limits [of Universe]—whatever, whenever or wherever they may be." [2] The book was dedicated to Alexandra and Allegra with Christopher Morley's beautiful line: *Your strange divinity still kept.*

Bucky worked on the book all through the summer of 1936. There can be no attempt to give a condensation of it here; the interested reader can go out and buy it for a small sum in any bookstore in America or England—it is selling faster than ever. However, certain of the ideas which are essential to Bucky's thinking can be briefly touched upon.

Inevitably, the first chapters are a plea for improving man by im-proving his environment, particularly his housing. Bucky very astutely described the difficulties a man would encounter if he went about ac-quiring an automobile the way he builds a house.

First the man (Bucky calls him Mr. Murphy) would bring the auto-mobile designer "a picture of how he would like the car to look, per-haps like 'a jinricksha of the Tang Dynasty . . . or a British corona-tion coach.'" That being decided, Mr. Murphy and the designer would choose all the different parts—motor, flywheel, frame, differential, etc., from manufacturers' catalogues. When they had made their selections they would get four or five local garages to bid for the job, and pick one of the bidders because of his price or because he had "built grandfather's

2 *Nine Chains to the Moon.* R. Buckminster Fuller. J. B. Lippincott Co., Philadelphia, 1938.

velocipedes." Naturally, as soon as they started building, Mr. Murphy would have to get a bank loan, and a building permit from the local town council, and insurance; all of these people would insist on changes and bury him in red tape, and probably demand a bit of graft on the side. Then the craft unions would have their say.

If the car ever got built it would cost at least $50,000 and probably would not run, or if it did, would do so badly. It is easy to see that is no way to build an automobile. Bucky felt it was no way to build a house. His own prescription for mass-produced housing was now only about fifteen years ahead of the times, as evidenced by the tremendous torrent of factory-built trailer-houses that has ravaged the countryside since World War II.

Another important concept, central to Bucky's philosophy, was expounded in the chapter called "The Phantom Captain." It begins with Bucky's famous mechanistic description of Man—"a self-balancing, adapter-base biped," etc. But Man is far more than that. All the elegantly designed, intricate mechanical structure is merely an "imbecile contraption" without the guidance of the Phantom Captain, who has neither weight nor sensorial tangibility. The Captain is the metaphysical fragment of the universal intelligence which is in every human being, the real persona of each individual, of which the perceivable body is merely a mechanical extension, hardly more closely associated with him than the steering wheel of the automobile he drives.

Bucky calls the brain the Captain's executive officer: there simply to supply him with information and transmit his orders to the body's mechanism. When the corporeal man-mechanism wears out, the Captain simply "abandons ship," and continues as an indestructible pattern of integrity.

The Captain has not only "an infinite self-identity characteristic but, also, an infinite understanding," understanding being an intuitive, nongraphable awareness of perfection, or of infinity, or of truth, which serves as a universal yardstick relative to which any sense experience may be evaluated. But, since perfection is never attainable in reality, it becomes a *time direction*. This indicates the meaning of the phrase *Never Never Land*. "Children dream truly," Bucky notes.

Although Bucky, at that time, may not have read Emerson's famous essay, his Phantom Captain closely resembles the great transcendentalist's "oversoul." Emerson says, "The soul in man is not an organ, but animates and exercises all the organs; it is not a function, like the power of memory . . . but uses these as hands and feet; is not a faculty, but a light; is not the intellect or will, but the master of intellect and will. . . . A man is the facade of a temple wherein all wisdom and all good abide." [3]

Bucky devoted considerable space in the book to Albert Einstein, who had "a powerful influence" on him and upon whose thinking he had based much of his own philosophy. He had been tremendously impressed by an article Einstein had published in the New York *Times* in 1930 in which he said that scientists were rated as great heretics by the church, but they were truly religious men because of their faith in the orderliness of the universe. Einstein's beautiful, nonanthropomorphic concept of God as the great orderer of the universe moved Bucky deeply, and the great scientist's statement that fear and longing were the principle motivations of man impressed Bucky so strongly that he used them a great deal in *Nine Chains*.

In another chapter, which Bucky called "$E=MC^2=$Mrs. Murphy's Horsepower," he was, perhaps, the first person to explain Albert Einstein's theory of relativity succinctly (in a ten-dollar telegram to Noguchi) in terms that a layman—a highly intelligent layman—could understand. Also, he outlined its possible application to everyday life and described what he felt the world would be like when Einstein's discoveries were applied practically. All this led first to a terrible disappointment, and then to one of the greatest intuitive experiences of Bucky's life.

Bucky finished *Nine Chains* in the autumn of 1936. He showed it to Christopher Morley, who was amazed and enthused by its profundity and originality. Morley, who had published some forty books with Doubleday, was just moving to J. B. Lippincott. He said to Bucky, "I think Lippincott should publish this."

With Bucky's consent Morley told Frank Henry of Lippincott about *Nine Chains*. Lippincott agreed to publish it. Bucky thinks that this was less because they felt any enthusiasm for the book, or even understood it, than because they wanted to please their new author, Morley, who was such a valuable "property." In fact, to show how little they comprehended it they eventually brought it out in a copper-colored jacket, thinking it appropriate since by that time Bucky was working for Phelps Dodge, the great copper mining company.

[3] *Essays,* Emerson.

The copy editor in charge of the book came to the chapter containing Bucky's "tentative" cosmic inventory and then to the chapter on Einstein. As a result Bucky received a letter from Lippincott saying that it was well known that Einstein had said that there were only ten men in the world capable of understanding his ideas. The editors had looked at the list, and other lists of savants, and had failed to find Bucky's name on any of them. Therefore, they felt they would be guilty of "charlatanry" if they published his book, and were very sorry they must decline to go ahead with it.

This was a devastating blow to Bucky. Like all new authors, he had fantastically high hopes for this book into which he had poured so much thought and, yes, emotion. In his fervid imagination he had pictured it sweeping the world with a new revelation of truth. Now to be accused of charlatanry was like lye on his brain.

In desperation he sat down and wrote to Lippincott saying, "almost facetiously," that Doctor Einstein was now living in Princeton and why did they not send the typescript to him? Bucky says, "Really, I did not think any more about it."

One day months later, when Bucky was working at home, he received a telephone call from Doctor Morris Fishbein, who said, "Doctor Einstein is coming in from Princeton to spend this weekend with me in New York. He has your typescript and would like to talk to you about it, if you are free to meet him here."

Bucky says, "So you can imagine, I did not have any other engagement."

That evening Bucky went to Doctor Fishbein's residence on Riverside Drive. It was one of those old-fashioned apartment houses with an ornate marble-floored lobby and a creaking elevator that carried him to the proper floor. There he was shown into a long drawing room with a high ceiling and tall windows overlooking the river. Doctor Einstein, looking smaller than life like a very wise gnome, was sitting at one end of the room surrounded by people standing around him against the walls and even extending out into the hall. As Bucky was taken through the crowd and introduced to the great scientist, he says, "I felt as I had never felt of anyone before; there seemed to be almost an aura about this man."

Einstein rose immediately saying, "We must talk together," and led Bucky to a smaller study. There was a table with the typescript of *Nine Chains* lying upon it underneath a lamp. Einstein sat down beside the table and Bucky sat on the opposite side. Einstein began the conversation by telling Bucky that he had read the book and approved of his analysis of how his philosophy affected his formulations, and that he was going to advise Lippincott to that effect.

Then Doctor Einstein said, and Bucky remembers every word exactly because this was one of those highly charged moments of life when the spoken word is deeply recorded on the memory cells by the powerful current of emotion: "Young man, you amaze me. I cannot conceive anything I have ever done as having the slightest practical application. [He was, of course, referring to Mrs. Murphy's Horsepower.] I evolved all this in the hope that it might be of use to cosmogonists and to astrophysicists in gaining a better understanding of the universe, but you appear to have found practical applications for it."

One can easily understand how powerfully these words affected Bucky. For he had been called a nut and a crackpot so often, had been treated with contemptuous amusement by serious scientists and philosophers and engineers, and called a charlatan by his own publisher. And, now, the greatest scientist in all the world not only acknowledged the accuracy of Bucky's exposition of his recondite theories and philosophical principles, but actually declared that he had contributed a new understanding of the practical possibilities of Einstein's discoveries to the great man himself. It was the ultimate accolade.

Years later, when the secrets of the Manhattan Project were revealed in that apocalyptic flash of light over Hiroshima, Bucky thought of that good and gentle man with whom he had talked in a quiet room over Riverside Drive; thought of the innocence of that extraordinary intellect which had unlocked the secret of the atom, yet had not conceived its fearful uses. By then Bucky knew the story of Einstein's going to President Roosevelt to warn him of the appalling potential which Lise Meitner and Otto Frisch had discovered by applying Einstein's energy equation to producing theoretical fission. Bucky thought of the unprecedented secret research which Einstein's talk with Roosevelt had set in motion, resulting in that first practical application of Einstein's principles to earthly affairs in the sky above a small, unsuspecting Japanese city.

"Because of our talk that evening," Bucky said, "I had this extraordinary insight into the agony this beautiful man must have suffered, knowing he had brought this thing about; and now, for all the rest of his days, he was in terrific pain because of his responsibility as a scientist."

Having clarified Einstein, at least for an informed readership, *Nine Chains* touched, though only briefly, on Bucky's theory of energetic-synergetic geometry and then proceeded with an outline of the whole history of the human race, and how it came under the dominance of its rulers—the priests and the Great Pirates. Using man's basic motivations of longing and fear, the priests, understanding a little more about general principles than their disciples, used this knowledge to exploit the fears of the masses through the application of those principles to primitive magic, while manipulating them through their longing for a better world by promising them heaven. Meanwhile, the Great Pirates, through their command of the sea, operated outside man-made laws, which did not extend much beyond the beaches, thus becoming outlaws and gaining dominance by their control of world trade.

Bucky describes the gradual enlightenment of the masses, while at the same time their rulers managed to retain their autocracy by keeping always one jump ahead of them so that the improvement in living conditions, brought about by man's increasing advantages gained by ever more sophisticated tools produced by industrialization, accrued mainly to them. The whole system was, according to him, based on the assumption of scarcity, of there never being enough to go around.

The tremendous advances of science and its application of industrialization in the nineteenth and twentieth centuries have, Bucky passionately believes, rendered this fear of scarcity irrelevant for the simple reason that, if properly managed and utilized, present industrial and agricultural techniques could easily provide not only enough of everything for every living inhabitant of the earth, but ample means for a much larger population. This is only obstructed by outworn traditions, fear of change, and lack of imagination or the will of mankind to succeed as Universe clearly intends them to do.

Bucky considers that these obstructions are placed in the way of progress by the economic system built upon the ownership of land and the "false" accounting methods foisted on the masses by the masters of capital. In order to acquire land, the basic essential of existence in an agricultural economy, people had to give collateral to the warrior chiefs who had seized it by force. In primitive societies this collateral was in the form of cattle which, since they multiplied naturally, produced "dividends" for the lenders. This, at least, made some sense. Later, when the borrowing took the form of money or capital, the lenders demanded and received interest. To Bucky's mind this was both false and immoral because money does not regenerate itself by natural increases. He hates the interest system with the fanatic intensity with which the twelfth-century Roman Catholic Church regarded usury, as it was then called.

By this means the former rulers, the priests and the Great Pirates, metamorphosed into capitalists while still controlling the productive capacity of the world through a hydra-headed monster which Bucky calls "Fincap" (finance capital).

Though Bucky's recording of history is, in the words of one of his greatest admirers, "wildly erratic" in regard to particulars, the general principles he derives from his study of it have a certain validity from which viable conclusions and new directions for the course of mankind can be charted.

These are but a few of the ideas distilled from Bucky's brain into the pages of *Nine Chains,* and its present recognition as a classic derives from the fact that Bucky had succeeded in completely clearing his mind of the barnacle growth of generally accepted "facts" that were factitious. After his deliberate "unlearning," he viewed the universe with the clear eyes of a highly intelligent child whose vision was not distorted by preconceived prejudices. What he saw was, indeed, remarkable.

With Einstein's letter in their hands Lippincott went ahead with *Nine Chains,* which was published in 1938. It did not then make the big combustion that Bucky had envisioned in his euphoric moments. In fact, it fell into the literary pool with the impact of a withered leaf. *Newsweek* gave it a fine review: "A three-ring circus—high wire acts, blaring bands, clowning and all—with one man as the whole show. . . . This book is at once a guide book and a dream book of the future, a purge of the past, a debunker of architecture, economics, politics . . . this ruddy-faced, gray-haired inventor is no nut. Great stuff!"

The other reviews ranged from feeble to derisive. Nobody much bought it. For Bucky was, as usual, too far out. But people were beginning to catch up with his ideas. *Nine Chains* would become a classic, as Bucky became a world pundit.

CHAPTER XIII
NO CHAINS

BUCKY has described the summer of 1936 as a low point in his and Anne's life. Not the lowest—the night by Lake Michigan was that—but they were scraping bottom. From that time on their course turned ever upward; not in one serene, ascending curve—life with Bucky could never be serene—but in mountain peaks and deep ravines that never quite reached the nadir. A graph of it would look like a chart of the Dow Jones average in a turbulent bull market.

Bucky had a gift for making new friends, at once fascinating them by his brilliance and endearing himself to them by his genuine warmth, his eager acceptance of affection. Among those he had acquired recently was William H. Osborn. Bill Osborn was a big, ruddy-faced gentleman—the word is used precisely—who was that rare combination of a splendid sportsman and a man of venturesome intellect. Like everyone imaginative and intelligent enough to understand what Bucky was saying, he was enthralled by the coruscation of ideas which erupted from Bucky's mind like the stream of sparks from steel in contact with a grindstone.

Osborn was a power in the great Phelps Dodge Corporation—his mother had been a Dodge—which was beginning to move out of its traditional business of mining copper into the wider field of manufacturing copper products. He decided that Bucky would be a valuable source of new directions for the company. In the autumn of 1936, Osborn offered Bucky the position of Director of Research with Phelps Dodge. It paid a handsome salary.

Bucky's job was to help create this new research department and pour out ideas from his fecund brain that might evolve into new devices for the company to manufacture. Despite one abortive project Phelps Dodge got their money's worth, not only from new inventions, but from the publicity Bucky's original conceptions generated and the ideas he threw off which other men seized upon and carried through.

His first big contribution was a new type of brake drum, made of solid bronze and fitted with hard rubber insets so designed that it rapidly dissipated the heat generated by braking. This eliminated the grab and fade caused by overheating in existing braking systems, thereby cutting in half the deceleration time. The Fuller bronze brake established the metallurgical principles of the now widely used disc brakes.

He also devised the oxyacetylene, melted-tin-ore centrifuge that made it possible to process hardhead tin ore which had heretofore been impossible to refine.

Bucky's most widely publicized spectacular for Phelps Dodge was the Dymaxion bathroom. It was basically a refined version of the prototype he had built for Standard Sanitary, this time made of copper, of course! It consisted of two compartments—tub-shower and lavatory-toilet. Its four basic sections were designed to be dye-stamped out of sheet metal. The lower halves of both compartments were copper sheet coated with a noncorrosive alloy of silver, tin, and antimony; the upper halves were made of aluminum sheet with an interior surface of synthetic resin colored to individual taste. Plumbing connections were standard; easily hooked up to water pipes and drains, as were the electrical connections. There were electric resistance strip heaters and a fan for cooling.

The whole Dymaxion bathroom occupied a floor space of five square feet, could be manufactured for about three hundred dollars, and weighed only 420 pounds, about the weight of one conventional bathtub. Bucky intended that it should ultimately be made of plastics—not then perfected—in which case it would have weighed and cost even less.

Having learned his lesson at Standard Sanitary, this time Bucky was careful to sell the ideas to the plumbers' union first. So persuasive were his arguments concerning the vastly increased work opportunities such inexpensive mass-produced bathrooms would provide, that in their official magazine, *The Ladle,* the union came out for it enthusiastically.

All in vain! Standard Sanitary, which was one of Phelps Dodge's largest customers, was so terrified by the plumbers' former reaction that they talked Phelps Dodge out of putting it into production. Bucky thought it was just due to the inertia of the housing industry as a whole.

However, Phelps Dodge did build thirteen prototypes, all but one of which were sold. Chris Morley loyally bought two for The Knothole; the Osborns took one or two, and one ended up in the hydraulic testing section of the Bureau of Standards in Washington, which certified that it complied with all requirements of the United States building codes.

Naturally, the Dymaxion bathroom would not have appealed to everyone even if it had been put into production. Very tall men found its five-by-five dimensions too confining, though they fitted Bucky well enough. And an architect friend of his said of its ultimate development as a self-contained unit, "Bucky thinks people ought to get weighed sitting on a toilet seat, brushing their teeth with a cake of soap and taking a shower with a fog gun. But I ain't gonna. I just ain't gonna."

As always, when Bucky had a spectacular new device to exhibit, he had a marvelous time. He mounted one of his bathrooms on a pickup truck and drove all around the East Coast showing it off. The author happily recalls tearing through the more sedate streets of Lawrence in the truck with Bucky at the wheel, assorted Hewletts in the bathroom, one of them sitting on the john, and streamers of toilet paper flying out behind.

Because it was never put into production, the Dymaxion bathroom was generally considered just another of Bucky's failures. But not by him. He was perfectly justified in considering it a resounding success, because it worked, and proved out the principles from which it derived.

Nor did it engender any bitterness between Bucky and the Phelps Dodge officials. As long as he proved his point, Bucky did not care tuppence whether it made money or not, and the Phelps Dodge people realized that Bucky had delivered the goods, and that their decision to abort it was not his fault. Until Bill Osborn died he remained Bucky's devoted friend.

Phelps Dodge officials often had great difficulty reading Bucky's reports. He had carried his theory of navy days that he "would rather not be understood than be misunderstood" to extremes. In his meticulous endeavor to be absolutely precise he had evolved a labyrinthine prose style involving the use of esoteric Latin- and Greek-root words that few people could understand; *Time* magazine later christened it "Fullerese."

His oral discourses were, and have remained, easily understandable because his sensitivity to audience reaction immediately informs him when he is losing their interest and he automatically readjusts to their limits of comprehension. But when writing, he has no such check on his lack of intelligibility.

On one occasion Bucky handed a report for the board of directors to his immediate superior. Several hours later the official came back in despair. "This completely defeats me," he told Bucky, "and if I can't understand it, heaven knows, the board can't. Do something!"

Bucky read it to him, breaking up the long sentences into short lines, pausing after each to make sure his audience understood. "I get it now," the official said. "See if you can write it that way."

Bucky took it and, without changing a word, wrote it in the form of a prose poem with each line containing a single thought. It was far more easily understandable. As an example of how this worked, consider a typical Fuller sentence from his book *No More Secondhand God:* "So amplified in degree are these quantities of motion, captured by faithful extension of both ends of the sensibly charted scales beyond the sensorial limits, as progressively to place a working measure of the original omnipotent power within man's conscious control."

In the book it is written:

> "So amplified in degree
> are these quantities of motion
> captured by faithful extension
> of both ends of the sensibly charted scales
> beyond the sensorial limits
> as progressively to place
> a working measure
> of the original omnipotent power
> within man's conscious control." [1]

This is not exactly easy reading, but it is far more comprehensible than the prose version.

In the case of the Phelps Dodge report, Bucky's superior agreed that it was now quite understandable. "But," he said in horror, "it is *poetry!* I can't get the board to read that."

[1] *No More Secondhand God,* R. Buckminster Fuller, Arcturus Books, Carbondale, Ill., 1963.

He and Bucky worked out a compromise version in which the sentences were broken up by dashes, stars, asterisks, and parentheses.

This was the beginning of Bucky's couching his more esoteric thoughts in verse form. Whether it is poetry or not is a matter of sharp controversy among critics. Some enthusiastically say it is; others that it is nonsense in doggerel form. Evidently Bucky's alma mater is among the ayes. In 1962 Harvard awarded him the Charles Eliot Norton Chair of Poetry.

During all those summers, Bucky, Anne, and Allegra managed to spend at least one month on Bear Island. But maintaining it had become a financial drain. Bucky had been able to contribute virtually nothing except the pleasure of his company, and other members of the family were hard pressed by the depression.

When Mrs. Fuller died Rosey took over the management of the island. Though she had not blown her inheritance, her income was very small, and Leslie, who had divorced Neddie Larned and married Nelson Borland, Jr., could not help much. However, Rosey staunchly sustained it for the family. To save money she even spent one whole winter on the island, an experience almost comparable to Admiral Byrd's lonely vigil on the South Polar Plateau. However, Rosey said she would not have exchanged her memory of that winter for a pleasure dome in Xanadu.

In the late thirties and early forties things became so stringent that Rosey even took in boarders to help defray expenses. Anne, despite her distaste for the rugged life, sportingly stayed there on several occasions to help out with the chores. The experiment was hardly a resounding success. Bucky says, "Rosey was so tender-hearted and charged so little for room and board that I think her boarders often cost her more than they paid."

Eventually the island was made into a corporation, with shares held by every member of the family down to Mrs. Fuller's great-grandchildren, each contributing proportionally to its upkeep. By whatever means, Bear Island was preserved for the family, especially for Bucky. This is the important thing; for on it he has, year after year, renewed his strength to continue his strenuous vocation of explorer of Universe, reorganizing civilization for the benefit of all peoples.

In 1938, Ralph Ingersol Davenport, managing editor of *Fortune* magazine, came to Bucky with such an attractive proposition he could not turn it down. "Mitch" Davenport offered him the job of technology consultant (idea man extraordinary) and writer at a salary of $15,000 a year. In those times this was quite magnificent, and the work was exactly suited to Bucky's temperament. It proved to be a fertile field.

Members of *Fortune*'s staff say that, contrary to general expectations, Bucky turned out to be "a very soldierly employee." He came to his office promptly on time, stayed there until closing, and kept busy all the time writing long memoranda that were quite difficult to understand. Patricia Divver Lynch, who was one of the top editors, says: "I often went down to his office to talk with him. He just bubbled like a fountain, he had so many ideas, he never ran dry. Never! Everything was new; he never repeated what he said yesterday. Bucky was difficult for me to understand when he was talking about scientific things, even more difficult when he wrote about them. The more pedestrian financial reporters did not understand him at all. But his architectural things and inventions made great sense to me. I thought his house on a pole was a splendid idea. I would have liked an office building like that because everybody wants to have an office next to the managing editor. If you put him in the center of a circular building then everybody could be next to him." [2]

Mrs. Lynch did not know about Bucky's hexagonal dwelling units, which would have accomplished this purpose.

There were many brilliant editors of *Fortune* who became Bucky's friends, such as Charles J. V. Murphy, John Chamberlain, and John Jessup. John Cort of *Time,* who became devoted to him, was another. Bucky did not write many articles while he was there, though he contributed to several, including a brilliant piece on national resources, illustrated with Dymaxion projection maps [3] showing the location of minerals, sites for dams, oil wells, and the great deposits of oil shale under the mountain states, which are just now technologically possible to extract profitably, and the population density. It was a modest forerunner of his World Game, an exhaustive inventory of the resources of the entire earth.

Though Bucky did not write many articles, the whole staff was electrified by the sparks that flew from his brain. While he was at *Fortune* the Business Department made one of its periodic checks on efficiency

[2] Mrs. Patricia Divver Lynch (now Dagg) to the author.
[3] Described later.

and productiveness. They looked into Bucky's reportorial output; then went to Davenport and asked, "What does Mr. Buckminster Fuller write for his $15,000 a year?"

Davenport replied, "It doesn't matter."

"Doesn't matter?"

"Look you," said Davenport: "as managing editor I have to have new ideas every single, solitary day, and sometimes I just dry up. So I send for Bucky; and Bucky comes in and talks for about two hours. By the time he leaves I have more ideas than I can publish in the magazine in ten years. He recharges my batteries, and he's worth twice what he's being paid."

While Bucky was on *Fortune* he was working on and refining many of his own ideas, especially about the progress of humankind through the advantages gained by the tools of industrialization. To clarify them in his own mind and for others, he made enormous historical charts of the progress of all the history of inventions and discoveries from earliest recorded history to the present, allowing one-quarter inch for every year. Every time there was a new discovery the chart went up one increment so you could see the acceleration of energy-utilizing events. In 1938, Bucky gave a lecture on the charts at the Bureau of Standards in Washington. The charts went completely around the walls of that big auditorium. They were color coded. The most completely abstract intellectual generalizations were in purple and so down the spectrum to mere mechanical inventions, which were in red. Bucky says, "Looking at the charts you could see that the purple of the mind was well over the red of matter. Every time an advance in technology was made it could be traced back to the thinking that had gone on well before it. As you moved around the room you could walk along in history and sort of feel the rate of gains mankind has made."

As Bucky has written: "Every time a man uses his know-how, his experience increases and his intellectual advantage automatically increases. Energy cannot decrease. Know-how can only increase. Wealth which combines energy and intellect can only increase with use . . . the faster the more!"

Bucky was also refining and expanding his theories of energetic-synergetic geometry, which he calls "nature's geometry." As the basis for this he reached far back into the ancient history of mathematics, back before Archimedes (d. 212 B.C.), back before Euclid (who taught in Alexandria about 300 B.C.), back to Pythagoras (d. 550 B.C.), who was entranced by triangles and discovered the tetrahedron, the octahedron, and the icosahedron.

The basic premise of Bucky's dynamic geometric system was that there was no such thing as infinity. He accepted Einstein's curvilinear *finite* universe. Therefore, there was no such things as a straight line, because it would continue to nonexistent infinity. This knocked Euclidean geometry into a cocked hat except as a convenient means of inexact measurement.

He also affirmed that nature always worked in whole numbers—chemical elements always combine in "beautiful whole numbers," H_2O, never π, for example. This eliminated such irrational numbers as pi (π) and alogon (the diagonal of the square), which straggle off infinity in an infinitely repeated gaggle of numerals also only useful as a convenient means of inexact calculations.

Finally, Newton's static universe—"a body persists in a state of rest," etc., was clearly false since science had discovered that there was no such thing as either a body or rest, only nodes or quanta of energy. Bucky wrote one of his strange little poems about this:

> Newton was a noun
> And Einstein is a verb
> Einstein's norm makes Newton's norm
> Instant universe
> Absurd
> A body persists.
> In a state of rest
> Or—
> Except as affected—
> Thus gravestones are erected!
>
> Non-simultaneous, physical universe
> Is energy, and
> Energy equals mass
> Times the second power
> Of the speed of light
> No exceptions!
> Fission verified Einstein's hypothesis
> Change is normal
> Thank you, Albert!

Bucky says: "I don't think Nature is using any of the constants men have been using. The constants came about by people making a very arbitrary choice of starting with the cube, and I don't see any cubical crystals; some may look cubical, but they never are.

"I said, 'Nature is not operating on the basis that man is trying to make her work on. She is operating quite clearly on a rational basis. I think she is using models, and man simply picked the wrong model—the cube which requires perpendicularity.'

"I said: 'I think Nature has a superb, rational coordinate system and I am absolutely intent to find it. So I went on to what is sometimes called vectoral geometry.'"

As a first step in devising his new geometry, Bucky, using pingpong balls as spheres, packed them as closely as possible around a central sphere. He found that they do not form a supersphere, but a polyhedron with fourteen sides; this is a vector equilibrium because the value of its radial vectors (lines of force) is exactly the same as that of its circumferal vectors—it is in perfect balance. A single-layer vector equilibrium has exactly twelve spheres. Another closely packed layer around the first takes 42 spheres, and to form a third layer 92 spheres are required.[4] Ninety-two is the number of unique atomic systems called elements, and the heaviest element, uranium, is number 92. Now, if you add the numbers in the three layers together—12,42,92 —you get 146, which is the exact number of neutrons in a uranium atom. Add another 92 and you get 238, the number of nucleons in a uranium atom.

If you remove the center sphere from a vector equilibrium it closes down to an icosahedron—a twenty-sided "solid" structure. If you continue to contract it, you get an octahedron—an eight-sided figure, and this can be split into tetrahedra. All polyhedra can be subdivided into component tetrahedra, but a tetrahedron, which is a triangular pyramid having four equal sides, cannot be subdivided into component polyhedra having less than four faces. It is indivisible. It is "the minimum prime divisor of omni-directional universe," for it encloses the minimum volume with the most surface of all polyhedra. (The sphere encloses the most volume with the least surface.)

Therefore, Bucky wrote a first principle: "The tetrahedron is the basic structural system, and all structure in the universe is made up of tetrahedronal parts."

---

[4] This process can be repeated indefinitely without changing the shape of the structure.

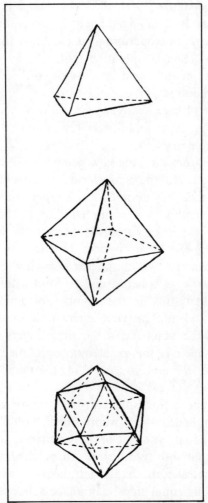

From top to bottom, tetrahedron, octahedron, icosahedron.

It is not the intention here to endeavor to describe Bucky's system of synergetic-energetic geometry as differentiated from conventional static geometry. It will suffice for the present to state that, working from those general principles, he made many unique mathematical discoveries which were later confirmed by such pragmatic proof as the discovery by doctors A. Klug and J. T. Finck of Birbeck College, London, of the icosa-geodesic structuring of the polio virus with the probability that all spherical viruses have similar arrangements of proteins; and, more importantly, by Nobel Prize winner Linus Pauling's documentation of the basic omnitetrahedronal constellations characterizing not only all of organic chemistry, but also all of the combining patterns of metallic atoms.

Bucky himself was to prove some of his own geometrical discoveries in the structure that made him famous.

Bucky says of his work: "You see, I was looking for the coordinate system of nature, and I was absolutely confident that I had found that system. I still am, and I think that in later years I will be most remembered for the fact that I found nature's coordinate system and it will be possible to make models of it.

"The most important thing about it is that for centuries scientists have been saying that 'Nature is not using models, because there is a fourth dimension, energy, but you can't make a model of the fourth dimension. It is so abstract as to be immodelable.' This brought about the enormous dichotomy between the humanities and the sciences. The humanities people simply could not understand what the scientists were doing, because the scientists could not show them in models or drawings, and the humanities people could not understand their abstract and unreal mathematics. Right there is the basis of C. P. Snow's assumption of the two intellectual worlds and the great chasm between them. I later told C. P. Snow about my mathematics, and he agreed that they might really span the chasm.

"But I am perfectly confident today that tomorrow you will be able to see little children being able to do nuclear physics in model form because that is the way Nature is doing it. She is not static, she's dynamic, and the models make it clear now, how she can do these things dynamically."

While Bucky was living in the unusual security of an assured income, and doing all this high thinking, he did not yet retire to plain living. On the contrary, he continued to drink copiously and to enjoy gregarious occasions. However, he adopted a form of exercise to keep his magnificent body in shape. Some twenty years before the Kennedys, he took up jogging—he called it dog-trotting.

In Manhattan's Central Park, lovers strolling through a summer evening—it was still quite safe in 1939—would be startled by the sight of a stocky figure in a sweat shirt and undershorts pounding around the reservoir. In Lawrence, where Bucky still frequently went on weekends, he imbued a whole group of Hewletts and their husbands and friends with the habit of this exercise. They might be sitting around in Martin's Lane convivially drinking at midnight or later, when suddenly Bucky's "vectors" would overpower the restraining circumferential forces, and he would shout, "Come on, Dog-Trot Club, time for a run!"

Stripping off their jackets and pants the whole pack would follow him through the quiet lanes and lighted thoroughfares on a three- or four-mile run. The inhabitants, returning from formal dinners in tuxedos and evening gowns, would stare a moment and then comment, "It's that crazy Bucky and his friends."

In New York Bucky continued to acquire ever more friends as his more comfortable circumstances permitted him a wider scope. Inevitably, Clare and Harry Luce were among them, as well as many of the Time-Life people. Another man who became an intimate was Hailey Fisk. Fisk was a lively young fellow with red hair, pale blue eyes, and no noticeable abundance of brains, who moved in New York's most fashionable circles. He became devoted to Bucky, who, as he always did, returned this affection in full measure. At some point in their friendship he invited Bucky to join the Racquet and Tennis Club. Bucky eagerly accepted.

Why he wanted to join a club whose membership was almost entirely composed of rich, empty-headed, sporting society characters with no social consciousness and an antediluvian political orientation considerably to the right of Herbert Hoover is one of the apparent paradoxes of his character. It is doubtful if he went to it twice a year, and certain that he met few congenial spirits there. Yet, on further examination, there appears an emotional explanation.

It must be remembered that Bucky's failure to make any of Harvard's fashionable clubs had made a wound on his psyche whose cicatrice remained, and still remains after fame and fortune beyond the reach of most men have come to him. Rejection was the thing that hurt him most. The Racquet Club was one of the most fashionable in New York, indeed, in the whole country. Ergo, to be accepted by it was to show those snobbish Harvard boys of long ago that they had made a bad mistake.

While discussing Bucky in the unlikely role of clubman, it is convenient to consider his present affiliations of that type; they are much more sensible. Eventually he resigned from the Racquet Club and joined the Century Association, which is equally swell, but whose membership is far more intellectual and which owns the finest private library in New York. He also belongs to the New York Yacht Club —a natural because of his love of sailing—and the Somerset Club of Boston, which gives him an excellent base of operations in his native state. In addition he belongs to the Coffee House, New York; the Cliff Dwellers Club, Chicago; the Northeast Harbor Fleet, Mount Desert, Maine; and the Camden Yacht Club, Maine.

Bucky continued to knock out inventions almost casually during this period of philosophical-mathematical-sociological mental activity. In 1940, for example, he designed, but did not build, a contraption he called "The Mechanical Wing." Designed to fit on a triangular A-frame, two-wheeled trailer to be towed behind an automobile, it was "a compact mobile package in which the essentials of contemporary U.S. living can be transported to a Vermont farmhouse, a lakeside campsite, a weekend or vacation house, or incorporated into a permanent dwelling." [5] In a space no larger than a small powerboat Bucky concentrated all the necessities for luxurious living in the wilderness. To wit: A Dymaxion bathroom with hermetically sealed waste packaging and chemical disposal apparatus; a diesel engine air-compressor, electric generator, and water heater, and a kitchen and laundry unit with sink, laundry tub, electric range, refrigerator, and storage space for dishes and silver. All you needed was a tent and you were in business anywhere.

Though the whole package was never marketed—heaven knows why!—Bucky's A-frame carrier became the small boatman's favorite vehicle for transporting his craft.

Just at the end of this period Bucky designed his first shelter which was actually put to use. In the early summer of 1940, he and Christopher Morley were driving through Missouri near Mark Twain's Hannibal. Glistening in the sunlight across the level fields stood a cluster of circular corrugated steel grain bins. The sight of them fired a spark in Bucky's imagination that was a combination of intuition and his consistent preoccupation with housing. "Do you see those grain bins over there?" he asked Morley.

"Yes," said the writer. "Kind of pretty, aren't they?"

[5] *Architectural Forum,* October, 1940.

"They are," Bucky agreed. "They could also be the most efficient unit for a small prefabricated house now available for mass production by present industrial methods. You could house a small family in one at a cost of about a dollar per square foot of floor space."

As Morley looked dubious, Bucky launched into an enthusiastic, explanation of why and how: "A cylinder encloses considerably more space than a cube of the same wall area; ergo, less material is needed. Properly capped by a roof or fitted lid, the cylinder would be inherently rigid and require no bracing, as those bins are. Their natural streamlining would cut internal heat loss to a minimum and the circular shape produces the most efficient distribution of internal heat."

Bucky added imaginative details of how insulation could be obtained by introducing fiberglass between the outer walls and an inner plywood lining; windows made like portholes—he always thought in terms of ships—would not weaken or clash with the circular walls; a dozen other refinements. The circular plates and the lid could be shipped anywhere and quickly bolted together on the spot.

As Bucky expanded on this theme, Morley, like everyone who ever heard him in the first bright flash of a new idea, glistened with enthusiasm. "Why don't you make them yourself?" he asked.

"Because I haven't got the money."

Morley became very serious. "Look," he said, *Kitty Foyle* has made me a sinful amount of money. It's just pouring in—book, paperback, movies, everything! Let me finance it."

Ordinarily Bucky, the burnt child, would have been wary of again accepting money from an acquaintance for one of his projects. But Morley was a true friend—one to be trusted beyond cavil. "Let's do it," Bucky said. "First we'll find out who makes those things."

The war in Europe, which Bucky had long foreseen because of what he considered the greed and stupidity of financiers and politicians, had begun the previous fall (September, 1939) with the invasion of Poland by the Nazis. For a time after the fall of Warsaw, while the German and Allied armies had sat in fortifications just looking at each other, it had seemed as though the United States would not fight in this one, though Bucky thought otherwise. However, in April, the Germans had taken Denmark and Norway. Even as Bucky and Chris Morley were driving through Missouri, the Nazi armies were sweeping through Holland and Belgium toward their lightning invasion of

France. From smug complacency Americans had suddenly launched a panic preparedness program against the time when they, too, might be attacked. Thus was Bucky's new idea almost aborted and as suddenly saved.

The Butler Manufacturing Company of Kansas City, Missouri, turned out to be the best equipped for Bucky's purpose. As he headed west Bucky was feverishly making engineering drawings in his fine-lined style of the details of his new house, his mind racing ahead of his pencil, evolving ingenious problem-solving devices.

As finally turned out by the Butler Company under contract with the newly organized Dymaxion Company of Delaware, the Dymaxion Deployment Unit, as Bucky later named it, was a perfectly circular structure twenty feet in diameter made of corrugated galvanized steel lined with wallboard to the inner side of which fiberglass insulation had been laminated. The lidlike roof, fitted tightly all around for strength, had a translucent ventilator on top which could be raised or lowered. The foundation was a circular brick floor covered by a layer of corrugated steel covered with one-half-inch Celotex insulating boards on top of which was a layer of hard-pressed Masonite.

The interior was divided into three pie-shaped rooms by heavy, fireproof curtains strung on wires, which could be drawn back to make one large room. The round portholes were glazed with acrylic plastic, the first time it was ever used for this purpose. A small circular bin was hitched on the back of the main building for utilities and bathroom.

The DDU, minus the bricks, weighed only 3,200 pounds, about as much as a medium-sized car, and with Montgomery Ward furnishings, including a kerosene stove and refrigerator, was priced at $1,250.

Bucky always built things in an unorthodox way. Like the 4D house, this one was erected from the top down. First the roof was assembled and hoisted up on a specially designed pole. Then the top sections of the walls were bolted together and to the roof and hoisted up. The lower circle was installed by the same procedure. Then the mast was removed.

On a hot day in August, 1940, the prototype was erected outside the Butler factory, and their engineers, headed by President E. E. Norquist, came to inspect it. They studied it with admiration. "Now let's go inside," said Norquist.

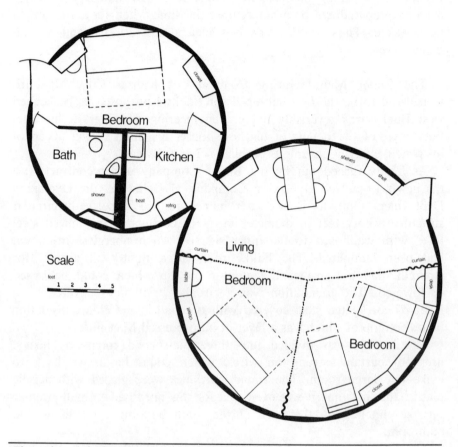

Floor plan of double Dymaxion Deployment Unit.

The temperature was over 100° and the sun-heated steel walls of the house almost burned your hand. "No thank you," said one engineer. "You'll fry in there."

Norquist was a sport and went in anyway. Then he shouted, "Hey, it's air-conditioned!"

Very cautiously the others followed. It was, in fact, much cooler inside. Bucky was laughing in high delight. The house, was, as he had expected, air-conditioned by nature. The superheated air rising from the steel walls created a vacuum under the house which sucked cool air down the ventilator.

Dymaxion Deployment Unit, 1940.

The vicissitudes of the DDU began when the British government ordered some for troop housing, then cancelled the order due to priorities of shipping space for weapons. Manufacture of it began for cheap civilian housing as Bucky had intended. But the crash rearmament program of the United States forced the government to ration steel: there would be none for experimental civilian housing. Bucky and the Butler Company thought they would be forced to abandon the whole idea.

Then there was a sudden dramatic change. Great Britain was now fighting alone against the Nazis, who had conquered France and were continuing their victorious advance through the Balkans and Greece. The United States Government was openly supporting England by all means "short of war," and greatly enlarging its own perimeters of defense. This meant that small bodies of American troops and technicians must be stationed in far-off places where housing was unavailable. Some bright character in the general staff realized that the DDU, so light that it could be shipped by air, and easily erected at any spot on the globe, would be ideal housing for these cadres. A unit was installed in Haynes Point Park in Washington for study by the military. They looked at it, and saw that it was good.

Moving as quickly as government can only in wartime, Butler Manufacturing was accorded top priority for steel and orders for as many DDUs as they could turn out running twenty-four hours a day.

The units were soon pouring off the assembly lines, and being shipped all over the globe. Bucky insisted that each shipment should include a tool kit and the special sectional mast used in erecting them. They were used at radar installations on remote Pacific islands and in other distant places. A small city of them was built on the coast of the Persian Gulf for the use of American pilots and mechanics who were assembling and flight-testing American war planes sent there by ship to be flown on to Russia who had now (June 30, 1941) been attacked by Germany. These DDUs were air-conditioned and lighted by electrical hookup to generators on an American ship moored alongside the pier.

When the United States entered the war after the Japanese attack on Pearl Harbor on December 7, 1941, an enormously increased war production produced a stringent shortage of steel. No more was available for housing, even for troops. The Butler Company's priority was cancelled and the production of DDUs ended even more abruptly than it had begun. But thousands of them had been profitably built. To his surprise, and almost against his principles, Bucky—and Chris Morley —had made money—not a lot, but some.

After the war, as always with Bucky's attempts to improve housing for mankind, the domes ran head-on into building codes and zoning restrictions. No matter how popular domes were for auditoriums and other large enclosures, the individual homeowner had enormous difficulties in building one to inhabit personally unless he lived in a very remote area, or one managed by an extraordinarily intelligent and flexible board of supervisors. Thus, the domes became a symbol of Bucky's continuing battle against the rigid rules of the construction establishment, in which he has been joined by thousands of people who want to break the shackles that capital and labor have fastened on debt-ridden homeowners in the name of protecting them against shoddy workmanship and cheap materials. So far very few dome-houses have been built.

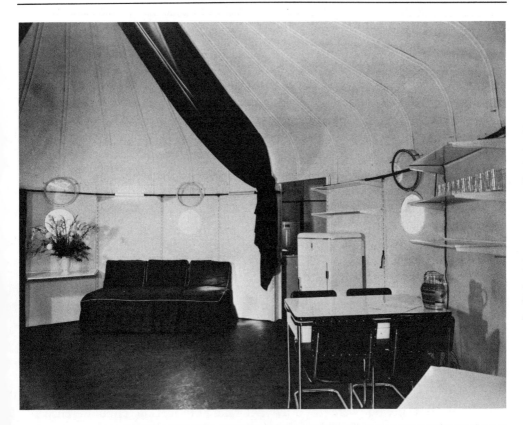

Interior of Dymaxion Deployment Unit furnished as a home, 1940.

It was during this summer of 1941 that Bucky decided to stop drinking forever. Though he was very busy with the DDU, he was thinking of many other things and constantly refining his concepts of the design revolution. And he was talking to anyone who would listen about his great design for the future of mankind, which, in his dedication to it, had become a holy crusade to him, a feeling that was intensified by his emotions concerning the useless war that was being fought. He says: "I found that my drinking was interfering with the design revolution; because when you are drinking, even if it doesn't distort the sense of what you are saying, people think it does. They think you are just babbling. I realized that you cannot drink and be taken seriously as a prophet of the future. So I stopped."

Just like that, Bucky stopped drinking. And ever since that day his habits of both eating and drinking have become more and more ascetic, much as the saints of old gave up all worldly vanities for their dedication to God. He eats, not for enjoyment, but merely to keep himself in the best possible physical condition.

He has also given up all other stimulants except very weak tea. He believes this flushes out his system and he drinks forty or fifty cups of it every day. Wherever he is, except on the lecture stage, a kettle is always kept boiling and the teapot close by his hand. "Hot water would do as well," he says, "but it is so insipid. I just put in enough tea to give it a faint flavor."

The tea does, indeed, keep his system flushed out. He goes to the bathroom about once an hour. Concerning this habit he made one of his humorous little sketches, neatly framed for his sister-in-law, Hope Hewlett Watts, which is reproduced herewith:

One of the things Bucky was conceiving at this time was a new kind of map of the world. Projecting an accurate flat map of something that is spherical like the earth is fantastically difficult, so difficult that it had never been done successfully. The maps generally in use were based on the projection first made by Mercator back in 1569. In the Mercator projection the meridians of longitude are straight lines running north and south. But on a globe the meridians converge at the North and South poles. At the equator they are approximately 69 miles apart. But if you were to draw a circle 360 feet in circumference around the North Pole, the meridians of longitude would be *one foot apart*. It is easy to see that carrying them up from the equator in straight lines produces increasing distortion, until in the Arctic it is absurd. On a conventional map Greenland looks almost as large as South America, when it is really no larger than Argentina.

Various attempts had been made to achieve less distorted projections—orthographic, stereographic, external perspective projections, etc. *The Encyclopaedia Britannica* of 1952, ignoring Bucky, states flatly, "It is impossible to retain throughout the proportion of lines or areas or equality of angles. . . ." It goes on to state that if some areas are accurate, others must be distorted. Bucky decided that in his future world of extreme rapidity of transit such distortion would not do.

He started with the tremendous handicap of not having studied spherical trigonometry except for the little he had picked up in navigation courses in the navy. In any event it would have required days, perhaps months of calculation, in those precomputer days. Bucky decided to work it out empirically. He proposed to base his map of the world on the principle of a three-way great circle grid, which mathematicians said could not be done. While he was still in Kansas City he had the Butler mechanics make him two "beautiful copper hemispheres" so accurately machined that they fitted one inside the other as perfectly as a universal joint. He explained:

"Being pure hemispheres the edge of one became a great circle ruler and I could take any two points on the inner one and bring the outer one to that and this edge made an absolutely perfect great circle ruler because a great circle is a line formed by a plane going through the center of a sphere. So the hemisphere was a plane going through the center. Now, with this I was able to lay out my map with squares and triangles—60-degree edges on all squares; all the triangles were 60 degrees of arc. Working very, very carefully on the inner hemisphere with an extremely sharp scribe I would make my mathematical points. Then I would take my great circle ruler and scribe the great circle between those points very, very accurately. I did the spherical triangles within one degree of accuracy. I had 60 intervals along the edge of the triangles and I connected those with my great circle ruler and it made a three-way great circle grid of perfect triangles."

Though it was done for the map, this was the inception of the geodesic dome; for Bucky said to himself, "If I can ever do the mathematics of this, I feel that I can make a completely triangulated spherical structure. I think the same grid can be worked there. If I have tension between the legs of the triangles they won't spread under a load. Therefore I can load any one point on a sphere and it will distribute the load through tension to three other points and on to hexagons— [made up of triangles] and icosahedrons. At each vertice [point] the load will be distributed three ways so in no time the load will become so diffuse it will not in any way jeopardize the structure. I haven't done it yet. I'll have to do that by trigonometry. . . ."

Meanwhile, Bucky worked out his map of the world using triangles,

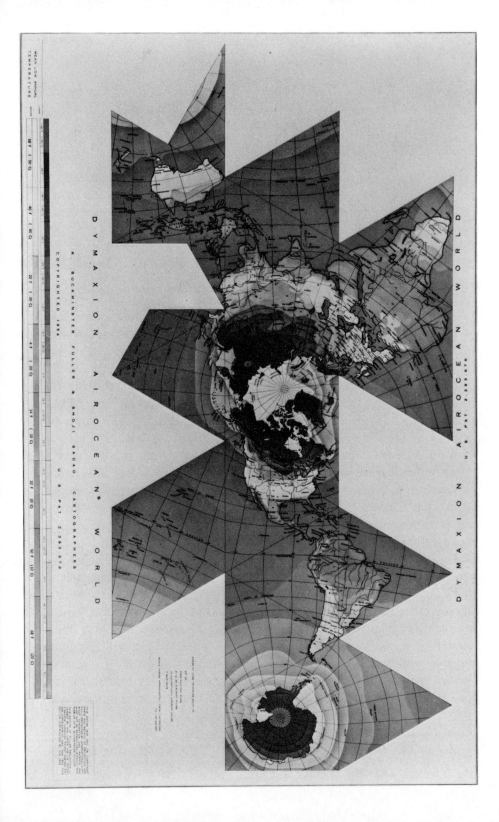

DYMAXION AIROCEAN* WORLD

R. BUCKMINSTER FULLER & SHOJI SADAO. CARTOGRAPHERS

COPYRIGHTED 1954

U. S. PAT. 2,393,676

DYMAXION AIROCEAN WORLD

U. S. PAT. 2,393,676

MEAN LOW ANNUAL
TEMPERATURE

and squares very accurately measured. These triangles and squares with portions of the globe upon them were then cut out of paper so they could be fitted together in any perspective—the view from the North or South Pole, or from one great continent or another, or the ocean world. They could also be fitted together to make an icosahedronal vector equilibrium—a twenty-sided globe. Thus, one could study different routes or angles; and in other variations one could chart the density of populations along parallels of latitude; or mineral belts, or fertile agricultural lands. But the main great point of Bucky's map was that, although there were slight distortions in all areas incident to projecting a sphere on a flat surface, no single area was distorted in sacrifice to another, and the proportion of lines, areas, and angles was retained throughout, which the *Encyclopaedia Britannica* said could not be done.

Bucky offered the Dymaxion Airocean World Map, as he called it, to the editors of *Life* magazine, with whom he had consulted once a week during his time on *Fortune*. They assigned his close friend Gerard Piel of the beer family to write the explanatory article. Piel went through a great deal of discussion with the scientists and mathematicians, who were brought in by *Life* as consultants, before they dared to publish the Dymaxion map. They unanimously said in a derogatory manner that it was "pure invention"; that Bucky had somehow fudged it.

In spite of this, *Life* concluded that it really worked and decided to publish it anyhow. That issue (March 1, 1943) sold 3,000,000 copies, the greatest circulation *Life* had ever attained up to that time.

The derogatory remarks made by the scientists redounded to Bucky's benefit when he applied for a patent on his map. His patent attorney told him that in 1900 the United States Patent Office had ruled that it was impossible to patent any further cartographic projection, as all the possible mathematics and projections had already been exhausted. However, Bucky pointed out that: "We have three noted experts, who say this map is 'pure invention.' Even though they said it in a negative way, it is the best possible testimony to prove to the patent examiners that it is really an invention."

Bucky got his patent.

← *Dymaxion map of the world.*

CHAPTER XIV

BUCKY TURNS HIS BACK

EVEN though Bucky believed that all wars were irrational and unnecessary and that World War II, like the others, had been brought on by the intrigues of Fincap maneuvering for control of the fictitiously scarce resources of the earth, he was sufficiently shocked by the genocidal policies of Hitler and the barbarity of the Japanese, and also influenced by his latent patriotism, to want to play a part in the defense of his country. In addition he could see that the design revolution would be set back by centuries if the totalitarian powers won.

Impressed by the success of the Dymaxion Deployment Unit and the interest in the Airocean World Map, people in high places were at last beginning to take Buckminster Fuller seriously. Late in 1942, he was offered the important post of Director of the Mechanical Engineering Division of the Board of Economic Warfare. He eagerly accepted it.

Leaving Anne in their apartment in New York because Allegra was still at Dalton School, Bucky headed for Washington. The capital was jammed and running over with people brought there by the immense expansion of wartime government activities. Bucky could not find a place in which he could afford to live, which bothered him less than it would most people. "You might find an empty barn or warehouse or something like that," a friend said to him.

"That's all right," Bucky said cheerfully. "I brought my bathroom with me."

He had driven over in the Dymaxion bathroom truck.

Bucky eventually wound up in an apartment over the garage of the Yugoslavian Embassy, 2222 Decatur Place. Anne stayed on in New York until Allegra finished the year at Dalton School, and then joined Bucky at Decatur Place. The following year Allegra went as a day scholar to Miss Madeira's fashionable school in a Washington suburb.

The work at the Board of Economic Warfare was challenging and Bucky performed it efficiently. In 1944 he was promoted to Special Assistant to the Deputy Director of the Foreign Economic Administration. However, it was neither sufficiently creative nor did it consume enough time to fully utilize his prodigious energy output. Midway in 1943, he embarked on an exciting creative project which saw him working in Washington by day and moonlighting in New York nights.

Some time before this, Gerard Piel, who had written two stories for *Life* on Henry J. Kaiser, had introduced the great industrialist to Bucky. Kaiser was evidently greatly impressed by Bucky, for soon after the latter went to Washington Kaiser called him up and asked if it would be possible to design a car that would have certain specifications such as a high rate of acceleration, seat four people, and greatly undersell the cars then on the market. Bucky said, "Will you hold the wire while I do a little calculating?"

In a short time he told Kaiser, "Yes, it is possible."

A few days later Kaiser called Bucky at home late one night and told him that at a dinner for important industrialists he had told them that the big thing after the war was automobiles, and that he was going to go into the business with a brand-new type of car. "Now, I've committed myself," Kaiser then said. "You said it could be done and I want you to design it for me."

Bucky said, "Give me twenty-four hours and I'll let you know."

The next day he went to Milo Perkins, Executive Director of the BEW, and asked if he could do the job for Kaiser in his spare time. Perkins had no objection, though he thought Bucky would find it impossible to get engineers to help him.

So Bucky accepted Kaiser's proposal. In New York he interested Walter Saunders, a young engineer, and the latter's architect partner, in the project. They had a beautiful house they had rebuilt on 72nd Street and were willing to work at night with Bucky. After the day's work in Washington, Bucky would take the five o'clock train to New York, work with his partners all night, and return to Washington on the first morning train. He slept on the trains. Bucky says, "That is all the sleep I got."

In exactly one month the three men had made all the engineering drawings and had constructed a full-scale mock-up of the car. It was a three-wheel design, which had front-wheel as well as rear-wheel steering, so it could move sideways like a crab into a parking space. It was to be powered by individual, very light, hydraulic turbine engines, which Bucky had designed, mounted on each wheel.

At Kaiser's suggestion Bucky set up the mock-up and laid out the drawings in a suite Kaiser had rented in the Waldorf. Then the industrialist, his son, and top engineers came to inspect it. They were all enthusiastic and Kaiser said, "I'm going to go ahead and produce it."

After some excited planning, Kaiser asked Bucky how much he owed him so far. In his almost willful financial innocence Bucky said: "I am not in business. I don't feel like doing it that way. I'll simply give you my costs."

He added up the amount he had paid his assistants for their night work, the rent of the office where they had worked, and the amount of his fares back and forth to New York. The entire cost of producing the completed design and the full-scale mock-up came to approximately $2,500. "When I think back on it," Bucky says, "so small an amount was really preposterous."

Then Kaiser said, "You have designed this thing for me, and have charged nothing for your services. How do you want to share in it?"

"I'll just leave that up to you," Bucky replied.

Very warmly Henry Kaiser said, "My best friends have all said that to me at one time or another."

It was then arranged that Kaiser would build a prototype out on the Coast and that Bucky would join him there when he was ready to start, if he could get Milo Perkins's permission to go. "Everything looked fine to me," Bucky said. "but when Kaiser walked out that door, it was the last time I ever saw him."

Milo Perkins considered that building a car with such advanced technology would be a very important initiative for American industry after the war. He agreed to give Bucky leave of absence whenever Kaiser sent for him. Bucky waited for the word, and waited and waited. . . .

The only contacts Bucky had with the Kaiser Company were through young Kaiser and a company representative named Schleptner. They told him that Kaiser's method of operating was to set up the original project, after which his representatives and engineers would follow through. Kaiser, they said, paid no attention to what happened after the inception of a project. This naturally made Bucky uneasy.

Then he learned from Milo Perkins that Kaiser had hired Alexander Taub, the man who had designed the current Chevrolet engine, to work on the project. Furthermore, Taub proposed to put an engine of his own design into the car. Bucky was horrified. The engines he had designed weighed only a few pounds; the Taub engine weighed six hundred pounds—more than the whole car as Bucky had designed it. With that weight everything would be out of balance; the specifications for parts too weak. It simply would not work.

Then Bucky got queries from the Kaiser engineers concerning his springing plans for the wheels; his design for the steering mechanism, etc.—evidently they were designing something.

Bucky telephoned Gerard Piel, who had meantime left *Life* to become head of Kaiser's Public Relations Department. "Gerry," he said, "you introduced me to Henry Kaiser; and something very strange is going on out there. I designed this car; I didn't get paid anything for doing it except expenses. I was supposed to go out there and build the prototype. I've had experience in this because I have built prototypes of three cars and I would know how to do it. Quite clearly they are working on a car because the engineers have been calling me and that makes me feel that something very wrong is going on."

Piel said, "I'll talk to Kaiser."

Following this conversation Piel wrote to Bucky that absolutely nothing was going on. Then came more inquiries which made Bucky protest to Piel that he was sure they were producing a car. The next letter Bucky received came from Henry Kaiser himself in which he said, "I've called the whole thing off and I am taking my losses like a man."

Bucky did not learn the whole story of the doublecross until after the war when he read a magazine article about the new Kaiser car—a purely conventional vehicle which was a disastrous failure. The article said that Kaiser had tried to build a Dymaxion car designed by Fuller and that it had run into a tree and been smashed up, proving that it was no good.

Bucky felt, quite rightly, that he had not only been defrauded but traduced. Of course the car was no good—with that big engine it had to be. But in addition to the deceit and bad faith, the use of his trademark and name on a car he had not built had brought discredit upon it—and Bucky. He had no redress. For one thing he was too busy by then on other, more important projects. Bucky was especially hurt by Piel's betrayal of their friendship. He said, "It was a bitter kind of thing. . . ."

When he finished the design of the Kaiser car, Bucky's social life in Washington became very interesting. To take the place of the Three Hours for Lunch Club there were the Thursday Luncheons at the Cosmos Club. There he became very friendly with Vannevar Bush and other scientists from the Manhattan Project, and various exiled Europeans who were working in the American war effort. Of course they did not talk about their supersecret projects, but they could discuss general principles. Bucky found them intellectually stimulating and they reciprocated. It was another step in his self-education, which was continuing and, perhaps, will not end even after he becomes an indestructible "pattern in integrity."

In the Board of Economic Warfare Bucky learned of a very serious problem that threatened the vital production of war planes. At the start of the mass production of the fighters and the big four-engined bombers, the techniques of automobile manufacture had been tried. It turned out a lot of airplanes but they were not really first class. Bucky says: "It was absolutely preposterous to build airplanes by the Detroit method of having huge dies to smash metal into the desired shapes. You could not do it as accurately as was necessary. In England and Germany there had been an enormous war-accelerated improvement in design and our first planes were just not as good as theirs. There were enormous losses when they first went into action."

As a result, manufacturing was returned, as far as possible, to the regular airplane companies, especially for the great new superfortresses —the B29s. Large factories were hastily built by Boeing in Wichita, Kansas, where there were already smaller airplane companies. Wichita went from 100,000 inhabitants to 200,000 in one week. People had to sleep in three shifts in beds. The factories were running twenty-four hours a day, and so were the moving picture theatres, to accommodate workers who came off the evening shift at midnight, had a bite of dinner, and went to the movies at 3 A.M. It was a crowded, miserable existence for them and, even more important, the workers felt insecure. For they realized that when the war was over there would be no need for so many planes and they would be out of a job. "Why put up with this lousy life and end up on the street when we can go somewhere else and get a job that has a future?" they asked themselves.

Because of this reasoning the ratio of quits over hirings, as the manufacturers called it, became so precipitous that it threatened the maintenance of production schedules. It looked as though the B29 program might founder. Something had to be done.

Bucky learned of this situation first from his old friend Grover Loening, who had built Vincent Astor's plane and gone on to great success with the Loening amphibian. He had sold his company, which had become Grumman, and he was now head of the Aircraft Production Division of the War Production Board. Indeed, everybody there was terribly worried about the situation in Wichita; they were searching anxiously for something that would give the airplane workers a sense of job security.

The 4D Dymaxion house suddenly became the answer. Bucky could redesign it so it could be manufactured by an airplane company with comparatively little retooling. There would be a gigantic need for housing after the war. It might become a great new industry in which thousands of skilled workers would find jobs. It was a natural.

Bucky became the man of the hour. His old friend Clare Boothe Luce had introduced him to Herman Wolf, who was a public relations man for labor on the War Production Board, and Wolf arranged a meeting with Walter Reuther of the CIO as well as Harvey Brown, president of the International Association of Machinists, the airplane workers' union, and other labor leaders. The IAM council was particularly enthusiastic about the project as they were not only patriotically concerned about falling production in Wichita, but worried about the fate of their members after the war. Bucky consulted with them as to which airplane company had the best labor relations. They told him Beech Aircraft of Wichita.

In the summer of 1944, Bucky and Gregory Bardacke, who was also a labor representative on the War Production Board, went to Wichita to see Jack Gaty, who was vice president and general manager of Beech Aircraft. Gaty was a slim, trim, expensively dressed man in his early forties with strong features, voltaic gray eyes, and a precision-machined mind. Contrary to wartime usage he would not allow the federal government to purchase the great machines which Beech Aircraft needed to fill the huge war production orders, but insisted on merely renting them. He wanted Beech to be under no obligation to government. He was such a strong proponent of free enterprise and so fanatically opposed to governmental interference with business that he and his company kept free and clear of such a "socialistic" subsidy.

One would suppose that Gaty's extreme right-wing views would produce an immediate conflict with Bucky's antiestablishmentarianism. It did not. For Bucky was so completely apolitical that he admitted no difference between left and right. To him all politics were both so corrupt and so totally irrelevant that he completely ignored them, and could work happily with men of all shades of opinion so long as they knew their job. He and Gaty became, and remained, warm friends.

At the moment of their first meeting Jack Gaty said that he was profoundly uninterested in manufacturing "prefabricated houses." Bucky was profoundly irritated by the implication that his was a prefabricated house. He says, "It was evident that Jack Gaty thought of me as an industrial designer, who would take an airplane and make the seats more comfortable and change the decor and paint stripes on the sides to make it look prettier."

So Bucky began to talk at the rate of seven thousand words an hour —maybe eight. And he talked for at least four hours, by the end of which time Gaty had changed his opinion of both Bucky and his house. He was impressed by Bucky's bathroom; and by the plans for the house; by Bucky's knowledge of the kind of tooling that would be needed and his knowledge of production engineering. Most of all he was impressed by that Niagara of ideas.

At the end of four hours Jack Gaty said, "I'd like you to talk to my workers."

He called a quick meeting of the shop stewards and all the workers who could get into the Wichita headquarters of the International Machinists Association. After Bucky had talked to them for several hours everyone agreed that the project was worthwhile if a prototype could be produced at Beech. After this discussion Gaty said: "What are we waiting for. Let's go!"

A preliminary agreement was signed that night.

Bucky went back to Washington and, in his spare time, incorporated the Dymaxion Living Machines Company—later changed to Fuller Houses, Inc. R. Buckminster Fuller was chief designer and engineer. The president was Herman Wolf. Other officers were Gregory Bardacke and Bucky's secretary at the BEW, Cynthia Lacy, whom he made vice president and secretary of Dymaxion Living Machines. The company was capitalized with 15,500 shares of stock at $10 par value. Fuller held 5,500 shares, Beech was given an option on 1,000 shares, and the remaining 9,500 were sold to "the public," which public consisted mostly of friends of the officers, among them several members of Herman Wolf's family and many people he knew in the labor unions. Harvey Brown became a member of the board of directors. The charter was so worded that Bucky's 5,500 shares gave him a veto power over production of the house. He frankly said: "If, and when, adequate time and money and know-how have been put into the Dymaxion houses, they will be installable anywhere in the world as quickly as a telephone. But it will take time, probably until 1952. Ergo, whatever we can do in 1944 must be thought of as gestative functions. The time is premature to think of this new industry as a commercially exploitable undertaking."

Therefore, the stock was sold on the basis of "consider your money thrown away." The sales argument was that its purchase was to be considered a contribution toward solving the postwar housing problem and not a financial investment. In other words the "ice cream soda clause."

In October, 1944, the officers of the company resigned their government jobs and moved en masse to Wichita. There Bucky had another conference with Jack Gaty in which they settled the details of the production of a prototype. Bucky says: "Jack did not want his own production upset, so he agreed to fix up a disused building that was in rather poor shape. They put in new beams so the roof would not fall on our heads. It was big enough to build the prototype inside."

Remembering his experience at Bridgeport, where his mechanics had staged a slowdown for fear of losing their jobs, Bucky said to Gaty: "I want six of your best mechanics. You have 20,000 people working for you so you can spare them. And if they are your very best they will not be in fear of working for me, for they will know they can have their old jobs back."

Jack agreed that this was reasonable. After various other points were settled a formal contract was drawn up and signed. Then Gaty had Bucky talk to the workers again, not only just those at Beech but to as many of the other workers as possible. Such was his enthusiasm that they envisioned not only building a prototype at Beech, but a great new industry of housing that could be produced in airplane factories.

A few weeks after Bucky got to Wichita, Jack Gaty called to him. "Come here! I want you to see this curve. It's an absolute must."

Gaty showed him the graph of hirings and quits. The down-curve that had made everybody so concerned had swung upward so sharply that it looked like a mountain peak rising from a valley of despair. In Washington the Air Corps people were ecstatic. That was one problem solved.

With an Air Corps contract for two prototypes and the highest priority for materials, work was begun. Bucky imported Arthur Hewlett from Lawrence in a managerial capacity and his young friend Edgar J. (Sonny) Applewhite as director of personnel. For Bucky was an incorrigible nepotist, not from greed or to spread the wealth among his family, but simply because he trusted those he loved.

As it was built under Bucky's direction, the new Dymaxion Dwelling Machine was a vastly improved version of the original 4D house. It, too, was hung from a mast by steel cables, the ends of which were anchored in the ground, but instead of being hexagonal it was perfectly round, 118 feet in circumference. The walls were made of sheet aluminum stamped out by dies designed by Bucky with the help of Beech engineers. Completely around the house at eye level was a broad sheet of plexiglass slightly tinted to obviate glare, with pull curtains for privacy. The domed ceiling was sixteen feet high. On top of the outside of the dome was a big, streamlined ventilator, which swung with the wind like a weathercock, designed to furnish natural air conditioning like the Deployment Unit, but much more effectively.

The bow-shaped living room, occupying about a third of the interior, had a stainless steel fireplace—because Bucky loved open fires and recognized their contribution to the ambiance of a house. There were two bedrooms, each with a Dymaxion bathroom, and a small kitchen. Ample closet space was provided and an unusual amount of storage space on motor-driven revolving shelves. The floors were made of tapering plywood strips between converging aluminum floor beams. The color of the neoprene silver lining of the ceiling dome and walls could be changed at whim by colored lights directed at it from oval drumheads in the partition units. There was an infinite number of amenities and engineering refinements invented by Bucky's fertile brain to make housekeeping easier and protect the interior environment.

He had originally figured that the 4D house should weigh 6,000 pounds. The Wichita prototype weighed almost exactly three tons.*

* A conventional house of the same size weighs about 150 tons.

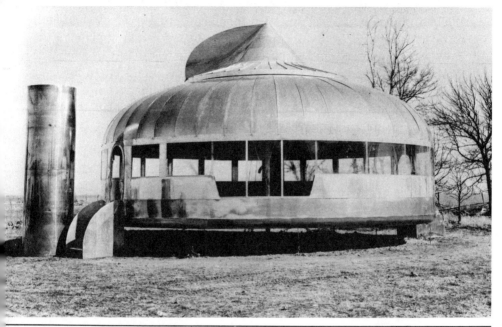

Prototype of Dymaxion Dwelling Machine being built at Beech Aircraft, 1945.

No single component, no beam or rib or panel, weighed more than ten pounds and each could be lifted by a man with one hand, leaving the other free to fasten it in place. All the components of a disassembled house, including the mast, could be packed in a packing case of less than 300 cubic feet for shipping by air to any place in the world. The retail price of the house would be $6,500, about a dollar a pound, or the cost of a Cadillac, at that time.

The amazing thing about this Dymaxion Dwelling Machine, in spite of its dismally mechanistic name and its mass-production components, was its elegance and cozy comfort. The blue-tinted aluminum of its circular exterior seemed to harmonize with the sky, while its carefully planned and mellowly decorated rooms were both pretty and surprisingly welcoming.

Another surprise to everybody—including Bucky—was the quality of its acoustics. Marian Anderson, who tried them out by singing in the prototype, said that never before had she heard the sound of her voice flow *around* a room.

The Dymaxion Dwelling Machine was exhibited to the public in Wichita in October, 1945. Between then and February many thousands of people from all over the country came to see it and applaud. Publicity was widespread and enthusiastic. *Fortune* featured it in an article illustrated by luscious color photographs. All this produced an amazing flood of 37,000 *unsolicited* orders, many of them accompanied by checks. The stock of the renamed Fuller Houses, Inc., went to twenty dollars a share on the over-the-counter market. Naturally, this was when Bucky's troubles began.

Interior of Dymaxion Dwelling Machine, 1945.

His difficulty was that everyone suddenly saw a chance to make big money. A highly successful Philadelphia entrepreneur named William Wasserman bought a thousand shares and temporarily became chairman of the board for the purpose of arranging the financing for mass-producing the house. Herman Wolf and the labor people were as anxious as the capitalists to profit by the bonanza they saw glittering before their eyes. Due largely to Bucky's integrity—intransigence they called it—the glitter was fool's gold.

The Beech engineers figured that to begin mass production—machinery, sales organization, setting up dealerships, the whole intricate, expensive business of starting a big new industry—$10,000,000 capital must be raised. The financiers decided to do this by recapitalizing Fuller Houses, Inc., by issuing 750,000 shares at a par value of $1 a share. The original shares were exchanged at a ratio of one for ten, leaving 595,000 shares to be sold to the public at $10 a share, automatically making the original issue worth $100 a share—a nice profit! This would produce $5,950,000. The rest could be had by borrowing from the banks or selling first mortgage bonds. The U.S. Government was ready to help with a big loan. If Bucky had chosen to sell out at this point he would have made half a million dollars.

Everyone apparently ignored Bucky's genuine moral repugnance for this type of financing and they had forgotten his original statement that building the prototype must be thought of as "a gestative function. The time is premature to think of this new industry as a commercially exploitable undertaking." As usual, they did not think he mean it. But he *did*.

The story of just what happened to Fuller Houses depends on whom you talk to. Bill Wasserman says: "No matter how hard we tried or what pressure we used, we could never get a finalized plan from Bucky. Every time we thought we had one, he would come in with a whole new variation on the design. For instance, if there were rumors of unrest in the plumbers union, he would insist on his self-contained, shit-packaging john, which nobody had invented yet, not even Bucky. I admire his brilliance and humanitarian philosophy; he's a great man; but he was impossible to work with." *

To get rid of Wasserman, Bucky offered to buy him out at par. Wasserman gladly accepted and told all his friends to unload Fuller

* William Wasserman to the author.

Houses, which most of them did, including Jack Gaty who sold out Beech's 10,000 (new) shares at a handsome profit.

Bucky was deeply disturbed by this attempt to capitalize on his invention. Because the whole thing was premature he considered the financial shenanigans nothing more than an attempt to bilk the public, or, at best, a deluded effort to anticipate the necessary time sequence of gestation which, by his reckoning, was twenty-five years from his 1927 conception of the house, which would therefore not be viable until 1952. He says:

"What I was really developing was a good prototype which was fine for the Air Force, who could handle it. But it was not ready for the general public. People wanted to buy; but there was no industry to distribute the houses. In a sense what went on was almost scandalous. Legally there was no fraud whatever intended, but to me it seemed inherently very corrupt because of what I knew about it.

"There were a number of people who wanted to come in and take over the business and put up the ten million. The politicians in Washington were willing to back us to get the house into production. Herman Wolf wanted to get it going. And I kept vetoing. I said, 'It is not ready. Here are all those orders, but who is going to install it? The present building industry won't do it.' The plumbers say they are the only ones licensed to hook it up to the city mains and the electricians say they are the only ones licensed to do the wiring. Both unions say: 'If you bring in a house with all the plumbing and wiring all done we won't have any business left. We can't handle it unless we can take all the wiring and plumbing apart and put it together again.'

"Also, the houses would have to be delivered by a very special truck, rather like a telephone truck, and we had no such trucks and no capable distributors.

"Hundreds of people came to us who wanted to be distributors, but I kept showing them that they did not have the capability of putting this thing up. It was not premature as a demonstration of a principle, or for the Air Force; it was exactly right for them. It was technically very successful, but we were nowhere near in a position to go into mass production, and sell them to a lot of people. Because we could not deliver. And it's just not honest to sell people something you can't deliver.

"So," Bucky says, "I was forced to do just what I had done before in Bridgeport; to shut down solvent. Nobody made any money."

There was a blazing row with Herman Wolf, who felt that Bucky was deliberately preventing him and the union people he had persuaded to invest money in the enterprise from reaping their just gains. In fact, Wolf was so enraged that he made the fatal mistake of trying to drive a wedge between Anne and Bucky. He burst into the Fullers' home one day when Anne was alone and said to her, "I think you should know that Bucky is having an affair with so-and-so."

To his amazement Anne turned on him furiously, saying: "You have no right to say such things about Bucky to me. And even if it were true, it's none of your business."

Bucky has long ago forgiven Wolf, but Anne and Allegra never will.

Other stockholders were furious. They were justified from their point of view as, perhaps, Bucky was from his.

In fact, it is very difficult to assess the rights of the situation. Was Bucky completely objective in vetoing the great plans? Or was it just due to his emotional and intellectual disgust with Fincap and all its ways that made him magnify the difficulties? There was a tremendous demand for the house. The United States Government, anxious to get a new industry started to provide employment in the postwar uncertainties, and to relieve the acute housing shortage, was willing to back it with millions. Financiers were ready to provide the organization, and engineers the know-how. Might it not have been a spectacular success if Bucky had enthusiastically brought his genius to bear upon the very real problems?

But Bucky could feel no enthusiasm for a project primarily designed to make money. He could not force himself to play that game. There can be no doubt that he genuinely believed it would be ethically wrong for him to associate his God-given competence with that type of organization; gambling with the credulity of people on the chance that the promoters could pull it off on a heads-we-win, tails-the-public-loses, and we-win-anyhow basis. Again, as before, he felt that it would betray his ideals and falsify his covenant with himself to work selflessly to the betterment of mankind. God, or the Great Intelligence, helping him, he had to do it his way.

Once again he turned his back on a fortune and walked away.

CHAPTER XV

GEODESIC INTUITION

WHEN Bucky had left Washington for Wichita, Anne had gone to stay with Arthur and Natalie Hewlett in Woodmere, Long Island, leaving Allegra to finish her last year as a boarder at Miss Madeira's School. After the Arthur Hewletts joined Bucky in Wichita, Anne rented an apartment at 6 Burns Street in Forest Hills, Long Island. It was a pleasant though small apartment in a far from fashionable suburb, but it was conveniently located midway between New York and Lawrence. "I liked it," Anne says, "but Allegra thought it wasn't classy enough." Bucky never cared where he lived. The Fullers lived there longer than anywhere else in their married lives—over fifteen years until the apartment was finally burned out.

Allegra had grown up to be a very pretty girl with cobalt blue eyes under long dark lashes, good features, and a golden creamy skin. She was quite small, having inherited Bucky's stocky figure. "She is all Fuller," the Hewletts say.

When she graduated from Miss Madeira's School, she spent that summer of 1946 studying ballet with Balanchine in New York. This was not a girlish whim but a long-term interest in the dance in all its aspects. Every summer she had studied different techniques with a variety of teachers. Sometime during the summer of 1946 Bucky came east for a talk with his daughter about her future.

Bucky says: "I thought Allegra was going to be an engineer, because she used to enjoy mathematics so much; and she enjoyed talking to me about my search for the coordinate system of nature. She was an extremely good critic of my mathematical thinking. For that reason I had entered her for MIT. I was very thrilled when they agreed to take her, because at that time there were only six girls in MIT."

When he talked to Allegra, Bucky sensed her lack of interest in becoming an engineer and her genuine love of the dance. So, hiding his disappointment, he told her: "I can see that I am really pushing you to be an engineer. You don't want that, you want to be a dancer."

Allegra nodded, and Bucky said, "Why don't you give up the idea of going to school altogether and concentrate on what you really want to do?"

Allegra did that, working with Balanchine at the New York School of Ballet for two years. But just dancing was not enough for her. Because she had lived in an atmosphere of intense intellectual excitement all her life, she found her fellow students rather dull. There was a great deal of sitting around waiting to go on, and all the girls seemed able to talk about was the best place to buy their stuffed-toe ballet slippers or the technique of ironing a tutu.

She thought of her father's great long charts of the upward progress of man; and she thought of doing something of that sort about the history of the dance. So, without giving up Balanchine and the School of Ballet, she began spending more and more time in libraries getting data about the dance. At about that time Lincoln Kirstein and Edward M. M. Warburg, who were helping to finance Balanchine, gave their great collections of terpsichorean memorabilia to the Museum of Modern Art. Knowing of Allegra's intellectual interest in the history of the dance, the curator in charge of these collections asked her to help organize and catalogue them. So, for the last part of her time with Balanchine, Allegra was also putting in a full day's work at the museum. And learning a great deal.

In an unexpected way Bucky profited by his daughter's enthusiasm for the dance and her evolving theory of it as a means of communication. During the years from 1932 to 1943, Bucky had not given any important lectures; he had dropped out of sight in that field. In 1943, he had been asked to explain his theories to a gathering of scientists who were guests of the Board of Economic Warfare at the Cosmos Club in Washington. From that time on, partly due to the publicity about the Dwelling Machine, the demand for him grew. Naturally, Allegra went to hear him on several occasions.

She loved her father very much and understood even his recondite phrasing, but she noted that other people often did not. So one day she gave him an illuminating piece of advice.

"Father," she said, "you were brought up as a New England gentleman, and they are taught that it's not good form to make flamboyant gestures. So when you lecture you stand there stiffly with your hands at your sides, just talking; and sometimes people don't get it. But when you talk to me alone you use your hands most expressively. Now, from what I have learned about the dance I know that arms and legs and body movements can be a marvelous and fundamental method of communication; and I believe that you could communicate with your audiences better if you would only *let yourself go*."

Bucky said, "Allegra, you're absolutely right."

That was the beginning of Bucky's frenetic—and endearing—style of platform expression. He starts quietly enough with simple words and phrases, but as he warms up and becomes more esoteric, he begins moving. His stubby hands form triangles and circles, his arms rotate or come together to make tetrahedra and octahedra. As he becomes more deeply involved, his legs take up the rhythm so that sometimes he is dancing all around the platform, his whole body expressing the principles of very energetic-synergetic geometry, or whatever he may be talking about. As Allegra foretold, and Norman Cousins observed when he spoke of people understanding Bucky "by osmosis," he does communicate his thoughts far more clearly by illustrating his speech with body language.

The scrapping of the Wichita project inevitably brought Bucky down in people's thinking; *Fortune* unkindly observed, "Fuller is down the flush." Of course they were quite wrong. For Wichita had been to him merely a wartime detour, though a vitally interesting one, from the mainstream of his thinking, which more and more concentrated on the mathematics of his synergetic geometry and how he could apply the general principles he had discovered to specific matters. For, as he often says, "Philosophy gains validity by the practical application of its general principles."

He was already conceiving a spherical structure based on the three-way great circle grid. He had intuitively realized that it could be done; but since it must be done with absolutely scientific accuracy, his previous empirical methods would not suffice. He says: "Between my jobs at *Fortune* and the BEW, I had managed not to be quite as impecunious as I had been. Though I had spent most of the money, I had a few things I could sell and we had an apartment at the very low rent of seventy dollars a month. So I said, 'I am just going to buy the time—I don't know how long it will take—but I am going to buy the time to fully comprehend spherical trigonometry. Because if you are going to build a dome based on geodesics and triangles you are going to have to be absolutely accurate, near enough would not be good enough.' So I invested the time—two years—1947–1948, and just really worked on my mathematics. And I got it!"

In a way this resembled Bucky's great decision of 1927 to concentrate on thinking. But he did not carry it to such lengths. For one thing, he did not feel silence was necessary. He was not now clearing rubbish from his mind, but merely studying a new discipline. He knew "what sounds he wanted to make," so he kept right on talking to anyone who would listen. More and more people were anxious to hear him. In 1947 he lectured at the American Institute of Architects in Cleveland, Dartmouth College, the Municipal Housing Show at Portland, Maine, and the Institute of Design in Chicago, besides many lesser places.

Thus he came from Wichita to the little apartment in Forest Hills to turn it inside out, but not upside down, since he regards the words up and down as purely fallacious when referring to the spherical system known as Planet Earth, where there is logically no up or down but only in and out. In fact, he later wasted a powerful amount of thought trying to find accurate substitutes for sunrise and sunset, such as "sunclipse" and "sun sighting," though these expressions failed to satisfy his poetic sensibilities.

In any event, the apartment became a combination study, workshop, and classroom and therefore a shambles. Anne made no complaint. Her serene faith in Bucky could not be shaken by any apparent failure, and her belief that her particular function in Universe was to help him in his life's work had survived worse confusion and would be triumphantly vindicated sooner than she expected.

As might have been surmised, Bucky rapidly mastered the principles of trigonometry, making some improvements on conventional doctrine as he went along. He did not wait, however, to complete the course before beginning to build models of the vision he had when he first scratched out the coordinates of that three-way great circle grid on the copper sphere that Butler had made for him.

He was to call his supreme invention the geodesic dome, because parts of great circles are technically known as geodesics and the dome was half a sphere based on great circles crisscrossing to form triangles or tetrahedra evolving into octahedra and icosahedra.

In his thinking about a dome as a dwelling, Bucky developed the historical theory that man's first habitations were domes—the natural domes of caves and the vaulted branches of trees. These *visible* geometric natural structures were but "manifestations of the invisible, because of the infra-sensorial structuring of nature's universal dynamic mathematical cellular agglomerates." Thinking about the narrow limits of man's sensorial apprehension compared to the enormous range of the macro- and micro-modules of Universe, Bucky came intuitively to one of his basic conclusions: "The physical and metaphysical are altogether one reality."

As he reconstructed the history of housing Bucky put it in two categories. The first was the natural dome which man later imitated by building conical huts or igloos, or up-ending the inverted dome bottom of his primitive basket-boats or dugout canoes over his head to keep off the rain. This evolved into the stone domes made of wedge-shaped blocks of the early seafaring peoples of the eastern Mediterranean, the domed tombs of Greece, and the Roman domes like that of the Pantheon.

In the second category were buildings based on the cube, which, according to Bucky, were inferior because horizontal crossbeams are comparatively weak. As he points out, the walls and columns of ancient buildings remain standing long after the roofs have fallen in. But the Grecian tombs, the dome of the Parthenon, and the ancient domed buildings of Istanbul, the Near East, and India remain intact. In modern times the only building to survive at ground zero in Hiroshima was a domed structure.

With his love for wordplay Bucky makes an argument for man's innate feeling that the D-om-e is H-om-e, by citing words with the root syllable om-domus (God) domicile and the fact that man travels through life from the W-om-b to the T-om-b. However, he merely points it out and is willing to accept "negative reactions."

As has been noted, before Bucky ever went to Washington or Wichita, his dome had been gestating in his mind. He even conducted some crude experiments while he was working with Beech. In his two years of study in Forest Hills, the idea became all-consuming. It was not only an intellectual development from the general principles of synergetic-energetic geometry, but an intuitive insight as well, a transcendental glimpse into the Great Intelligence.

As he explained it: "When I had worked out my three-way great circle grid of perfect triangles for the map, I realized that it would be possible to make a spherical structure or dome, which is a half sphere, formed by thirty-one great circles around a sphere, crisscrossing each other to form perfect triangles of varying sizes. The surface triangles of a sphere are the outer parts of a tetrahedron. So I had all these tetrahedra and they all go to the center of the sphere; they cannot come apart. Now supposing I cut off the points leaving only the triangles; and I have tension bands on the outside; they still can't fall in or get out, they are like triangular corks. Cylinders have parallel lines, which do not help each other; they let infinity in, and with my map I had learned that you never do anything with infinity. The triangles are a closed stable system so this distortion, this infinity thing, cannot get in.

"Nothing could be more fundamental to my feeling that it would be possible to develop a three-way great circle grid, and if I did so it would have structural strength without any precedent in history.

"The reason for this is that whereas parallel structures do not help each other, my grid of triangles with great circle tension bands would transfer a load to all parts of the structure. The bigger it was and the more triangular or octet trusses were involved, the more the load would become diffused and therefore more easily taken care of. In other words, a load upon any particular part of the structure would be absorbed by the strength of the entire structure through the tension bands. Therefore any section could be made infinitely lighter than it would have to be if it stood alone, as do parallel columns and beams."

The scientific wording of this is: "As the number of trussed faces of symmetric polyhedra are increased through the hierarchy of great circle arc . . . and chord-trussed solids, the number of vertexes and edges increase, providing more dispersed structural interactions for resisting concentrated loads and also more and shorter chords, thus providing increasingly favorable slenderness ratios for the compression columns. . . .

"Therefore, theoretically (and as far as it has been tried—practically) the size of a clear span structure is limited only by the relative alloyed coherences of the metallic atoms," Bucky wrote in 1967. "We may therefore consider clear-span geodesic, tensegrity spheres in the magnitude of two miles diameter as now realizable. . . ."[1]

In Forest Hills Bucky began to build small domes using various materials and different variations of the basic geodesic structure, and they generally worked. Then, in 1948, he was invited to go to Black Mountain College for the Summer Institute where he had delivered a lecture the previous year.

[1] *Ideas and Integrities.*

Black Mountain had been a remarkable innovation in education when it was founded by John Andrew Rice and a small group of idealistic artists and scholars in 1933. Located in the hills of North Carolina near Asheville, it was a sort of educational commune, an experiment in community education based on pure democracy and freedom from formal academic structure. Its atmosphere in some ways resembled those of the communal experiments of Brook Farm and New Harmony in New England, without their religious connotations. Many of its rustic buildings had been built by the faculty and students themselves to plans supervised by the great Walter Gropius of the Bauhaus in Berlin. In its time it had attracted some great teachers of art, music, and literature, and sent forth graduates who made names for themselves in their various disciplines.

By 1948, it was suffering the disintegration due to the clash of ideals and personalities that had also afflicted those other communal experiments. However, the summer institutes still attracted brilliant, uninhibited intellectuals, and the 1948 one was especially scintillating.

Bucky knew he would love it as he and Anne drove down the rugged road that was hardly more than a trail into a narrow valley enclosed by steep, forested hills. Unpainted wooden buildings crouched beneath the trees beside the quiet water of aptly named Lake Eden. It was a truly Edenic setting for intellectual experiments and the creation of beauty. The Fullers made many fine new friends and found some old ones there—the Josef Alberses, who had come from the Bauhaus fifteen years before, he to teach painting, she to instruct in the ancient art of weaving in very modern designs; Willem and Elaine de Kooning; the Theodore Dreisers, who came from Boston; Charles Burchard of the Harvard School of Design; John Cage, the composer; Peter Grippe, the sculptor; Erwin Bodky, pianist and harpsichordist; Edgar Kaufman, Jr., of the Museum of Modern Art; Isaac Rosenfeld, author of *Passage from Home;* Merce Cunningham, dancer-choreographer; and sculptor Richard Lippold, who had been so anxious to come that when told the place was full he wrote Albers to say that he had bought a hearse to bring his wife and two children down, in which they would sleep if the college would "lend them its plumbing." The members of that star-studded faculty, including Bucky, were given room and board, $100 for traveling expenses, and $25 a week.

There were seventy-four eager and highly intelligent summer students for Bucky to enthrall by his priceless benefice of hope for the future through benevolent technology. Martin Duberman in *Black Mountain* [2] writes: "Fuller carried on a nonstop talkathon sleeping only two hours at a time [a nap every six hours]." The students were carried away by Bucky's enormous energy and promethean excitement, though some of them could not understand him. Even as brilliant a man as Arthur Penn spoke of Bucky's vision as "practically palpable" but "not one I could reproduce even for a minute . . . just absolutely extraordinary." [3] John Cage wrote, "The work and thoughts of Buckminster Fuller are of prime importance to me. He, more than any other to my knowledge, sees the world situation—all of it—clearly. . . ." [4] The de Koonings fell in love with Bucky and he with them. They became, in Bucky's words "great friends, really extraordinary friends . . . Bill is a very, very wonderful thinker." But Bucky thought some of de Kooning's pictures "confusing." History does not record what de Kooning made of Bucky's five-hour lectures.

One thing that pleased Bucky was the tradition of Black Mountain that faculty and students were constantly together at work and play and meals, thus obliterating the academic chasm inevitable in more conventional institutions. To be exposed constantly to the challenge of those keen, uncluttered minds, to be one of them, was a constant delight to him, and to them as well. Many of that ardent Black Mountain band look back through the years at that summer, with Bucky spouting ideas like a nonstop geyser, as the motivating inspiration of their entire lives.

The informality of dress and demeanor enhanced the sense of ageless comradeship. Daytimes, faculty and students alike wore overalls or blue jeans—no unusual thing now, but remarkable by the academic mores of 1948. However, mindful of its image in a world as yet unaccustomed to hippie costumes, Black Mountaineers wore jackets and ties or dresses at night; and at the Saturday dances at night women usually wore long dresses and an occasional black tie appeared. These things were customs, not rules, for theoretically there were no rules at Black Mountain, only a consensus of faculty and students as to what sort of behavior was best for the college.

For the same reason, cohabitation between the sexes was sternly frowned upon. On one famous occasion when a boy and girl student had spent the night in an otherwise empty building, a joint committee

---

[2] *Black Mountain* by Martin Duberman, E. P. Dutton & Co., New York, 1972.
[3] *A Year from Monday* by Arthur Penn, Wesleyan University Press, 1967.
[4] *Black Mountain*, op. cit.

of faculty and students met to consider whether expulsion was in order. The whole thing was dropped when the girl offered to produce a doctor's certificate that she was *virgo intacta*. This now old-fashioned posture consorted well with the puritanical attitude toward sex which was one of Bucky's inherited hang-ups despite his personal divergencies from strict observance. Just another of his paradoxes.

Probably Bucky's greatest triumph of that summer, and certainly the most fun he had had in a long time, was his appearance in the leading role in the faculty play. This was another Black Mountain tradition along with concerts, dance recitals, and impromptu readings. With all that talent available, these were often exciting occasions.

That summer the play was the comedy with music, *Le Piège de Meduse*, Englished rather roughly as *The Ruse of Medusa*, by the French avant-garde composer-playwright Erik Satie as translated by Mary Caroline Richards. It had been staged only once before, in France in 1913. John Cage and Merce Cunningham, who were producing it, gave the female lead to pretty Elaine de Kooning and "persuaded" Buckminster Fuller to play the comic role of Baron Meduse. Cunningham himself choreographed and danced "the mechanical monkey," with a magnificent tail designed by Lippold. Bill de Kooning painted the scenery.

Rehearsals were rather disappointing at first, and Bucky was particularly stiff. He learned his lines right off—he could memorize almost at a glance, but his delivery was dismal. His burgeoning role as prophet of the future appeared to have made him self-conscious about his dignity, and he said rather pompously, "I can't put on an act. I like to do my own thinking, not to speak somebody's lines."

Cage and Cunningham called in Arthur Penn, who had been writing his own drama all summer, as play doctor. Penn added some very funny improvisations to the script which relaxed the cast, except Bucky who, in Penn's words, was still "gravely muted." One day Bucky admitted that he was afraid of making a "damn fool of himself." To break this down Penn invented a series of improvisations in which he and Bucky did make damn fools of themselves. He told Duberman, "We skipped around, did giddy things, laughed artificially and rolled on the floor." [5]

Suddenly it all became great fun. Bucky reverted to that joyful time when he used to delight in playing the buffoon at the impromptu Hewlett theatricals at Martin's Lane.

[5] Ibid.

The night of the performance he was magnificent. In dress shoes and spats, flapping gray flannel pants, an outsize cutaway, polka dot waistcoat, white socks, Pickwickian collar, and a very tall white high hat, he played the role like a combination of Groucho Marx and Emmett Kelly. There is a prodigious picture of him doing an abandoned dance with Merce Cunningham's mechanical monkey. Mouth wide open, emitting a manic roar, goggles glittering frenziedly, he looks a little like a bald-headed gorilla. The play was a smash hit.

Bucky said ever afterward that the experience helped him immensely to let himself go in his lectures.

Bucky's serious project for the summer was to build the first big geodesic dome, fifty feet in diameter, with the help of the students. Its design would be a beautiful geometric pattern of three different types of triangular trusses in various pastel colors. He had brought with him a carload of aluminum alloy venetian blind strips for the compression members, and planned to get the rest of the material in Asheville.

Bucky worked on the dome all summer, doing long, intricate calculations all night long when mere mortals were asleep. Eventually the complex calculations for a large dome took him and a young assistant, Donald Richter, two years to complete, working with nothing but an adding machine, as they could not afford a mechanical multiplier. Fortunately the calculations only had to be done once, because they could be extrapolated for domes of any size.

In September the great day arrived. In a pouring rain Bucky spread the makings out in a rough field. His student assistants tore around in the downpour, hitching bits of it together while faculty and students, having abandoned work for the day, stood on a hillside with raincoats and umbrellas waiting to cheer the great event.

They had no chance to cheer. When the last bolt was in place and the tension applied the dome struggled briefly upward, sagged, and collapsed in a sodden heap. Everyone was intensely sympathetic, but Cunningham later told Duberman that "it didn't put Fuller off at all." And Bucky himself explained to the author of *Black Mountain* in 1969 that he deliberately built it too weak in order to find the critical point at which it would collapse, and that it was "predicted to fall down." [6]

This is typical Fuller after-the-fact rationalizing, and Bucky appeared unconcerned because his ego would never let failure in, any more than infinity—he did not believe in either. Certainly he had known from his

[6] Ibid.

calculations that the dome might not work, but equally certainly he had hoped it would. The truth would seem to be that he had tried to do what Starling Burgess would have called a "botch job" with inadequate materials—he would have used better ones if he could have afforded them.

In the winter of 1948–49 Bucky had a busy speaking schedule, lecturing before the architecture and engineering sections of the University of Illinois, and at the Architecture and Design School of Chicago, North Carolina State, the Illinois Institute of Technology, the Architectural School of the Chicago Art Institute, Hull House in Chicago, the University of Toronto and, at last, at his own alma mater, Harvard University's Graduate School of Design. His most important affiliation was with the Chicago Institute of Design. There he and the engineering students built a number of domes of different designs, "all of which worked," says Bucky.

In the spring Bucky received an urgent plea from N. O. Pittenger, who had succeeded Josef Albers as rector, to return to Black Mountain as Dean of the Summer Institute. Although he was now getting a fee of $1,000 per lecture, Bucky agreed to take the job for a salary of only $800 for the six weeks, which was all the college could afford.

Duberman wrote: "Black Mountain barely made it through the summer of 1949. Pittenger, Natasha Goldowski, Ray Trayer, and Bucky Fuller . . . stitched together a fabric that just managed to keep the body decent . . . Fuller's task was first on the agenda and he carried it off with his usual aplomb." [7]

Black Mountain was, in fact, in the terminal stage of institutional leukemia brought on by too many intellectual egotists in its bloodstream. Bucky gave it a temporary shot in the arm by bringing with him most of the summer art staff, among them John Wally and Emerson Woellfer of the Chicago Institute of Design, who taught drawing, painting, and sculpture while their wives taught ceramics and photography. Other disciplines were taught by well-known figures attracted by Black Mountain's former brilliant reputation.

Bucky also brought along nine young engineer-designers from the Institute to help him build his newest dome. It was a fourteen-foot-diameter hemisphere made of aluminum aircraft tubing with a vinylite skin. Unlike the dome of 1948, this one went up in a hurry and stayed

[7] Ibid.

up all summer. To prove its strength Bucky and eight of his engineers all hung from it like monkeys.

Another technical triumph was the first structure built on the principle of tensegrity, a Fuller-coined word, derived from tension—integrity. According to the books, student sculptor Kenneth Snelson built a tensegrity mast after hearing Bucky deliver a lecture. Thus are myths made. In fact, Snelson had been very close to Bucky throughout the preceding summer—"a sort of father-son relationship," he says,[8] and had absorbed many of his ideas. He went on to make a career out of tensegrity sculptures.

Tensegrity Dome skeleton, 1953.

[8] Kenneth Snelson to the author.

This type of construction still relied on the triangular components, but instead of the compression members or struts being joined at their vertices as in the classic dome, they were hollowed out and strung on a wire (or string) tensional network. The diagonals of cubes form tetrahedrons. If you eliminate the cubes and run tensional wires through compression members from the centers of gravity along the radii to the vertices you get a tetrahedronal structure in discontinuous compression and continuous tension. Struts thus seem literally to float in the air, though held in place with enormous strength (for their weight) by the tensional network.

Snelson's 10-foot mast worked brilliantly. It could be raised vertically or held out horizontally, inducing much greater stress with never a quiver. It could be forcibly twisted out of shape, only to spring back like a dimple pushed in a derby hat, with its hollow sticks, apparently devoid of support, triumphantly maintaining themselves like the Indian rope trick. Even someone looking right at it could not believe it was possible. It was, in one student's words, "an act of faith."

Despite the ominous atmosphere in which it began, the Summer Institute was a great success. Bucky's only setback was when he chose a young student to read aloud one of his two-hundred-page technological-metaphysical poems. It is recorded that by the time the man finished half the audience was asleep and the other half wished they were.

However, when Bucky himself spoke, no one slept—or even coughed. No matter how long the discourse or how recondite, students and faculty alike sat on the edges of their chairs with rapt attention to every word. This was in part due to the charisma which suddenly invested this stocky little man as he carried his audience with him from earth to the ultimate nebulae of the cosmos, then brought them whirling home through intergalactic space to a safe landing on earth with the practical applications of the universal principles he had explored. As always, when he lectured, he was "thinking out loud."

Most of all, the excitement Bucky engendered was due to his inspiring message that man was intended by the Great Designer to be a success, as was every other feature of that elegantly intricate, finite system known as Universe. If humankind failed, it would be due to their own stupidity in not acting in accordance with the general principles governing Universe, which they could discover by using their God-given intellects. If they should fail, it would be no more than a slight setback for the Great Designer because there were, without a shadow of a doubt, trillions of other intellects working on billions of other planets to forward His ultimate purpose.

However, Bucky did not anticipate failure for humanity. They were, he told his audience, designed to succeed and they were well on the way. In an exhilarating peroration to one of his talks he said, "Man has now completed the plumbing and has installed all the valves to turn on the infinite cosmic wealth [of inexhaustible energy]."

Like those other students of the previous summer, the boys and girls who listened to him in the echoing wooden assembly hall found their youthful cynicism dissipated, their lives made meaningful, and their minds expanded. This last was important above all because the mind is one thing on earth which, once enlarged, never again quite retracts.

Another thing that enchanted those boys and girls was that when Bucky came down out of the empyrean and off the platform he became one of them. Because he believed in them far more than he did in the sages of society, and because back there in Chicago in 1927 he had cleared the rubbish of outworn stereotypes from his mind and relearned how to look at things with the sensitivity of a child, he was forever young—their compatriot, not their senior. He played with them and joked with them and he genuinely *loved* them.

As Bucky drove away from Black Mountain for the last time, young V. V. Richard stood by the roadside with the others, waving frantically; feeling something important gone from her life yet always to be with her, enriching her years however many they might be. "I can see him still," she said, "in the back of that old, open convertible, waving good-bye to us with one bare foot." [9]

[9] V. V. Richard to the author.

CHAPTER XVI

THE APOTHEOSIS
OF THE DOME

EARLY in 1949, prior to his last summer at Black Mountain, Bucky and Anne were driving down to North Carolina State College, where he was to give a series of lectures. As he drove expertly at high speed along the narrow Virginia roads, he was thinking out loud. "I am absolutely confident about the geodesic thing now," he said. "After our experiments at the Chicago Institute and the completion of my calculations, I know it really works. But I have exhausted all our money and we are not getting enough from this lecturing to move very far—I keep spending it all. I don't know how to go on."

"How much will it take to get the thing going?" Anne asked.

"About thirty thousand dollars," Bucky answered.

"Then go to me," Anne said. "I can lend it to you."

In Bucky's words, "Anne had inherited another legacy. So she sold all her IBM stock for $30,000 and loaned the money to me. Had she kept it she would have been a millionairess now. On the other hand, on two different years when the radome program was at its height, our income was over a million dollars; and since then I have been averaging two hundred thousand dollars a year. Every bit of it I continually put back into my work—the World Game and the other research projects. But Anne realizes that we've had much more than if we had a million dollars. What really counts is what we have done for humanity. That is the payoff and it is incalculable.

"Somehow or other Anne was sure that I had really learned how to do this thing, and that it would really count. Boy, she was great!"

Almost lyrically, Bucky described his progress from then on: "For the first time I was really independent, not having backers to bother me with their greedy demands; and I said, 'I will now undertake to go ahead.'

"Only $30,000, but it made all the difference. Out of this came the bigger domes that proved my theories. I would buy two or three thousand dollars' worth of material and the students would help me build them—bigger and still bigger domes."

In 1946, Bucky had chartered the Fuller Research Institute dedicated to implement:

"Commonwealth pertinent, individually conceived, intuitively urged and spontaneously joined search, research and enterprise in the borderline realm of 'just not impossibles,' where transcendentally in altocumulous thought—cloud, orderly trending concepts accrue, differentiate and integrate. . . ."[1]

Into this Institute Bucky channeled most of his lecture earnings. In 1949, he organized Geodesics, Inc., which was to handle manufacturing and patent royalties of the domes. Later came Synergetics, Inc., which dealt with design and research for private industrial operations; and Plydome, Inc., his personal research and development company.

In February, 1949, the U.S. armed forces were first made aware of the geodesic dome when a small, thirty-one-great-circle necklace structure of tubular beads and a continuous internal cable net was set up in the garden of the Pentagon. It could be folded up in a small package, or rapidly erected by tightening the cables, which caused it to rise into a hemispheric dome. It attracted a great deal of attention but no orders for the time being. This was all right with Bucky, who was not ready for commercial operations.

The first really big dome (50 feet in diameter) was built in Montreal in 1950 by Bucky's former students at the Chicago Institute, Don Richter and Jeffrey Lindsay, assisted by Ted Pope, under the auspices of the Canadian Division of Fuller Research. Canada was chosen because aluminum alloys, which were still under wartime rationing in the United States, were decontrolled there. Other domes were built of wood, plaster and wood, and later of plywood or cardboard. They all worked.

People were beginning to take note of the domes and consider them for actual use. In 1951, a small two-frequency hyperbolic-parabola dome with an outwardly tensed "Hypercoat" skin, especially designed for Arctic conditions, was sent to Baffin Land, Labrador. It was high time to get a patent.

Bucky described the process: "I went to Donald Robertson, who had

[1] The Fuller Research Foundation, 1946–51.

succeeded in getting me the first real patent on the World Airocean Map. He is a very brilliant patent attorney who had been chief attorney for the Aluminum Company [Alcoa]. He got some beautiful patents on the geodesic dome. The first patent was applied for in December 1951, and was granted in June 1954, but, of course, the dome was protected from 1951 on.

"It was a fantastic patent. The moment domes became big business, the great companies like General Electric and Kaiser wanted to build them; and came to see me about doing so on a royalty basis. I sent them all to Robertson. He told me that each of their patent attorneys had said to him, 'Of course, the first thing my clients wanted me to do was to find a way to get around the geodesic patents, but I couldn't do it; they are so superbly drawn.'

"If I had not had those patents," Bucky said, "you never would have heard of me."

The very first big break Bucky ever got came in 1953, which happened to be the fiftieth anniversary of the Ford Motor Company. Out at the great River Rouge Plant stood the perfectly circular Rotunda building around a court that was open to the sky. During his last years old Henry Ford had spoken wistfully of building a dome over it so that the court could be used in any weather. In 1952, his grandson, Henry Ford II, conceived the idea of building such a dome as a tribute to his grandfather and a commemoration of the anniversary. Young Henry consulted his engineers, who scurried off to confer with the leading architects. The answer was, "It can't be done." The most efficient conventional dome with the ninety-three-foot diameter needed to span the circular court would weigh 160 tons. The steel-framed, stuccoed, fluted walls of the Rotunda would collapse under such weight.

Ford was not a man to give up easily; surely in these times of engineering miracles a way could be found. Someone suggested calling in Buckminster Fuller.

This was not as desperate a measure as it would have seemed five or even two years before. For Bucky's stature had been growing steadily. Not only had the experimental domes aroused a great deal of interest in architectural and engineering circles, but Bucky's synergetic geometry and his cosmic viewpoint were commanding serious attention. In 1951, for example, he had given major addresses at no less than twenty-four universities and institutes, among them such towers of prestige as Harvard, the Boston Architectural Center, the U.S. Air Force Institute of Technology, American Institute of Architects centers in Detroit, Cleveland, and Chicago, and the University of Illinois. In addition, for the past four years he had conducted courses at what *Time* magazine called "the archbishopric of practical science in America," the Massachusetts Institute of Technology. Bucky arrived there each time dragging a carload of models, tools, domes, and other items. The *Architectural Forum* had recently published an enthusiastic technical article about the geodesic domes.

So Ford engineers came to Bucky to ask if he could build a clear span dome ninety-three feet in diameter, and how much it would weigh. Bucky answered the first question immediately; of course he could. The second question took a little time while he conformed his two-years' series of calculations to the specific problem. Then he gave them a figure they almost refused to believe—eight and one-half tons.

The deal was made. Bucky gave the Ford Motor Company the right to manufacture the dome under his direction on a royalty basis. When the matter came before the Ford Board of Directors they—and many of the Ford engineers as well—were "gravely and most visibly skeptical." Fortunately, Henry Ford II had some of the venturesome spirit and open mind that had led his grandfather to dare such innovations as a car for the masses, the first automobile assembly line, and the "revolutionary" concept of paying a minimum wage of five dollars a day, which, of course, eventually made the whole mass-production American industrial economy possible. Ford rammed the contract through.

Bucky was never happier than in his work for Ford. Way back in 1918, old Henry Ford had become the only industrialist he really admired because of his imaginative solutions of the problem of mass-producing the Eagle Boats and his humanistic attitude toward his employees. Now Bucky found the grandson equally admirable.

The Ford contract did not give him much time. Signed in January, 1953, it called for the dome to be in place in time for the stockholder's meeting in April. Bucky's figure of eight and one-half tons was, he thought, heavier than it needed to be, but on this first big contract he could afford to take no chances. Instead of the simpler great-circle-grid construction he decided to use the octet truss—a word he coined from octahedron-tetrahedron. This consisted of struts joined by X-shaped terminals united in such a way as to weave around the hub nuclei, forming the four planes of a vector equilibrium so that a load applied to any one point was immediately distributed radially outward in six directions and thence throughout the entire system. Bucky had made the first octet truss with toothpicks and dried peas in kindergarten in 1900; he patented it in 1961. These octet trusses were then riveted together to form the triangular or tetrahedronal elements of the great dome.

Bucky's calculations indicated that the Ford dome would require 19,680 struts about a yard long, each weighing five ounces. The holes at the ends for the rivets had to be spaced within a tolerance of five one-thousandths of an inch—normal tolerances in building construction are *one-eighth of an inch*. This was done by making up special punches on indexing lathes to an accuracy beyond the capacity of the human eye. Once made, the punches perforated the struts at high speed. They were color-coded with bits of tape so all the workmen had to do was to rivet them into triangles and join these to larger triangles.

Like so many of Bucky's structures the dome was built from the top down as a rotating, hydraulically elevated umbrella. The workmen stood on a wide bridge thrown across the Rotunda court from the surrounding circular roof. No great cranes or heavy machinery were required since twelve-foot sections of octet truss complexes ready to be riveted into place weighed only four pounds.

The dome was completed in four months, two days before the deadline. Covered with a transparent skin of polyester fiberglass, it came to just under the calculated eight and one-half tons. It weighed only two-and-a-half pounds for each square foot covered. Even this was clumsy compared to a transportable dome Bucky later designed for Ford, which was twice the diameter of the Rotunda Dome, and weighed only five ounces per square foot covered.

The Ford directors and stockholders at the meeting and the thousands of tourists who came to see it were enchanted by the Rotunda Dome. Seen under the clear fiberglass cover against the blue of the sky, the lacy network of concentric rings balancing compressional and tensional forces in elegant mathematical perfection of structure had the ephemeral grace of a gigantic spiderweb. It was as beautiful as the groining of a Gothic cathedral, perhaps more beautiful, because it did so much more with less.

Suddenly, it seemed, all the world wanted geodesic domes. Bucky was not in the least surprised—he reckoned that people had at last caught up with his thinking. His friends were dumfounded to see one of Bucky's fantastical inventions really hit the jackpot.

Looking upward through the octet trusses of the Ford Rotunda Dome,
1953.

All during this time of intense work on the domes, Bucky's family life was very stable and happy. Anne was living contentedly at Forest Hills, and Bucky was able to be home a great deal more than he had been during the years of the war and Wichita. When he went off to give his courses at MIT or to his lectures Anne often went with him, and in summer he was frequently able to get to Bear Island for a month or more, and sail the boats he loved so much.

In 1947, he had bought the *Nitana* in which to teach Allegra to sail. She was a racing sloop eighteen feet on the waterline, twenty-nine feet overall, which had been champion of the M.B. Class in Buzzards Bay from 1932 to 1936. Bucky and Allegra had great fun in her.

After two years with Balanchine's Ballet, Allegra began to "hunger for further intellectual development." She found that at Bennington College, which was then inaugurating an experimental educational program, she could major in the history of the dance. Bucky, who had lectured at Bennington and knew the president and many of the professors, easily arranged to get her a scholarship.

Allegra had a brilliant scholastic record at Bennington. Her final thesis, which made Bucky inordinately proud, was on the dance as a means of communication. In it she theorized that the dance had originally been used by small savage tribes as a means of indicating to possibly hostile strangers their intentions, either peaceful or warlike, or their specific needs. And she discovered that in cold northern countries the signaling movements were generally made by the legs of the dancers, while in warmer countries, particularly in Asia, these ideas were conveyed by arm movements. When other means of communication superseded the dance it became formalized into religious rites and aesthetics.

Allegra's most original contribution to the subject was the idea that now, when television made possible the almost instantaneous projection of images throughout the world, the dance might again become an important means of communication, overcoming the language barrier that kept peoples apart, by telling each other what they really felt, not what the politicians were saying.

Bennington's new system, later widely copied, had an "in period" when the students studied on campus in the conventional way, and an "out period" when they went out into the world, got a job, and learned by doing. Following her natural bent, Allegra decided to spend her out period in moving pictures. She got a job with the International Film Foundation where she had as her cameraman Kenneth Snelson, who had built that first tensegrity mast at Black Mountain. More importantly, she met and fell in love with a brilliant young director named Robert Snyder, who later became an Oscar winner. This caused some unusual discord in the Fuller family.

Anne did not like the idea of her beloved daughter marrying Snyder. Bucky says, "It certainly was not antisemitism." But of course, he could be wrong. For Anne had been brought up in Lawrence, one of the most violently antisemitic communities in the entire world, and while intellectually she was entirely free of that sort of prejudice, deep in her subconscious may have lurked a residue of her childhood indoctrination.

Bucky feels that Bob Snyder may have offended her by his first approach to her about marrying Allegra. "He went to her, not to me," he says, "and he talked to her in a way that the Old World does talk about what parents might be able to do for a young couple when a good man takes their daughter as his wife."

More likely, however, what really disturbed Anne was the idea of her daughter marrying into the moving picture world. For she had never known it, and was filled with the natural prejudices aroused by lurid stories of Hollywood life, and the "ephemeralization" of the institution of marriage in that community. In the society to which she belonged by birth, and even among the serious artists and writers she had known, and among the scientists who gathered with her husband, there was a generally contemptuous attitude toward Hollywood. People who went there were often thought of as having "sold out."

In any event, Allegra did marry Bob Snyder at Bennington on June 30, 1951, with her father's approval and her mother's rather reluctant consent. It turned out very happily, although, according to Bucky, "Anne gave Bob a tough time for several years." But she finally came around.

From 1953 on, the dome business was booming. Many of the great universities in the United States put up domes, either for experimental or practical purposes. These domes were made of various materials from plyboard to plastics and even paperboard. Bucky designed other domes for special purposes such as the fifty-five-foot dome built under license by Berger Brothers of New Haven for the Air Force. It had a quilted double skin filled with air which provided such excellent insulation that a smaller version of it was later floated on an ice island to the North Pole, providing a comfortable shelter for personnel carrying out important scientific experiments.

Small playdomes for children to climb on were put into mass production in 1957, and became a regular feature of schoolyards and playgrounds all over the country. Other special designs included a corrugated aluminum structure built by Bucky and students at the University of Natal at Durban, South Africa, for the Zulus, whose grass-thatched huts were constantly being eaten by their cattle. Many small domes were built by campers seeking seclusion in forests where other structures were impracticable—you could put up a dome in a tenth of the time it took to build the crudest log cabin.

In the nature of things Bucky's biggest customer was the Defense Department. In 1954, at Orphan's Hill in North Carolina, Bucky watched a Marine Corps helicopter lift a thirty-foot-diameter wood and plastic dome off the ground and fly away with it at fifty knots. There was no trouble caused by wind resistance because of the dome's natural streamlining. Thus he finally accomplished his 1927 dream of completed shelters delivered by air.

That first Marine Corps dome was followed by over three hundred others, including a design that was assembled by untrained marines on a beachhead in 235 minutes, and a three-helicopter hangar that one helicopter flew from the deck of a ship to the beachhead. Others especially designed were two domes installed at Wilkes Land, Antarctica, and another situated at the South Pole during the geophysical year of 1957.

Bucky's very best customer became the United States Air Force. In the 1950s, the cold war with the Communist countries became steadily icier, and, as Russia developed the hydrogen bomb and her giant missiles to deliver it, the Defense Department began to build the DEW Line (Distant Early Warning) 4,500 miles long just above the Arctic Circle in Canada, to provide at least fifteen or twenty minutes warning of a surprise nuclear attack. These radar installations required housing to shelter them from the fierce polar storms. This was very difficult to provide because the structures enclosing the large revolving radar scopes had to be free of metal so the microwave beams could freely penetrate them. At first the Air Force tried pneumatic igloo-shaped housing, inflated with compressed air. When the hurricane-speed gales hit them, the wind-created vacuum sucked them out as you would blow out a candle, ruining all the equipment.

In 1954, the Air Force turned to Bucky to ask if he could design a dome of materials pervious to microwave beams, which could withstand winds up to 200 mph, could be flown in a package to the construction sites, and be erected in twenty hours, which was all the time that they could count on between storms. Geodesics, Inc., came up with a dome made of diamond-shaped polyester fiberglass struts and a fiberglass skin. A small, thirty-foot-diameter dome was built by Lincoln Laboratories, the developer of the DEW Line for the Air Force, and erected on Mount Washington. In a two-year test it withstood winds up to 182 mph, and did *not ice up*. Radar beams went through it without distortion.

This test proved that geodesic domes were the answer to the DEW Line problems. Bucky says: "The program was going to be a very big thing entailing enormous amounts of money, and some of the big corporations wanted to be in on it. The Air Force people came to me and said: "We have to get these things into mass production. What are you going to do about it?"

"I told them I did not have the capital to manufacture the domes and they said, 'We know that. That's why we want to know what you propose.'

The first Radome installed by the U.S. Air Force above the Arctic Circle in Northern Canada, 1956.

"I said, 'I'll license any reputable manufacturer to make them, and I will make the royalties very reasonable so it won't block you at all.' They said, 'That is such a generous attitude that we [as government] will back you in protecting your patents.' "

So the deal was set. General Electric became the prime contractor. The "radomes," as Bucky named them, were fifty-five feet in diameter and forty feet high. They were mounted on high steel platforms built over the operators' huts. The first one was erected by an Air Force crew in fourteen hours, thus beating the specifications by six hours. Not one of them has collapsed in the Arctic storms.

Industry was not long in following government in finding uses for geodesic domes. Don Richter, who had gone to work for Henry J. Kaiser, had set up a microdome in his office. Kaiser saw it and asked, "What's that?"

Richter explained at some length, giving an enthusiastic account of the domes already in use and their enormous possibilities. Henry J. was sold. As a result the Kaiser Aluminum Company acquired the right to manufacture the domes on a royalty basis.

The first Kaiser dome was designed as an auditorium for Henry Kaiser's Hawaiian Village in Honolulu. It was an aluminum-skinned structure 145 feet in diameter, manufactured at the company's Oakland, California, plant. When Kaiser heard the dome had arrived in Hawaii he took a plane to Honolulu in order to see it go up. He was too late. By the time he arrived the dome was already built and filled with an audience of 1,832 people listening to a concert given by the Hawaiian Symphony Orchestra.

The statistics are: The dome was erected in twenty-two hours and within twenty-four hours of the arrival of its components in Honolulu the concert was over. The conductor said the acoustics were "the best in my experience."

Kaiser Aluminum built many other domes at prices ranging from $50,000 to $190,000, among them the municipal auditorium at Virginia Beach, the Citizens State Bank in Oklahoma City, and the elegant Casa Mañana Theater-in-the-Round at Fort Worth, Texas.

Many other companies applied for licenses to construct geodesic domes. By the end of 1959 there were more than a hundred licensees. One of them, North American Aviation, built a 250-foot-diameter dome for the American Society for Metals at its Cleveland, Ohio, headquarters.

Concert audience seated in first Kaiser Dome in Honolulu twenty-three hours after its disassembled components arrived in Hawaii.

Designed by John Kelly, it was a gossamer net arching over the society's buildings, gardens, and pools. Kelly regarded this structure as "a realization of Fuller's concept of advancing technology's overall trend to invisibility." [2]

The biggest dome built in the 1950s was constructed by Bucky's own company, Synergetics, Inc., for the Union Tank Car Company at Baton Rouge, Louisiana, in 1958. The company needed a plant big enough to run a whole train of cars into for rebuilding and reconditioning with a huge span of clear space for shunting and turntables.

[2] *The Dymaxion World of Buckminster Fuller* by Robert W. Marx, Southern Illinois University Press, 1960.

This "roundhouse" was the largest clear-span structure in the world at that time, with a diameter of 384 feet and a height of 128 feet. Its enclosed volume of 15,000,000 cubic feet is about twenty-three times that of St. Peter's Dome and it covers an area of 115,558 square feet. Yet it only weighs about 1,200 tons, approximately *two ounces* per square foot covered, and it cost less than ten dollars per square foot covered. That really is ephemeralization!

Meanwhile, domes began to be in demand throughout the world. This was partly due to the United States Government policy of using them as U.S. pavilions at various world fairs; a policy that made sense since they were not only the cheapest way of covering large areas, but the only uniquely American contribution to architecture since the skyscraper. The first one was planned for the International Trade Fair at Kabul in Afghanistan. The United States Department of Commerce signed a contract with Synergetics, Inc., on May 23, 1956. Designs, calculations, and engineering drawings for a dome one hundred feet in diameter with a nylon skin were completed in a week. By June 30, it was manufactured and packaged and shipped in a DC-4 to Kabul. Untrained Afghan workers under the direction of one of Bucky's engineers, using the color-coding system, erected it in forty-eight hours. It was the hit of the fair, outdrawing all the other exhibits, on some of which work had been in progress for months and at a far greater cost. The Afghans loved it because, they said, it was a modern version of the Mongolian yurt (tent) of their forefathers.

Though Bucky recognizes how much trade unions have done for labor and is himself a card-carrying member of the Machinists Union, he could not help contrasting the fast work on the Kabul dome with that on an exact duplicate of it built in St. Louis. Where the unskilled Afghans had taken forty-eight hours, skilled members of the Machinists Union, at $5.50 an hour, took *six weeks*. Bucky describes them sitting in pairs under beach umbrellas, smoking and talking while members of other unions carried things up to them or wasted time on other jobs. Then they would leisurely arise, stick in a few bolts, screw on the complementary nuts, and relax for another twenty minutes.

Bucky says that this is a method of distributing wealth without adding commensurate value to the product. But he does not blame the union men so much as the whole economic system which requires people to earn a living, often by false "make-work," when in his world of plenty they would automatically have an abundance of everything they needed and could take just pride in fast efficient work. In his words, "Production would no longer be impeded by humans trying to do what machines can do better."

The Kabul dome was such a marvelous advertisement of American know-how that the government began flying it, and other domes like it, hither and yon to fairs all over the world. They turned up in such unlikely places as Poznan, Casablanca, Delhi, Rangoon, Bangkok, Tokyo, Osaka, and many others. Two paperboard domes made by the Container Corporation of America and sent to the Tenth Triennial Design Exhibit at Milan won the *Gran Primo*, the highest award given to any participating country. When these domes began to melt in the steady rain, Bucky saved the day by ordering them covered by "bathing caps" of vinyl or aluminum foil.

The U.S. Pavilion at the International Trade Fair in Kabul, Afghanistan, 1956.

The most publicized dome of this period was the 200-foot-diameter "golden dome" built by Kaiser Aluminum as the United States Pavilion at the American Exchange Exhibition in Moscow in 1959. On seeing it Khrushchev made his much-quoted remark: "I would like to have Mr. J. Buckingham [sic] Fuller come to Russia to teach our engineers." Bucky has since spent a good deal of time in Russia working with scientists and engineers.

It was in the ultramodern General Electric and Whirlpool kitchens in the Moscow Dome that Khrushchev had his famous argument with then Vice-President Nixon. Donald Moore, who designed the Whirlpool kitchen, later became one of Bucky's assistants and closest friends.

The Moscow dome was purchased by the U.S.S.R. from the United States government and is now a permanent exhibit in Moscow's Sokolniki Park. The Russians were so interested in Bucky's ideas that in 1958 he was appointed by the State Department to visit Russia as a representative for engineering in a protocol exchange. At a dinner the Russians gave in his honor they said that they had been following his work for twenty-nine years, a long time before he was taken seriously in the United States.

By 1959, the geodesic dome had, indeed, been recognized, not only as a unique American contribution to architecture, but, in the words of *Time* magazine, "a kind of benchmark of the universe, what 17th-century mystic Jakob Boehme might call "a signature of God." [3]

[3] *Time,* January 10, 1964.

CHAPTER XVII

ACCELERATED TOING AND FROING

MOST of the millions that Bucky made out of the domes were promptly poured back into his expanding research organization for discovering further general principles of Universe and applying them for the betterment of mankind. The most elaborate of these efforts was the World Game,* a survey of all the resources of the local subsystem of Universe known as earth. Virtually none of the money remains in his possession. The last ambition he would hold would be to leave a large estate.

However, Bucky was not yet so totally dedicated as to neglect having a lot of fun spending some of the proceeds on himself and Anne, and also in making generous gifts to his less pecunious friends. Finding the author watching a black-and-white television set, he promptly asked permission to buy him the most expensive color set on the market, which offer was gratefully declined.

Suddenly Bucky turned up driving very expensive, fast foreign cars, though he continued to live in the little apartment in Forest Hills. The houses on Bear Island were completely rehabilitated (modernized? The Great Intelligence forbid!). He also bought Little Sprucehead Island and a share of Compass Island in his "microarchipelago."

Bucky's most extravagant purchase was the *Nagala,* a superb Swedish-built, thirty-square-meter sloop. Twenty-nine feet on the waterline, forty-three feet overall, with a tall, slightly raked mast and a highly polished wooden hull, she was so beautiful as to stop your heart. Being built expressly for racing, she had but a tiny cabin, sleeping two. When Bucky proudly showed her to Anne and his small grandson, Jaime Snyder (Allegra's son), the little boy looked at her accommodations and asked, "Where are you going to sleep, Grandma?" assuming that he and his doting grandfather would occupy the cabin.

---

* Described in Chapter XX.

Anne laughed and said, "It's all right, Jaime. I'm not going along."

The truth is that Anne cares as little for sailing as she does for rough-ing it. On the rare occasions when she consents to go out on the luxurious *Intuition,* a yacht Bucky bought in 1969, she promptly goes down to the cabin and reads a good book.

Needless to say, Jaime and Bucky had many marvelous sails on *Nagala,* and Bucky frequently raced her in his "thoroughgoing" all-or-nothing fashion in the New York Yacht Club cruises and against the fleets of the local Maine yacht clubs.

When Bucky traveled, which he did, and does, a great deal, averag-ing at least 100,000 miles a year, he lived far more luxuriously than at home in Forest Hills—he always stayed at Claridge's in London and, until he became so ascetic in recent years, ate copiously and well. Nevertheless, he once fed me one of the worst dinners it has ever been my misfortune to confront. We were all in London in the summer of 1963, and Bucky invited us to dine with him at a new Indonesian restaurant on the Brompton Road. The point was that its interior had been designed in a strikingly original manner by an architectural pro-tégé of Bucky's.

The company, besides Bucky and ourselves, was Bohemian—a tall, heavily bearded youngish man wearing corduroy pants, a sweater, and a black beret, who turned out to be Reiner Bonham, editor of the *British Architectural Forum,* the world leader in its field; his brilliant and charming wife, who happened to have lost a leg, and a group of topflight students of both sexes, various races, and variegated taste in costumes.

The conversation was quite literally out of this world; but the food should have been thrown out of it. The British are scarcely known for culinary perfection even in their native dishes; when they attempt the exotic it is a major disaster. Even Bucky, flying high in dithyrambic discourse, was forced to notice it. In an apologetic tone he said to me, "This is pretty bad. I'm sorry, I could just as well have taken us all to Claridge's."

My boggling mind tried to picture our entrance into that famous restaurant where everyone wears black tie at night—Bonham in his beret and corduroys; Mary Bonham stumping along on her crutches, and me on mine, followed by the assorted students in their bathless brilliance. Yet I was convinced that Bucky—and only Bucky—could have got away with it.

Bucky's chronofile records the steeply ascending graph of his world-wide recognition during those years. From Moscow to Tokyo and all places in between, he was in tremendous demand; his lecture fees rose to $5,000, most of which he poured back into research. Those who paid it got their money's worth, for he seldom talked for less than four hours and more frequently for five or six.

This remarkable recognition was not entirely due to the domes, though their publicity value gave it the initial impetus. Rather, it was due to the substance of his discourses. In a disillusioned world in which the thinking was preponderantly negative, his unique view of Universe, untrammeled by outworn platitudes of which he had disinfected his mind long ago, was gloriously inspiring, especially to students the world over. One thing that made his lectures so exciting was that they were never a repeat performance. He never knew what he was going to say; he just walked out on the platform and began to think out loud. Absolutely anything could come out.

Of course, his theme would always be consonant with the general principles he had discovered, or the inferences he drew from them. But each time he spoke he would add new refinements, and inferences he had not previously drawn would suddenly come clear. Rarely, but with electric spontaneity, he would actually glimpse a new general principle as his vocal thinking ranged far into the ultimate mystery of the cosmos. As he has said, "Development is programable; discovery is not." It is not something a computer or the human brain can make through calculation or ratiocination, for "knowledge is of the brain and wisdom is of the mind; discovery comes to the weightless, metaphysical mind as a flash of transcendental light. It is synergy, a sudden comprehension of the behavior of a whole system, totally unpredictable by the behavior of any of its components or subsystems, and therefore cannot be sought by empirical methods—since the brain cannot know what it is looking for—but only apprehended it as revelation by 'exquisitely prescient minds.' " [1]

The ultimate mystery of the universe is too profound and too complex ever to be grasped in its entirety by the human mind. It is "the maximum synergy of synergies." But each bright insight vouchsafed to man's intellect, each generalized principle recognized always accommodates to and works with, never contradicts, all previously discovered general principles. This proves the existence of an Intellect beyond the

[1] *Ideas and Integrities.*

powers of our apprehension. It is because this is so that the mystery will remain, but each true insight increases the leverage of humanity and their chance of becoming a success in Universe.

Thus these occasional insights that Bucky has when thinking out loud are not only tremendous occasions for him but for his entire audience. Even their explication after the event to other audiences, at second hand so to speak, are almost equally exhilarating. For each time he thinks about them he sees more clearly; and his listeners, hearing them for the first time, are enthralled by the freshness of the concept, which makes it all tremendously worthwhile.

In 1958, on his first trip around the world, Bucky stopped off in India where he had numerous speaking engagements. One day he made three speeches in New Delhi, in the morning, afternoon, and evening. At all three meetings he noticed a striking youngish woman dressed in exquisite saris, who usually sat in or near the front row listening intently, her large dark eyes refulgent with intellectual excitement.

At the evening lecture, Bucky used a little tensegrity sphere model, only about six inches in diameter, made of string and small turnbuckles. After the lecture he was presented to the lady, Mrs. Indira Gandhi, Prime Minister Nehru's daughter. She was so interested in the model that he gave it to her. Mrs. Gandhi asked him if he would come on Saturday to meet her father at their house. Bucky says, "I did meet him and we had a very extraordinary time."

At the appointed hour Bucky drove up the broad Teen Murti, the splendid avenue lined by imposing government buildings and official residences built by the British at a time when they expected their empire to last forever. At one end of it was the huge Vice-Regal Palace, with its golden dome and wide spreading wings, which had become the Indian president's house. Nehru lived at the other end in the former British Commander-in-Chief's residence, a massive red sandstone palace whose architecture has been described as "British monumental." Bucky passed through high, wrought-iron gates, which stood open all day long, and up a long driveway which curved around in front of the house between lawns and beds of brilliant flowers. Indian servants in white uniforms showed him into a high-ceilinged hall beyond which he could see another imposing hall, with long windows looking on a garden of splendid trees, green turf, and gay beds of English flowers. To his right was the receptionist's lobby with a round table and a statue of Mahatma Gandhi;

on the left through great double doors was the huge room where early every morning Nehru received the plain people of India who came to ask for his help, or for justice.

The servants led Bucky up a monumental staircase and through other elaborate public rooms to the smaller reception room of Nehru's private suite. There he was left quite alone.

Presently the door opened and Nehru slipped into the room. The "George Washington of India" was a slight, gentle man with a long, sensitive face. He was wearing the long white tunic with a rosebud pinned on it which has become known throughout the world as a "Nehru jacket." Silently he bowed to Bucky, making the Hindu sign of greeting with his hands folded palms together before his face.

Bucky made his formal, stiff little bow in return and, sensing what was expected of him, began to think out loud. Just what he said that day no one will ever know, for it was, as always, purely spontaneous. Nehru, who probably remembered it, is dead and Bucky cannot recall his words.

Though he has the deserved reputation for speaking at unconscionable length, Bucky is capable of holding to a time limit when circumstances enforce it. On this occasion he realized that the Prime Minister had a limited respite from the pressure of other business, so he held his discourse within reasonable limits. In the time he allotted himself he endeavored to give Nehru the essence of his philosophy and the logical reasoning on which it was based. During the entire period Nehru stood quietly intent, absorbing Bucky's words.

At the end of an hour and a half Bucky stopped talking. Once again Nehru bowed with folded hands and left the room. He had not spoken a single word.

Odd though this might seem, Bucky understood perfectly that Nehru wanted to keep his mind clear and uncluttered by irrelevant courtesy sounds to meditate upon the thoughts he had heard. It was the highest compliment the great Indian leader could have paid him.

As Bucky was leaving, Mrs. Gandhi stopped him and said, "Come to see us whenever you are in India."

So he had several other, more convivial meetings with Nehru, who was at pains to tell him that he had read all Bucky's books and admired him greatly. In fact, the unusual combination of scientific expertise and mysticism in Bucky's thinking accorded empathetically with Nehru's

English-trained, Asian mentality—the concept of personal survival as an indestructible pattern of integrity is not unlike Karma.

Bucky was in India in the winter of 1964, when its people were stricken by the news that Jawaharlal Nehru had suffered a stroke. He telephoned Mrs. Gandhi at once, who said: "Will you please come over right away? I'll send a car."

Even the Prime Minister's car had difficulty getting through the incredible mass of people outside the great iron gates, now closed, and packing the wide Teen Murti almost to the limits of vision waiting for news. Bucky hurried up the steps and through the rooms, peculiarly desolate now in their grandeur.

He was shown into Mrs. Gandhi's private sitting room. In Bucky's words: "Indira Gandhi came into the room with tears in her eyes and told me about her father's stroke. She was really absolutely forlorn."

Bucky gave her what consolation he could, speaking of his admiration for Nehru and their empathy. Then he says: "What do you talk about with somebody under those conditions? I said to her, 'If your father were not to recover would you try to carry on his political work?'"

"She said, 'Oh, no! I would not think of it; and I'm not suited to it. I do know much about it because I have been with him through it all, but I do not want to try to replace him.' It was clear to me that she meant it."

This emotional talk with Mrs. Gandhi gave Bucky one of his "strange insights." He felt that he had looked into her soul and found it pure.

When Nehru died in May of that year, Lal Bahadur Shastri tried to fill the vacuum his death had created in Indian leadership. He begged Mrs. Gandhi to accept the post of Minister of Information and Broadcasting in his cabinet. Nehru's sister, Krishna Nehru Hutheesing, has written: "This was the first time Indira broke down. Weeping, she told Mr. Shastri that she did not want any place in the government; she only wanted to work for her father's memorial." [2]

But Shastri was insistent. The Congress Party was in disarray; he needed Indira's name for the sake of unity, and at last she consented.

When Shastri died suddenly less than two years later, in January 1966, the situation was even worse. Strong men of the Congress Party like Krishna Menon and Morarji Desai, who had little in common with Nehru's ideals, were avid to seize power. To preserve her father's life-work, Mrs. Gandhi ran for Prime Minister and was elected.

[2] We Nehrus by Krishna Nehru Hutheesing with Alden Hatch. Holt, Rinehart and Winston, New York, 1967.

Bucky says: "They sucked her in. I wrote to her saying that because of my having had that extraordinary moment of being with her, I knew that what she was doing was not due to political ambition. Exactly the opposite! That she was doing it simply because of her dedication to her father and the wonderful ideals he had brought her up with, and her commitment to them."

Bucky added: "I realized that Mrs. Gandhi is not there with the usual drive that politicians have, the feeling that 'I can handle people's problems better than others can.' That was one of these two strange insights I have had—about Einstein and about Indira Gandhi."

So to Bucky Mrs. Gandhi remains the one politician whom he trusts and loves. It is indicative of his political innocence that it never occurs to him that after years of power she might have changed. So completely does he accept his "insights" as revelation, so total is his loyalty once given, that no matter what she did he would never think of applying Lord Acton's aphorism about the corrupting effect of power to her.

For him she remains as pure as Joan of Arc. But however much he may now be in error, it is certain that, in the emotion-charged moment in the Prime Minister's house, he saw her truly as she then was.

It is significant that Bucky's favorite politician is a woman. He regards women as being more in tune with Universe than men, more important to its functioning. Nature, he says, employs "discontinuous compression and continuous tension; for this reason compression is plural, tension singular." Life begins within a woman, with early life overlapping its mother's, the new wave emerging from within the older wave. Women are in continuous tension. Males are in discontinuous compression, fighting, jabbing, spearing. . . ."

Women were the inventors of civilization, Bucky believes. While the men were off hunting, exploring, having fun, and bringing home the kill, women kept the hearth fires going; planted crops, spun and wove, dried the skins and combed the wool for apparel, invented pottery; in fact, "they invented industrialization" by organizing the different tasks, inventing the tools to perform them, and consolidating the gains.

As long as primitive economy existed, men were important as providers and as fighters to protect these islands of civilization. But as industry became ever more complex and efficient, hunting grew more obsolete, while men's superior fighting ability was offset by the invention of gunpowder and then the revolver—the great equalizer. Thus men's functions became less important. So what did they do then, those discontinuous villains? They took woman-invented industry and ran it themselves as "a competitive weapon for augmenting widely ranging exploitations and plunder." Women were downgraded to the "sad state" in which they found themselves in the Victorian era.

However, Bucky believes that this situation is rapidly being reversed. For the last half-century women, particularly in America, have inadvertently taken over ownership control of a majority of the shares of the great corporations simply by outliving their husbands and inheriting the corporations. But they still let men run them through powers of attorney, trusteeships, and so forth.

Bucky believes that it is going to be different from now on: "Woman is now entering the ownership *management* of commerce and industry to an ever more important degree. By the twenty-first century she will have taken over full management of Spaceship Earth."

Bucky views the prospect with satisfaction. He writes, "Twenty-first-century woman will retain her tension-integrity continuity and will yet cohere the Universe. . . ." [3]

In 1959, Bucky changed his base of operations. He accepted an offer from Southern Illinois University in Carbondale to become Research Professor there at a salary of $12,000 a year and perquisites. The perquisites were far more important than the insignificant salary. They included an office and staff and a building in which to conduct his experiments and research, and to house his ever-accelerating chronofile, which he tentatively presented to the university.

In return Bucky agreed to deliver a few lectures and to hold seminars for students—at his convenience. There were virtually no limitations on his "toings and froings," as he called his dizzying circumnavigations of the globe. What Southern Illinois mostly profited by was the reflected splendor of his name. This was no small item. During Bucky's thirteen years there the university's student enrollment went from about 5,000 to over 30,000, only partly due to him, of course.

When the Fullers' apartment in Forest Hills was burned out, Bucky built a dome on a small corner lot in Carbondale as a home for himself and Anne. It was a small (thirty-nine-foot diameter) structure of blue and white plywood with tall door-windows facing in four directions. Privacy was obtained by a high board fence around the lot. There was a spacious living room ceiled by the airy hemisphere of the dome. The

[3] "Goddesses of the Twenty-first Century" by Buckminster Fuller, *Saturday Review*, March 2, 1966.

kitchen-dining room and utility rooms were under a cantilevered half-floor on which were the library-balcony, the two bedrooms and baths (not Dymaxion), and clothes closets.

The dome house was furnished in an odd blend of the very best modern-design furniture and some of Anne's beautiful antiques. It would seem a discordant combination, but it was not. Instead, the effect was serenely beautiful, even luxurious. Bucky explained this paradox: "Anything that is exquisitely well designed of any period harmonizes with things that are equally well designed no matter when they were crafted."

Living room of the Fullers' Dome House in Carbondale (Anne on sofa, Bucky at rear), 1963.

When Anne was asked what living in a dome was like, she said, "Well, of course, the only thing different is that you don't have flat walls. We had circular bookcases around the balcony; they were nice. The bad thing was you could not hang paintings because they would be just sort of dangling out from the curve. The only place I could put them was on the flat partition wall between the living room and the kitchen.

"The dome was very nice because we had enormous windows around the whole circle. We had the garden with a fence you could not see through although the air could come through, and there were lots of trees that screened and shaded us. So we used to be outdoors a lot. We would spend Christmas with Allegra in California and we always went away in the heat of summer."

Asked how she kept all those windows clean, Anne said, "Well, of course, I could reach them. So I used to have squeegies and spray the hose on them. It took about five minutes for each door. Those squeegies were great." [4]

Though Anne found her dome convenient and comfortable to live in, she was never exactly enthralled with Carbondale which, apart from the university contacts and resulting intellectual excitement when Bucky happened to be home, lacked most of the amenities of civilized living. For any sort of contact with the world of art, music, and theatre, which she enjoyed, she had to journey across the flat prairies and the Mississippi to St. Louis, or, preferably, even farther.

Bucky, who resembles Kipling's cat—"all places are alike to him"— except, of course, Bear Island—was so delighted at last to be living in one of his own domes that he wrote a parody of *Home on the Range* which he would sing, off key, at the slightest excuse:

> Let architects sing of aesthetics that bring
> Rich clients in hordes to their knees
> Just give me a home in a great circle dome
> Where the stresses and strains are at ease.
>
> Roam home to a dome, where
> Gothic and Roman once stood
> Now chemical bonds alone guard our blondes
> And even the plumbing looks good. [5]

[4] Anne Fuller to the author.
[5] Sung by Buckminster Fuller to the author.

Naturally, Bucky spent very little time in Carbondale, a nonconsecutive month or six weeks a year at most. Universities and learned societies all over the world were recognizing the profoundly original thinking of this man, who in ordinary academic terms had no education at all, only honorary doctorates and other intellectual honors. The very first one to jump on the Fuller bandwagon was North Carolina State University, which gave him the honorary degree of Doctor of Design in 1954. Michigan University made him a Doctor of Arts in 1955, and Washington University gave him a doctorate of science in 1957. Other degrees followed thick and fast—doctor of fine arts, Southern Illinois, 1959; humane letters, Rollins, 1960; letters, Clemson, 1964; three more doctorates in 1964, and so forth and so on. The year 1970 was a banner one with doctorates from the Minneapolis School of Art, Park College, Brandeis University, Wilberforce University, and Columbia College. That year Oxford University gave Bucky the ultimate accolade by making him a Fellow of St. Peter's College—a don. According to the old limerick, this meant he was entitled to a swan. But the honors Bucky prized most were those he received from his sometime alma mater, Harvard. As we have seen, he first lectured there in 1950. He was there again in 1960; this led to a rather amusing incident.

On that occasion his Harvard classmate and cousin-through-the-Fullers, novelist John P. Marquand, sat beside him on the platform. Years before, Marquand had been asked to contribute memories of Bucky for an article in *The Saturday Evening Post*. Influenced by his recollections of Bucky's less-than-glorious career at Harvard, and the family opinion of those days that Bucky was a no-good, irresponsible nut, Marquand wrote the *Post* a very derogatory letter. Bucky says, "He obviously didn't think much of me, but he said some very amusing things."

The night of Bucky's lecture at Harvard, it appeared that Marquand had not changed his views. He was fairly sweating with a terrific attack of stage fright on Bucky's behalf, fearful that he would disgrace the family. Bucky humorously described the scene: "John kept holding my hand. As more and more people crowded into the great hall, he kept saying to me, 'Bucky, do you realize that all these people are coming to hear you?'

"He clearly was trying to comfort me and strengthen me, and expected me to make an awful fool of myself. He only knew about my cars and my dome, and probably thought I was just a mechanic and could not possibly talk to these people."

Bucky did talk to "all those people" for about three hours. When he ended he received a standing ovation, not exactly a usual thing at Harvard.

Summing it all up Bucky said, "This apparently completely changed John's attitude toward me because he wrote a letter to our cousin Richard Fuller saying, 'I was completely mistaken about Bucky. He seems to be the greatest member of the family.' "

Harvard's change of attitude from 1914 was emphasized in 1962, when they invited Bucky to accept the Charles Eliot Norton Chair of *Poetry*. At the same time, the Harvard Chapter of Phi Beta Kappa voted to give the former dropout the golden key.

The extraordinary variety of Bucky's honorary doctorates—science, design, letters, law, arts, etc.—clearly indicates the universality of his disciplines. His recurrent theme, that the mistake of modern education is the production of specialists when what the world needs is men who see things whole, is never better exemplified than in his own self. The cliché of comparing him to Leonardo and Benjamin Franklin is so obvious that it is made in dozens of articles every year. But its banality does not vitiate its truth. Though he may never achieve their historical fame, the comparison remains valid.

Other recognitions of Bucky's accelerating fame came in invitations to join professional societies all over the world. Being an inveterate joiner—it makes him feel wanted—Bucky accepted many of them. They are as various as his disciplines, embracing astronautics, geography, metals, machinists, engineering, semantics, philosophy, ecology, ekistics, science, education, and the arts. Naturally, he belongs to numerous architectural societies, from the Royal Institute of British Architects to the Royal Society of Siamese Architects, et cetera, et cetera, as a former monarch of that country is reputed to have said.

Bucky's world-around traveling also accelerated. He was particularly popular in Russia and Japan. The fact that he was so apolitical and regarded politics as completely irrelevant enabled him to work harmoniously with people of any ideology. He says: "I am persona grata with all political camps because I am transpolitics. In fact, I could get out a joint manifesto with many extremists of both camps, radicals and conservatives, because they think alike in many things, and they think like me in many things."

In 1972, Bucky gave the baccalaureate address at the University of Virginia, the only time it has been given by a man who was not a Virginia graduate. He spoke of the sentimental attachment of the students to Jefferson because of his founding of the university. Most people nowadays pooh-pooh Jefferson as an old-fashioned liberal. "On the contrary," Bucky said, "Jefferson's truths were so far ahead of his time that Jefferson has not died. He is very much alive on the campus because his truths are still alive, and now becoming more manifest in the world."

Then Bucky gave them his favorite quotation from Jefferson, "The truth is not fearful."

At the dinner after the ceremony Bucky met William F. Buckley, certainly no Jeffersonian. However, as they talked they found many areas of agreement. Then Bucky in his blunt way said, "I would have assumed that I would not like you, but I find you charming."

Buckley laughed and said, "We should get out a joint manifesto."

"The extremists in both camps want to change things," Bucky says, "and in certain cases they are both right. Entropy, the second law of thermodynamics, implies change. It is the essential quality of an expanding universe and therefore should not, and cannot, be opposed. I think of Tennyson's verses:

> 'Not in vain the distant beacons. Forward, forward
> let us range.
> 'Let the great world spin for ever
> down the ringing grooves of change.' " [6]

Bucky continued: "It is the customs and traditions that seem so fine and valuable that may bring about bloody revolutions because nobody wants to change them. And yet they stand in the way of progress. Eventually, the United States will have to go, just as all great nations will have to go. If there is enough of everything to go around, fighting for patriotic reasons becomes murder instead of a praiseworthy thing."

With this philosophy it is no wonder that Bucky got along well with the Russians, even though he deplored their rigorous restrictions on independent thinking. This was particularly manifest at the Dartmouth Conference in Leningrad in 1964, where writers, philosophers, political

[6] *Locksley Hall*, Alfred Lord Tennyson.

economists, and scientists from both countries met to discuss world problems amicably in the hope of finding joint solutions.

Among the Americans present was Norman Cousins, liberal author and, at that time, editor of the prestigious *Saturday Review* (now of *Saturday Review/World* magazine). Bucky and Cousins became and remained "very great friends." Cousins gave the author a vivid description of the beginning of their friendship and of Bucky's principal contribution to the conference:

"Bucky and I sort of paired off at the conference. I had my daughters, aged fifteen and nineteen, with me and one of the things that fascinated me was the way Bucky was able to develop an empathy with them in a very short time; he completely hypnotized them. I remember coming into the hotel dining room in Leningrad for breakfast. After the greetings Bucky continued to explain to the girls some new theories in regard to electromagnetic lines of universal force. I was lost but they were not.

"At the conference, one evening was set aside at which each group would put up its futurist for the purpose of looking at life after the year 2000. The Russians were represented by Eugene Federov—spelled F-e-d-e-r-o-v—the head of the Soviet Academy of Science. Of course, the Americans put up Bucky—I'll spell that, too—G-E-N-I-U-S.

"It was a sort of intellectual gladiatorial contest and obviously each side wanted to show to advantage. The Russian spoke first. Federov was very good, as very methodically and very systematically, with supporting data, he talked about life in the year 2000—what the world population would be; what the world resources would be; and what the demands on those resources would be. It was a very impressive, cold turkey approach to the problem.

"Then Bucky spoke. As he usually does, he put his head forward, closed his eyes, clasped his hands and went soaring—and we went with him, piggyback on his magic carpet. He spoke for at least an hour and a half. Federov, who sat next to me, was entranced.

"Then, when Bucky completed his rarefied journey, Federov looked at me and said, 'The Americans win. No question about it! Mr. Fuller was magnificent. Never have I heard anything as daring, as really wonderful as this. Now tell me, what did he say?'

"This illustrates my point," Norman Cousins continued, "that it is not necessary to know exactly what Bucky says in order to grasp his essential meaning or to be elevated by his message. There is a quality of inspiration, and inspiration always transcends information. A quality of inspiration comes through in Bucky's presence or his words, especially when you have the two in combination, that has quite an independent meaning.

"1 would hate to be asked to summarize after Bucky gave a talk because that would be essentially the least important part of the transmission. The most important part is not transmittable, except by Bucky. And that is the sense that he clearly conveys, that it is possible to have a better world than we have today. That the universe is waiting to cooperate with us if only we know how to tune in properly to it and understand its laws as well as its allures.

"This is in the sense that there is a universal citizenship, or a citizenship of the Universe, beyond our existing parochial citizenships. And that there is a realm of cognition far beyond our limited horizons. Bucky becomes a master guide to this realm. I know no man who makes you feel so perfectly at home in the Universe as he does. . . ." [7]

[7] Norman Cousins to the author.

CHAPTER XVIII

GRAND STRATEGY

THE fact that Bucky, advocate extraordinary of industrialization, is also fervent for ecology superficially seems to be another of his paradoxes. It is not. For his kind of industrialization is based on ephemeralization and recycling. By doing more with less he would conserve the resources of Spaceship Earth and virtually eliminate pollution.

Bucky defines industrialization as "the extra-corporeal, organic metabolic regeneration of humanity." It consists of tools, specifically tools which are too complex to be made by a single individual, and which give man additional advantages in nature. These include words, tools which obviously require two or more people. "Industrialization is inherently comprehensive and omni-related to all humanity and all of humanity's ecological environment." [1]

The second law of thermodynamics states that all systems are radiating energy; they are entropic. But, since energy can neither be created nor destroyed, a balance must be struck somewhere in a finite though ever-expanding universe. The opposite of entropy is syntropy,* a gathering in, ordering, and consolidation of energy. Fortunately, our dark planet is strong on syntropy. Earth's own particular radiant energy star, the sun, is its prime source of energy. In addition billions of stars are giving off energy and a not inconsiderable portion of this reaches earth. Finally, earth picks up about 100,000 tons of stardust a year, and stardust is the intraverted concentrate of cosmic radiation because, according to Einstein, radiation and matter are behavioral states of the same phenomenon and have eternally regenerative terminal intransformabilities. Ergo, energy is powering into Spaceship Earth, if we only use it prop-

---

[1] "Letter to Doxiadis." Buckminster Fuller, *Main Currents in Modern Thought,* March–April 1969.

* Word invented by Buckminster Fuller.

erly. As Bucky said at Black Mountain, "Man has now completed all the plumbing and installed all the valves to turn on the infinite cosmic wealth."

In the course of Bucky's researches he has come up with some curious and startling statistics concerning our wasteful misuse of earth's resources. Take petroleum. By careful calculation he found that the amount of energy required to make one gallon of petroleum figured at the current price per kilowatt hour of electricity would cost roughly $1,000,000. At that rate one shudders to think of the cost of running one automobile for one day.

In order to dramatize our wastefulness Bucky sometimes cheats a little. A favorite saying of his is that at any given hour of the day in the United States 2,000,000 automobiles are stopped at red lights with their one hundred horsepower engines running, and, he adds, "This is the equivalent of 200,000,000 horses jumping up and down going nowhere."

The fallacy lies in the fact that the idling engines are only putting out about one horsepower, so it is 2,000,000 horses jumping up and down, not 200,000,000. That is still a lot of horses.

Other discoveries of Bucky's are that the amount of sulfur belched out of industrial chimneys in a year to pollute the atmosphere almost exactly equals the amount of sulfur taken from the ground for industrial purposes; that the amount of tin lying around aboveground in the United States is greater than all the tin left in all the known tin mines of the world; that the Bell Telephone system has enough copper in its obsolescent equipment to enable it, with its current excellent policy of ephemeralization, to supply all its ever-increasing system for the foreseeable future. The point is that his kind of industrialization would mean infinitely less pollution and waste. A balance could be struck with nature that could keep Spaceship Earth going full blast virtually forever.

Another telling point Bucky makes—and proves with statistics—is that in fully industrialized countries the birthrate automatically drops to about zero population growth. Therefore, he argues, if all the underdeveloped countries were fully industrialized, as they could be by intelligent use of the world's resources without taking anything away from the "have countries," the problem of overpopulation would simply disappear. Margaret Mead does not like his saying this; it undercuts her.

These are but a few of the reasons for Bucky's optimism about the ultimate success of humanity as a function of Universe; that function, as before noted, being syntropic, i.e., to produce order in an entropic system in accordance with the generalized principles which can be discovered by exercising God-given metaphysical intellects. Where he fails most dismally is in his plan for implementing these resplendent possibilities, in other words, the *political* system by which they can be brought to fruition.

Bucky would snort furiously at that; he considers politics a dirty word. For he does not realize that running any system, be it a government, an industry, or only a large farm, involves politics, if you accept the definition of politics as being the art or science of government. One of his favorite sayings is that if all the technicians and the machinery they operate were suddenly to be lost to the world at least two billion people would starve to death within six months. Whereas if all the politicians were shipped out in a very slow rocket to Jupiter, six months later the inhabitants of the world would probably be eating better than they do now. The catch is that the technicians would have had to metamorphose into politicians.

Bucky's plans for bringing about the happy circumstances he envisions are far less well thought out than his coordinates of the Universe. In one article he proposes that all the young architects of the world get together in an association to see to it that obsolescent methods of building are replaced by modern ephemeralization techniques. The illogic of this is evident when it is noted that Bucky has been fighting the architectural establishment all his life. Seeing their attitude toward his new approach, one boggles at the idea of a world run by a bureaucracy of architects.

At other times he states that when the peoples of the world are educated enough to realize that there would be plenty for all in a properly managed economy, they will force the politicians to turn matters over to the technicians who can do it. This still leaves the question of which technicians are going to make the decisions. Since they will indubitably differ violently among themselves, there has to be a person or committee to decide what is best to be done. And that is politics.

Another Bucky proposal—in the World Game—is to let computers make all the decisions, thus doing away with personal politics. But who is empowered to program the computers, which also can be made to speak with forked tongue?

Bucky's grand final solution is a form of instant democracy that would make the great protagonist of power to the people, Thomas Jefferson, revolve so violently in his grave as to produce an earthquake effect of 8.5 on the Richter scale and knock the University of Virginia flat. Instead of national citizenship, there would be world citizenship. Very good; with luck we may come to that. But he then proposes to hook every world citizen up to a giant computer by means of television. All great questions of world concern would be referred to the entire world electorate whose votes would instantly be recorded and tabulated. Bucky's faith in the innate wisdom and goodwill of humankind is so great that he believes they would make the right decision every time if they were properly informed without being misled by politicians.

That is the rub. Even though all the necessary information were fully available to every man—and woman—in Bucky's electronic utopia, how could he induce them to study, ponder, and vote upon it? Human nature being what it is, and people being as intellectually lazy as they are—even in the comparatively well-educated United States only about 65% of the electorate will stir their stumps to vote in a national election —why would the well-fed, well-cared for, lack-nothing people of his 99.95% perfect world bother even to push the right button?

It is Bucky's sublime faith in people that makes him so naïve in this area. In his moments of humility—and he has them in spite of what has been called his "delightfully unselfconscious egotism"—he says: "I am not a genius. I am a very average human being. What I have done any ordinary person can do. It is just because I am so average that I am a good example, a sort of norm of the potential in every newborn child."

Freed from fear of scarcity, with their longings assuaged by the rich opportunities that could be theirs, Bucky believes that people would develop all the sensitivities, the compassion, the wisdom and, yes, the love, which are his unique qualities. "Reform the environment," he says, "and human nature will do the rest."

One is reminded of Jean-Jacques Rousseau's Natural Man, and of truly idealistic Marxist doctrine that after the triumph of the proletariat was assured, the state would wither away. And one wonders. . . .

Though Bucky was so vigorously disseminating his philosophy with such a truly horrific schedule of toing and froing as would make the average man (as he thinks he is) collapse from sheer fatigue after no more than a week of it, he continued to pour out inventions for improving the environment and carrying out the design of Universe as revealed by his prescient intuitions.

One thing that he proposed and designed was a dome to go over an entire city, specifically the midtown part of New York from 64th Street to 22nd Street and from the Hudson to the East River. This was not as wild a flight of science-fiction as might be supposed. Bucky calculates that such a dome would reduce the energy loss of Manhattan approximately fiftyfold. This is because a sphere encloses so much more volume for each square foot of its surface than any other structure. The towers and other buildings of Manhattan are like the fins on an air-cooled engine, radiating heat, whereas the exposed heat-radiating surface of the dome would be only 1/85 of that. Conversely, in hot weather the dome would have much less heat absorption. Heating the surface of the great dome in winter would melt the snow. Melted snow and rain would run into huge gutters around it and be piped to reservoirs in Westchester instead of being wasted. Bucky calculates that the savings to the city in snow removal costs alone would pay for the dome in ten years.

He envisages a dome two miles in diameter and one mile high at its apex. Its skin would consist of wire-reinforced, one-way-vision, shatterproof glass, mist-plated with aluminum to cut sun glare while admitting light. From the outside it would look like a great glittering hemispheric mirror, while from the inside its structural elements would be as invisible as the wires of a screened porch, and it would "appear as a translucent film through which the sky, clouds and stars would appear." [2]

The circular lower rim of the dome would be mounted just below the tops of New York's tallest towers. In such a large dome the weight of the enclosed atmosphere would be almost equal to the weight of the structure with a differential of only 1/1,000. If the interior atmosphere were heated only one degree warmer than the outside air, the thing would actually float against its restraining cables like a hot air balloon. It would be far less costly to air-condition the entire city than it is to heat or cool individual buildings.

Bucky becomes poetic as he describes life in such a city. "Those who are familiar with the delights of covered city streets, in which outdoor restaurants and exhibits are practical (as in the great arcades of Milan), can envision the effect of a domed-over city, where windows may be open the year 'round and gardens bloom in the dust-free atmosphere." [3]

It was seriously proposed to put a similar dome over the New York

[2] "Why Not Roofs Over Our Cities?" by Buckminster Fuller. *Think*, January 1968.
[3] Ibid.

World's Fair of 1964. Pity it fell through! The perfect weather inside might have made the fair a success instead of the dismal failure it was. And the effect would have been great.

Another Bucky design for the almost perfect city is a huge, hollow tetrahedronal building like a latticed pyramid two hundred stories high capable of housing 1,000,000 people or 300,000 families, each of which would have a 2,000 square foot terraced apartment, with an additional 1,000 square feet for a garden. It would be, in effect, an open-truss-framework structured mountain whose sides would be covered with parked mobile homes. The interior would contain all the necessary machinery as well as vertical and horizontal transportation systems.

Composite picture of Dome covering midtown Manhattan, 64th Street to 22nd Street and river to river.

Because Bucky considers the ownership of land a feudal relic, stultifying to the owner because it ties him down when he should be completely mobile, and unfair to the vast majority of landless people, his almost perfect city would float on the ownerless sea. Its pyramidal apex would be 8,500 feet high and its three base edges would be two miles long. Because of its tetrahedronal structure it would be so relatively light that its hollow, box-sectioned, reinforced concrete foundations would float it easily. The city could be moored in triangularly patterned canals or anchored in the ocean at any point. It would be earthquake-proof and, because the hundred-foot depth of the foundations would be far below the turbulence level of the waves, "it would be a floating atoll with a harbor that is always calm and protected." [4]

Tetrahedronal City floating at sea.

Such a city would generate all its needed energy by means of atomic reactors, whose heat would run desalinization plants to provide it with plenty of fresh water.

Because of the tetrahedron's unique capability of being increased symmetrically in size by additions to any one of its four faces, the city could start as something small—say 1,000 inhabitants—and grow as

[4] "Man with a Chronofile. Buckminster Fuller," *Saturday Review,* April 1, 1967.

required. Such cities would permit new habitation possibilities on the watery three-quarters of the earth's surface.

In 1967, Bucky became president of the Triton Foundation and chief architect for the production of the Tetrahedronal Floating City for the U.S. Department of Housing and Urban Development. How-ever, changes in government policy aborted the project.

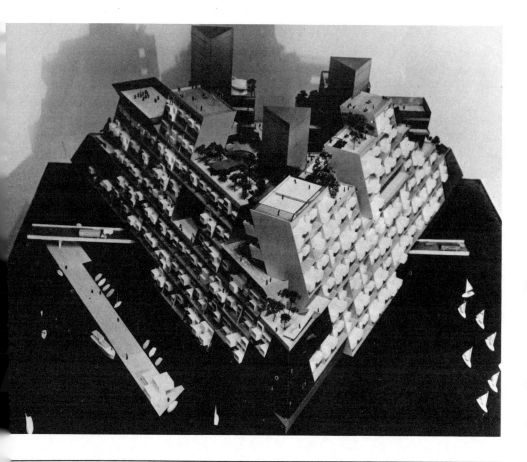

Tetrahedronal City

Some of Bucky's most inspiring experiences during the 1960s were the annual Doxiadis cruises. They were sponsored by that remarkable Greek ekisticist—planner of cities—Constantine Doxiadis, as floating symposia for men and women of international fame and highly intelligent, farsighted people of goodwill. They included representatives of many disciplines and vocations: philosophers, writers, teachers, planners, industrialists, scientists, and even politicians. They all boarded a ship at Piraeus, the port of Athens, and sailed around the Aegean Sea visiting one or more of the historic Grecian islands every day. Aboard the ship there would be morning and evening lectures by different eminent men and women, followed by group discussions of how this or that world problem could best be solved or, at least, mitigated. It was Doxiadis's idea that the ambient atmosphere of glorious ancient Greece would inspire creative thought and intellectual harmony. And it did.

Bucky was at his best giving and hearing the lectures, but not so good in the round table discussions. His inability to take part in the rapid give-and-take of group discussions has often been written of as an example of his supreme egocentricity. The difficulty has a physical explanation—he can't hear them.

Even as a young man, Bucky was somewhat deaf; as he grew older this malfunction became ever greater. Fortunately for him, as his deafness increased, so did the power of hearing aids which are now, with the use of transistors, exquisite examples of ephemeralization. With them he can hear any single voice—a man lecturing or someone conversing alone with him. However, the babble of many voices makes the tiny machines in his ears screech in a way that is pure torture. Ergo, his blank or pained expression during a general conversation.

Anne went with Bucky on several of the Doxiadis cruises, including the last one, called the Delos Symposium, in July, 1972. The theme of this symposium was "Action for Human Development"—a topic exactly suited to bring out Bucky's most stimulating ideas.

Norman Cousins gave a very amusing, highly typical description of Bucky on another trip, which he had from his close friend James Perkins.* On a certain day, Bucky gave an afternoon presentation. Cousins says: "Then they adjourned for dinner, but Bucky kept right on talking, not eating himself, and resumed in the saloon after dinner. Then he walked with the individual participants to their cabins. Finally he ended up with Doxiadis and Jim Perkins in the former's cabin long after midnight.

"As it was described to me, Perkins and Doxiadis, totally exhausted, looked at this man, who by now had been on this talking marathon for nine hours. You can picture it—Doxiadis getting undressed, Jim

* President of Cornell University.

Perkins slumped down in a chair, and Bucky sounding off his thoughts, exhilarated, fresh, energetic. And there was no doubt in either Doxiadis's or Perkins's minds that he could have kept on through the entire night, and he would still be fresh.

"What Bucky demonstrates to me in all this," Cousins said, "is that the key to longevity is creativity; the notion of degeneration of brain cells beyond a certain age is true only in the absence of creativity. Bucky, at seventy-seven, is proof of the theory that there is a limitless reservoir of potential intellectual activity that we carry around with us and most people in the course of a lifetime put only five or ten percent of it to work.

"Bucky still has a reservoir full and he's still using it. And this may be the most important discovery of all those he has made.

"It seems to me that there is a direct connection between creative thought and involvement in life and the production of epinephrine by the adrenal gland. When the challenge stops, the supply is turned off; the will to live atrophies and the body chemistry no longer functions. . . . Doctors are important merely as pain killers. Disease is combated by will. The proper prescriptions are written by the body itself, but only in the condition of balance and a state of grace. I've never known Bucky not to be in the state of grace." [5]

An earlier cruise had inspired Bucky to write a letter to Doxiadis in which he set forth what he calls his basic concepts of making man function as Universe intends. Woodrow Wilson had his Fourteen Points; Bucky has fourteen concepts. They are:

Concept one: *Universe*

Bucky always starts with Universe. This is his definition of it: "Universe is the aggregate of all humanity's all time consciously apprehended and communicated experiences."

Concept two: *Humanity*

The human is not an accidental onlooker "who happened in on the 'Play of Life,' but an essential syntropic function of Universe."

Concept three: *Children*

"Focus on new life. Since children are the hope of the future and 98% of the environment's positive or negative effects upon new life are wrought by age thirteen, it is obvious that effective work in advantaging life through environment can mainly be realized within the first thirteen years."

Concept four: *Teleology*

[5] Norman Cousins to the author.

Teleology by Bucky's definition means "the intuitive conversion by brain and mind of special case, subjective experiences into generalized principles . . . which permit the individual to reform the environment . . . so as to provide ultimately higher advantages for men," and to inspire others to do likewise.

Concept five: *Reform the Environment, Not Man*

Bucky's philosophy and strategy confine design initiative to reforming *only* the environment and *never* to emulate the almost universal attempts of humans to reform and restrain other humans by political actions, laws, and codes.

Concept six: *General Systems Theory*

Using the generalized principles he has discovered, Bucky says, "I always start all problem-solving with Universe, and thereafter subdivide progressively to identify a special local problem within the total of problems." He thus attacks it *comprehensively* and *anticipatorily*.

Concept seven: *Industrialization*

"Industrialization consists of tools." It involves "*all experiences of all men* everywhere in history." Bucky sees it as inherently comprehensive and omni-interrelated in respect to all humanity. And he believes that, though subsystems of it are run shortsightedly by selfishly motivated people, the whole works *inadvertently* toward ultimately providing all men with higher standards of living. . . . Because energy plus know-how is wealth, "the integrating world industrial networks mean ultimate access of all humanity to the total operative commonwealth of Earth."

Concept eight: *Design Science*

Design Science is concerned "with the scheduling of the complex interaction of the general systems events of industrialization." The rapid advance of technology in one field—air transportation, for example—must be "comprehensively integrated with all other vastly accelerating environment relationship transformations."

Concept nine: *The Service Industry*

"Humanity is gradually trending toward becoming Worldians." Therefore, the static appurtenances of life—houses, automobiles, even typewriters—will all be rented like telephones because of man's increasing mobility. Amplifying this thought in another article, Bucky foresees man's ability to deploy at will all over the earth and the solar system by means of autonomous structures made livable by our astronauts' life-support 'black box.'" And he adds, "Quite clearly, man, free to enjoy all of his planets . . . will also be swiftly outward bound to occupy ever greater ranges of the universe." [6]

Concept ten: *Ephemeralization*

"The acceleration of doing more with less . . . will complete the task of providing enough for all humanity within another thirty-four years . . . despite political systems that deliberately divide society and set one group against another." Bucky believes that without the interference of political systems it could be done in twenty years.

Concept eleven: *Prime Design Initiative*

Bucky believes that it is essential for the individual, invention-developing pioneer to maintain his economic initiative and not get tied up with the massive capital-cum-bureaucracy of large corporations, despite the leverage of their wealth.

Concept twelve: *Self-Discipline*

Instead of the obligation to make a living, Bucky substitutes the higher obligation of the individual's syntropic *responsibility* in Universe.

[6] *Playboy*, February, 1968.

Ephemeralization. Floatable cloud-structure spheres ½ mile in diameter.

Concept thirteen: *Comprehensive Coordination*

Comprehensivity instead of specialization is Bucky's key to successful design competence. His foremost self-discipline is never to try to sell one of his ideas to others. He will just design and test it, and wait for others, who need it, to come to him. He only goes where he is asked to speak because, if you force your ideas on people they listen unwillingly, but if they ask you to speak to them—especially if they pay a high fee—"they are very receptive."

Bucky incessantly engages in trying to make all his previous inventions obsolete by designing better ones.

Concept fourteen: *World Community and Its Subcommunities*

Bucky divides the ecological history of the human race into two chapters. The first chapter of a million years or so saw the scattering of humanity from its point of origin—Indonesia, he thinks—all over the earth into tribal units that became differentiated by various climatic conditions as regards pigmentation of skin, general appearance, etc. The second chapter—the last ten thousand years—saw these different tribes migrating *toward* each other and gradually eliminating the differences by crossbreeding. Thus we are now becoming genetically integrated—one race in one world. He believes that chapter three is just beginning, in which world man will realize his potential for success as a function of Universe through his accelerating mastery of "vast, inanimate, inexhaustible energy sources combined with doing more with less."

Bucky thinks that the United States, as "the theater of crossbred world man," best discloses the patterns coming upon all men; the patterns of total mobility. "The swift evolutionary changes taking place invisibly are about to uproot [man]. . . . All concepts of urbanization will become obsolete; only the Earth and the solar system will be his temporary home."

The "world shuttling" citizenship will converge for metaphysical exchange—for the brain and mind activities. They will deploy for physical activities such as field sports, work in factories, and for physical research in ecology, geology, archeology, and so forth.

Urbanism, according to Bucky, is "a world-embracing, entropic, volcanic physical explosion, countered at increasingly high frequency with the world-embracing, metaphysically contracting and information-concentrating system, which regenerates by broadcasting and publishing its progressively generalized concepts for regeneration of man's antientropic functioning—that fulfill his universe functioning."

This letter, condensed, rephrased, and summarized by the author, represents the distillation of Buckminster Fuller's "grand strategy" for humanity. He ended it on a characteristically humorous note:

> "Believe it or not, this is the longest letter I have ever written.
> "Faithfully yours. Finis
> "Bucky." [7]

[7] "Letter to Doxiadis." Buckminster Fuller, *Main Currents in Modern Thought.* March–April 1969.

CHAPTER XIX

ANNE'S TAJ MAHAL

In the mid-1960s, Bucky felt he was slowing down. By anyone else's standards he was still a lightning bolt, but this was not good enough for him. Taking stock of his situation he reasoned, "Either it is old age, in which case I can do nothing about it; or I am overweight,* in which case I can."

Seeking a method by which he would lose weight without loss of energy, he considered the various foods available to him. He reasoned that the energy of the sun was transformed into vegetation by photosynthesis. This process was then carried a step further by vegetation being eaten by cattle and transmuted into high-protein meat. Ergo, he would get maximum energy with minimum calories if he ate virtually nothing but lean beef.

The diet he adopted consisted of three-quarters of a pound to a pound of steak for breakfast, lunch, and dinner. At the two latter meals he ate a little raw salad and fruit for vitamins.† The cut of beef he prefers, because it has the least fat, is London broil. It is usually served in thin strips because it is so tough, but Bucky cheerfully chomps great hunks of it with his magnificent teeth.

The Fuller diet worked for Fuller. As the pounds dropped off, his youthful energy returned in its plenitude. He now weighs a trim 140 pounds, exactly the same as when he was a young lieutenant in the navy.

It might be supposed that this eccentric diet would prove quite a strain for Bucky's hosts in a time of astronomical prices for beef; but he is a most considerate guest. He insists on going to town and buying his own steaks in four-pound pieces—two days' supply. Furthermore, he cooks them himself in a frying pan. The author recalls going out

* Fuller weighed about 190 pounds.
† Fuller switched to cooked fruit when he developed diverticulosis.

to his kitchen one morning to find Bucky tending the sizzling pan and doing a soft-shoe dance in front of the stove in sheer youthful exuberance.

The year 1967 was the best and the worst for Bucky. That was the time when the most beautiful of all the geodesic domes so far built was opened as the United States Pavilion at Expo '67 in Montreal. Back in 1965, the U.S. Government had asked Bucky to help them plan their exhibit. He had proposed a giant World Airocean Map showing all the resources of the world, the peoples, their conditions and needs in a bird's-eye view such as he later envisioned for his World Game. When this was turned down he simply designed the great geodesic dome for them.

Bucky and Shoji Sodao, assisted by young architects and engineers from MIT, worked on the plans. Bucky had met Shoji when the young Japanese, then a student at the Cornell Architectural School, led Bucky's project of building a miniature earth on top of the Electrical Building at the university. They became fast friends and then partners in the dome-designing firm of Fuller and Sodao, Inc., at 12 Arrow Street in Cambridge.

Shoji, who was a summa cum laude graduate, has become Bucky's right-hand man whom he takes with him on all his most important design projects. He was a rather somber young man, though full of goodwill, always helping other students and completely devoted to Bucky.

Though Shoji is so modern in his architectural ideas, he is a great traditionalist in his personal life. For example, when he decided to marry he went about it in the ancient Japanese way even though he was born in America and fought in the Nisei Division in Italy in World War II. He contacted a go-between in Japan who made the arrangements with the prospective bride's go-between. "Go-betweens are like seconds in a duel," Bucky explained. Photographs were exchanged; then a meeting was arranged, and they became engaged.

That engagement lasted for twelve years. "I thought they would never do it," Anne Fuller says, "but Shoji came to Japan last year while we were there and suddenly the marriage took place. Shoji was forty-four; his bride was forty-two."

According to Bucky, it is an entirely fortunate marriage. "She is a queen," he says; "and from being so somber and serious, Shoji has become happy and carefree."

The plans Fuller and Sodao drew for the huge "skybreak bubble," as the three-quarters sphere of the Expo Dome was called, were like no other plans the builders had ever seen. For, except for a few details of the hubs where the compression members were joined in hexagonal radii, there were no drawings at all, simply tables of figures with which to index the machine tools that so accurately stamped out the stainless steel alloy components. From there on it was merely a matter of riveting them in place according to the color coding; it was all done with mathematics.

Since there could be no convenient bridge for the workers, as in the Ford Rotunda Dome, finding steelworkers willing to work two hundred feet above the ground without the security of a conventional steel-beamed structure under their feet presented a problem. It was solved by employing Mohawk Indians who did not mind dizzy heights with only the distant ground below seen through the delicate lattice of omnirepetitive triangles.

Another problem was the matter of overheating from the sun. This was ingeniously solved by Bucky. Instead of the customary plastic skin, the covering was made of thousands of separate triangular plexiglass panels so they could turn individually. They were operated by over two hundred and fifty electric motors hitched to a computer that was programmed to open or shut them in response to the weather conditions outside. Other panels were equipped with light sensors that raised or lowered shades as the sun in its diurnal passage commanded. The dome theoretically weighed approximately 600 tons; however, in conformity with Bucky's theory of the buoyancy of large domes, the weight resting on its foundations was considerably less than the total weight of its components when the air inside was warmer than the surrounding atmosphere.

The elevated monorail train, which carried visitors around Expo, ran right through "Bucky's Bubble," as some people called it: and the interior was filled with exhibits mounted on platforms staggered at different levels, carrying out the theme the U.S. Government had chosen: *Creative America*. The millions of visitors cared little for these sideshows; for they realized that the dome itself was the most creative thing America had produced in the last fifty years. Two hundred and fifty feet in diameter, tall as a twenty-story building, the great, iridescent bubble dominated the entire exposition. Imposing as it was from the outside, it was even more awesomely beautiful from within.

As one looked upward through its enormously high, clear hemisphere, which clouds and sky seemed almost to touch, the slender tracery of its structure looked as ephemeral as gossamer filaments.

Anne's Taj Mahal, the Expo '67 Dome.

On May 28, 1967, Bucky and Anne went to Expo '67. They were overjoyed by the acclaim they received, and particularly by overhearing the enthusiastic comments of the crowds as they walked through the dome's glittering interior. Bucky says: "It was a wonderful thing for the year of our fiftieth anniversary. To Anne the Expo Dome seemed to give validation to the extraordinary backing she had given me. To me it proved that the revolution on Spaceship Earth and the salvation for mankind that it would bring about would be gained primarily by design revolution and not by political revolution."

To Anne, Bucky said, "I have inadvertently brought about the production and installation of our own Taj Mahal as pure fallout of my love for you."

In this euphoric frame of mind they flew back to Kennedy Airport on Long Island and took a taxi to New York. On Queens Boulevard the cab smashed into the back of a truck and they were thrown violently against the front windows. Rotund Bucky bounced back with only a few bruises. Anne struck her head and was dazed. Crowds gathered, police cars and ambulances arrived with sirens screaming.

In a few moments Anne's head cleared and she shakily said she was all right. So, instead of going to a hospital, they went on to the St. Regis Hotel.

But Anne was more badly hurt than she knew. In the next few days she developed excruciating headaches and dizzy spells. Finally, she realized that something was terribly wrong.

Fortunately, Doctor T. I. Hoen, one of the great neurosurgeons of America, was a close friend of the Fullers. The moment Doctor Hoen was told of Anne's condition he ordered her to the New York University Hospital, of which he was the head surgeon. There tests showed that she had suffered a massive brain hemorrhage. Armed with his fantastic skill and inspired by his deep affection for his patient, Doctor Hoen opened Anne's skull and with infinite care drained off the coagulated blood and made delicate repairs. No one, not even Doctor Hoen, knew whether she would ever regain consciousness, whether she would live or die, or should she live, if she would be an inanimate heap of flesh.

Bucky was almost out of his mind. For all his dedication to his great mission, he felt he could not go on without Anne; she was, and always had been, his balance wheel, or in his sailor's phrase, his "anchor to windward." In this traumatic period, Gene Fowler wrote him a beautiful letter which gave him exceeding comfort:

Dear Bucky:

Anne is a woman of considerable strength. She will not leave you to continue alone. I have known for a long time that Anne's strength, beauty, and grace were in your work. It makes sense that this skybreak bubble should be, not a monument, but an embodiment of your love for her.

You have constructed something slightly tougher than a human being, but with the same beauty and grace; and knowingly set into materials torn from earth and shaped through our fires and minds a memory to outlast one remembered and then once remembering; knowing a woman large enough to be seen from space; and knowing men may enter and share.

More than the Taj, Bucky!

With love

Gene

Anne did not leave Bucky. Doctor Hoen's skill prevailed and she completely recovered to fly with her husband to further triumphs in what poetically speaking men still call the four corners of the earth, though they know these are but geodesic lines on the surface of a sphere.

Of their later life together Bucky, somewhat incoherent from emotion, says: "Anne is a woman who has constructed a world of her own, that she really feels right in, and she does not try to know how man learned words or what might be the construction of the universe. She has a universe of her own that works very well for her. And very deep faith. And an absolute commitment to love—when she loves she loves forever.

"Her universe contains many very beautiful conventions. In a sense I have sometimes violated what those conventions hold for her.

"For there is a force in me that makes me have to be comprehensive, to understand all the things I can about Universe—my universe that is so different from Anne's. I have heard people, whom I consider very good observers, say that when two people, who are as diametrically different as Anne and I, get married, it either cracks up right away, or turns out to be fantastically good. That is the way it has been for us.

"You have got to understand what's going on. She has knocked a lot of the nonsense out of me. Certainly one of the most beautiful things about our marriage is that each day now it gets more beautiful. We both are really just having a happier and happier time in life. It's very, very beautiful; you know, a fantastic kind of time."

CHAPTER XX

WORLD GAME

It was in the winter of 1969 that Bucky bought the beautiful yacht *Intuition*. He had driven from my house in Sarasota to the Morgan Shipyard in St. Petersburg and had seen her and loved her, and bought her, just like that, in an afternoon. She is a seventeen-ton, Morgan-built sloop, twenty-nine feet on the waterline, forty-four feet overall. Her lovely lines make her very fast. However, she is no racing machine, but a comfortable cruising yacht—skillfully crafted of the finest materials, with a roomy, well-furnished cabin and a convenient galley and head—capable of sleeping six in a pinch. Bucky had her fitted out with a superb suit of sails, and all the latest navigational gadgets including a ship-to-shore telephone that when she is there at long last links Bear Island to civilization, though it is used only in emergencies. He loves her like a cherished woman.

She was shipped by rail from Florida to Camden, Maine, where she was to be launched that summer of 1969. The night before, Bucky was inspired to write a poem about her—he could not name a boat in less than five thousand words. He sat through the night putting down the ideas that the word intuition quickened in him. Later he worked very hard revising it and amplifying it, and it was published as the title poem of his book, *Intuition*. The last few lines are, perhaps, the most extraordinary tribute to a sailing ship ever written.

> Again and again,
> Step by step
> Intuition opens the doors
> That lead to man's designing . . .

And because its design
Permits humanity to live anywhere
Around our planet's watery mantle
And because this sailing craft
We are now to launch
Is the epitome of design competence—
As manifest at this moment
In the forever mounting and cresting wave
Of design capability—
We herewith give
To this world-around dwellable
High-seas sailing craft
The name—INTUITION.

Intuition was to be launched by a heavy-duty crane to lift her off the big flatbed truck on which she had been transported to the shipyard. The little group of Bucky's closest kin and friends stood on the pier while Bucky recited those last moving lines; and his niece Sally Abbott, who had come over from Andover, Massachusetts, to perform the champagne-bottle-breaking ceremony, waited tensely.

Ironically, Murphy's law governing mechanical industrial tools—which Bucky refuses to recognize, holding that *anything that can go wrong will go wrong*—held good. The winch of that beautifully engineered, heavy-duty crane stuck. *Intuition* hung there a few feet above the planet's watery mantle until the following day.

Also in 1969, Bucky was invited to give the Jawaharlal Nehru Memorial Lecture in New Delhi. It was very difficult for him, not because he had no confidence in his ability to do so, but because the directors of the Memorial Fund insisted in knowing beforehand what he was going to say, so it had to be written down. It was the only one of Bucky's major addresses that he *read*. He solved the problem to some extent by thinking out loud into a tape recorder and having it transcribed. Then, of course, he went over the text and, as he always does with things he writes, made hundreds of corrections and additions in his spider-web handwriting, snaking in and out of the lines, running up the sides of the pages, doubling back to the bottom and flowing over onto the back of the page; and he included many algebraic formulae—a proofreader's nightmare.

The result, though not as spontaneous as his less formal style and more convoluted, was a remarkable and extremely condensed summary of his mathematical discoveries and philosophical thinking. Indira Gandhi, herself, made the introductory speech.

Through her, Bucky met and deeply impressed Karàn Singh, Minister for Civil Aviation and Tourism in the Indian government. Karàn was the former Maharaja of Kashmir, and was one of the first two maharajas to renounce their princely rank and become plain citizens of India. He and his beautiful wife became devoted friends of Bucky. Bucky once asked Karàn how they happened to get married. Karàn said, "You won't believe it, but it was a completely arranged marriage."

Bucky explains, "She was a princess of Nepal and he was then the Maharaja of Kashmir, the two extreme limits of the Himalayas, and their marriage was a dynastic matter. But it turned out to be very fortunate because they are both truly beautiful people and get on very well. Of course, they both became commoners."

Karàn Singh asked Bucky to design three new airports for the Indian government, at New Delhi, Bombay, and Madras. It was a challenge Bucky could not refuse, though it meant spending a month in India twice a year.

Bucky and Shoji Sadao have gone to India six times in the last three years. Of all the things Bucky has done—including his rapid passage from time zone to time zone (he carries three watches, one set at the time in the place he is, one at the time in the place he will be next, and one at Philadelphia time), the Indian trips were the most wearing. In summer it is often above 100°, and though most of the modern buildings are air-conditioned, whenever he went outside he was exposed to the infernal, humid heat. Bucky says, "I don't seem to mind the heat when I am there, but I find that it does play tricks on my insides." Which is his understated way of saying that it drains him physically.

In addition, there were enormous frustrations. At innumerable long meetings no one could make up their minds, and objections were raised to many of Bucky's brilliant intuitive solutions of the problems they encountered. In such group discussions his hearing aid howls and screeches at the multiple voices and he misses half of what is said. Though he dearly loves and admires his Indian friends, they are a difficult people to pin down. With their Asian politeness they at first agree to every proposal; and the next day they have second thoughts, then third thoughts, fourth thoughts, and tenth thoughts.

Despite the hard going, the final schematic plans were finished and accepted by the Indian government in the spring of 1973. But Bucky expects to have to return to India to advise on the actual building.

In compensation for his work, Bucky asked only that he be paid enough to cover his overhead for his research projects in the United States—that is, his total capability to earn money prorated for thirty-day periods. By the spring of 1973, he had received nothing beyond his expenses. For the Finance Ministry suddenly announced that they were going to tax his Indian earnings 60% as excess profits. "There was no profit, as such," says Bucky, "only enough to carry my research overhead. And the contract expressly stated that I was to be paid in dollars. To cut it down by 60% on a technicality would mean a serious loss to my research projects.

"Finally, things got so bad that I went to Indira and Karàn; and they immediately went after the Finance Ministry who have agreed to behave fairly well. But they have paid me nothing so far."

Bucky has organized two main institutions for implementing his grand strategy. The first he calls "The World Game"; the second is the Design Science Institute. The World Game is based on the techniques of the war games with their anticipatory forecasts carried out by the general staffs of the leading military powers of the world so as to be able to get there first with the most firepower. But in the World Game nobody loses, and all humanity wins. Its object is to make an inventory of the entire earth's physical and metaphysical resources and the needs of all its peoples; and then, with the aid of computers, to devise strategies to meet those needs abundantly.

The game was first played by Bucky and twenty-six students early in 1969 at the New York Studio School in a very amateurish way without computers. Bucky then set it up in his workshop in a two-story brick building at Southern Illinois University, where he began to compile the World Resources Inventory. As always, Bucky's planning considerably exceeded his financial resources. It included a world airocean map the size of a football field, which would be wired to serve as a giant visual display to show data concerning the world's raw and industrial resources, world conditions and events, together with world-trending and peoples' migrations and necessities.

Connected with it would be a $16,000,000 complex of high-velocity digital computers to evaluate the findings and strategies and display them on the map so that viewers from the balconies around the great dome building in which it would be housed could have a bird's-eye view of the exact condition of the planet at any given moment. This set-up was to serve as the central brain into which World Game extension groups throughout the earth would feed their information and ideas.

Bucky reckoned the total cost of the installation at $30,000,000. The fact that this amount of money was nowhere in sight did not dampen his ardor or give him a moment's pause. He believed that when its value became apparent to people everywhere the money would be made available. Meanwhile, he began on a more modest but still costly scale financed mainly by his own earnings.

As first organized Bucky had a staff of twenty, whose salaries he paid himself with help from SIU, assisted by numerous students at SIU and other universities throughout the United States and all around the world. The first World Game seminar was conducted by Bucky and Edwin Schlossberg, a young Ph.D. candidate at Southern Illinois, from June 12 to July 31, 1969. They worked toward developing research and design teams of students to deal effectively with the data and concepts necessary to the success of the great enterprise. Schlossberg said enthusiastically, "We were working at the frontier and each student was working at his frontier." [1]

Scenario Energy

Using Bucky's system of "energy slaves" (the amount of energy in kilowatt hours one man could generate in one year) they discovered that the "bare maximum" needs of the world in the year 2000 amounted to 1,242 energy slaves per capita per year or 15,000 kwh and 800 metric tons of coal or its equivalent (present U.S. need: 7,000 kwh per person). Once they knew what mankind would need they began to consider ways to provide it.

For this purpose they made huge charts of all possible sources of energy, including atomic reactors and undeveloped hydroelectric sources in Africa and South America. They combined these with the development of wind, tidal, and solar energy and the possibility of doing more with less, and came up with the temporary solution of a world-around electric power grid which would enable electric power to flow around

[1] "World Game Report." Gene Youngblood, *Los Angeles Free Press,* Dec. 26, 1969.

the world following the peak power load of each continent, thus utilizing the 50% of production capacity that now stands idle half the time.

Bucky found that the most promising *new* source of energy was wind power. He says: "The National Science Foundation has already made the pronouncement that wind power is our greatest resource for power—wind power is sun power, you know. It is going to take the place of fossil fuels and is quite adequate to meet all the needs of humanity. We will use power generated by windmills with the fuel cells that have come out of the NASA space program. These have 85% efficiency, compared to an internal combustion engine which has less than 25% efficiency. The windmills will generate electricity which will be used to separate hydrogen from water electrolytically and the hydrogen will be used to drive all our cars with no pollution at all. Meanwhile, the NASA-type fuel cells, also using hydrogen, will release all the electrical energy we need."

Bucky promptly began inventing more efficient windmills. As he points out, the use of windmills was discontinued just about the time when the aeronautical arts began to explore the principles of aerodynamics. Using this now advanced technology, he has been able to design far more efficient methods of utilizing wind power. Working with Hans Meyer, one of the world's great aeronautical engineers, Bucky built several test models on Little Sprucehead Island, including the Venturi model which is cowled like an airplane engine. Hans Meyer says, "To date [1972] we have developed a low-cost, highly efficient blade system and power transmission, and are now beginning work on hydrogen generation and compressed air storage." [2]

The Science Center in Philadelphia is presently backing the production of the first complete circuit of this kind. Bucky's students there are working on it under his direction and that of other scientists. At any moment now the citizens of Philadelphia will see a huge new Fuller windmill arise like a futuristic version of the trademark of the Netherlands on top of the new Electrical Building of University City Science Center.

Many other World Game "scenarios" have been developed throughout the years, involving enormous amounts of research, in agricul-

---

[2] Hans Meyer in *Buckminster Fuller Retrospective*, 1972.

ture, housing, transportation, clothing, and communications. (Incidentally, Bucky calls the press "our most polluted resource.") Though Bucky has never gotten his own personal $16,000,000 computer, he has spent a great deal of his own money buying computer time; and many sensible solutions have come out of the World Game, though no one has as yet been sensible enough to try them. However, an enormous amount of information on world resources and their improved use through ephemeralization has been stored in the World Resources Inventory ready for the world when it is ready to utilize it.*

Bucky says: "We are moving from the Industrial Age into the Age of Cybernetics. This is the most difficult transition in history because it has to be accomplished consciously, whereas the other transformations through which mankind has passed have been accomplished inadvertently."

Just as the World Game was beginning to accomplish great things, Bucky's situation at Southern Illinois became extremely difficult. The wave of student riots, which had originated in Berkeley in 1965–66, finally reached Carbondale in 1970, forcing the resignation of Bucky's dear friend and sponsor there, President Delyte Morris.

Bucky attributes this cycle of violence, which exploded like a string of firecrackers on campuses throughout the country, less to the hot war in Vietnam than to the cold war among the superpowers. He says, "With NATO, Russia, the United States, and China spending two hundred billion a year getting ready for Armageddon, we find very large funds—quite a few billions—assigned to making it impossible for the opposing economy to maintain any war production capability. And with the highly scientific technology involved, you cannot possibly have war production if you don't have universities. So huge sums of money were applied by both sides to try to destroy one another's universities, to destroy the students' confidence in the systems of education.

"They found that the university presidents were the most vulnerable of all the targets, because the president is just a money-raising man today, and he doesn't belong to the faculty and he does not belong to the students. They literally shot down a great many of the university presidents. I would not blame either side alone. The CIA was doing

---

* The data about the amount of sulfur going up in smoke almost exactly equaling the amount of sulfur mined came from the World Game.

it in Russia, and they were doing it here. The Russians themselves pointed out to me that they had a much greater advantage because our free press, which they didn't have, was used to build up enormous momentum.

"President Morris was a victim of this situation. He tried very hard to satisfy the demands of the students at SIU, but they did not want to be satisfied; they just simply wanted him out. They made things more and more impossible for him. They vandalized his house and worked up scandals, and finally got him pushed out."

When President Morris left, the whole ambience of SIU changed very rapidly. This was in part due to the financial crunch in which SIU, like all other great universities, found itself. During the fifties and sixties state legislatures and the federal government had been exceedingly generous with funds for institutions of higher education because the electorate equated education with success for their children. The ugly riots, the burning and vandalizing of university buildings, the threats to the very stability of the American system of government from the revolutionary attitude of the campuses, disillusioned the voters. They became less than enthusiastic about supporting a system which seemed to be turning their children, not into successful citizens, but into radical monsters out to destroy the values they still held dear. Responding to this 180° change in the wind of popular opinion, the legislatures tightened their purse strings as inflationary pressures sent educational costs soaring.

For example, the Illinois Legislature had voted $3,000,000 to finance Bucky's research, provided it was matched by another $9,000,000. This offer was quickly withdrawn. Worse still, the hundreds of tenured professors whom President Morris had brought in became fearful for their salaries; for even though they had tenure, that was only a kind of contract with the university which could do nothing unless the legislature provided funds. Like other faculties everywhere they became panicky, looking out only for themselves.

So Bucky found that instead of being considered an asset, he had become a liability in the eyes of those newcomers to the faculty. He sensed that they were organizing to ease him out, and themselves take over the momentum of his World Game and the Design Department he had developed for SIU without the expense of the large budgetary support he was getting. There was even a move on foot to take away the building provided for him by contract with the university. By thus cutting expenses, they hoped to ensure their own salaries. Bucky says, "I found it a very unfriendly situation."

This was something he could not bear, for despite his worldwide acclaim he still needed above all to be wanted. He says: "I found the community liking me very well—loving me. The old-timers could not have been more supporting, but I found it very unfortunate that I would suddenly be in university politics, which I have always avoided altogether."

In this stressful situation, Bucky thought of his friend John Rendelman, who had been the vice-president and the lawyer for SIU who had made the actual contractual arrangements with him. Rendelman had become president of the new SIU campus at Edwardsville, Illinois, near St. Louis. Bucky talked to him and conferred with the Board of Trustees of SIU. They all agreed that it would be appropriate for him to move his headquarters to the Edwardsville campus. Then, just as he was rather unhappily moving, a brilliant new prospect opened before him.

Martin Meyerson, president of the University of Pennsylvania, is a remarkable educator who has worked his way upward through the ranks of educational administrators over a period of some thirty years. Because of his wisdom and genuine empathy with the students he is one of the few academics who came through the bitter years of violence with an enhanced reputation. Originally from the Harvard School of Architecture and Planning, Meyerson went on to become the head of planning for the city of Chicago. Bucky met him there in 1948 when he went to teach at the Chicago Institute of Design. There was an immediate mental accord between them, and Meyerson asked Bucky to speak to his planners on several occasions.

Thereafter, they went their different ways, Bucky to MIT and on around and around our planetary spaceship; Meyerson eventually became dean of the School of Environmental Design at the Berkeley Campus at the University of California and then, because of his empathy with the students, chancellor of that riot-rocked institution. Throughout it all, he and Bucky continued their friendship, which was warmly renewed on the Doxiadis cruises—Meyerson went on eight of those scientific safaris, Bucky on all ten. Meanwhile, in 1971 Meyerson became president of the University of Pennsylvania, where, in

Bucky's words, "He is very greatly trusted and loved by the community and the students and the faculty and the trustees."

And Bucky added: "I found Martin a phenomenal man—I could understand how he could get on with the students. When Martin is sitting in the chair at any kind of meeting I have never known such comprehension of what is really going on; such a sympathetic attitude, but also an economy in getting people to the point without hurting them or offending them. He can really run meetings so they come out in logical ways and truly represent the consensus."

Meyerson had long wanted Bucky to be associated with a university he headed, and when rumors of the dissension in Carbondale reached him, he saw his chance. In this endeavor he was strongly seconded by President Harris Wolford of Bryn Mawr, who for several years had been urging Bucky to become associated with that college.

Their first attempt was abortive. When asked how much money he needed to conduct his World Game and other research projects, Bucky, with magnificent disregard of the financial facts of life replied casually, "Oh, three or four hundred thousand a year."

In some distress, Pennsylvania's representatives went to see Sonny Applewhite, who had retired as chief of personnel of the CIA to devote his life to organizing and editing Bucky's masterwork and mathematical testament, *Synergetic Geometry.* "It is something I have to do for Bucky," he says.[3] *Synergetic Geometry,* as is usual with Bucky's projects, is calculated to revolutionize mathematics and it took five thousand words just to summarize it.

Meyerson's representatives said to Applewhite: "We need Bucky, and we believe he needs us. But in these times we cannot finance such astronomical sums. Can you persuade him to be more reasonable or think of some way this thing can be arranged."

Applewhite was sympathetic and helpful. "One thing you could do is to find him a very nice place to live. He and Anne need a proper home and that might be an inducement."[4]

Eventually, the matter was worked out to the complete satisfaction of all concerned. Meyerson and Wolford, with some suggestions of support from the Rockefeller Foundation—which incidentally never materialized—developed a consortium which included Swarthmore and Haverford. Bucky had lectured at Haverford several times with Chris

[3] Applewhite to the author.
[4] Ibid.

Morley, whose father had at one time been its president. The first time Bucky presented the airocean map was at Haverford in the late thirties, and he also unveiled some of his new mathematical concepts there.

These four institutions became his sponsors. They were members of University City Science Center, being built as part of the redevelopment of what Bucky calls "a junky part of the city" in the thirties blocks along Market Street, by a consortium of twenty-six universities and colleges from an area extending as far south as Johns Hopkins in Baltimore. One of the new buildings, almost a block long, houses the great computers to service the twenty-six members of the consortium.

The four sponsors joined in arranging for Bucky to come to Science Center as what they appropriately call World Fellow in Residence. Science Center became his "immediate host," with offices in one of the new buildings. They also agreed to undertake the not inconsiderable business of moving tons of his research material, including the World Resources Inventory and the Chronofile, from Carbondale. They also agreed that he should have access to those marvelous computers for the World Game. Those were the splendid auspices under which Bucky made what he expects will be his final move.

It proved to be an exhilarating change of venue. In contrast to the unhappy situation that had developed in Carbondale, he found himself greeted by the universities, the City of Philadelphia, and the State of Pennsylvania in "the most extraordinary way." The university presidents not only arranged for him to lecture at all their campuses, but honored him with large banquets and small intimate dinners at which they made sure he would meet all their trustees and the ranking members of their faculties, as well as the community leaders of Philadelphia. Bucky's immense popularity with the student bodies, and the faculties as well, was extremely gratifying both to him and to those who had arranged to bring him there.

In April 1973, at a function in City Hall attended by two hundred leading citizens, Mayor Frank L. Rizzo made Bucky an honorary citizen of Philadelphia, an honor never before accorded to anyone except foreign heads of state. As the mayor presented Bucky with what looked like a slim gold cigarette case containing the beautifully designed insignia of his citizenship, he said with a grin, "If you get into trouble with my police just flash this on them and they will go away."

Bucky says, "Of course, I would never use it for that; but I must admit that in the old days I often used my badge as an honorary captain of the Aviation Division of the New York City police to get out of trouble."

Governor Milton Shapp of Pennsylvania also recognized Bucky's arrival in his state by sending the chief of the state troopers to escort him to Harrisburg for a luncheon at which he asked Bucky to become a member of the State Art Commission.

At the suggestion of Harris Wolford of Bryn Mawr, Bucky was asked to take part in planning Philadelphia's role in the celebration of the Bicentennial of the signing of the Declaration of Independence. Bucky says: "It is of great importance in Philadelphia because, of course, this is where it was done. The people here are completely committed to the idea of saying something to the world; they would like what they do to be metaphysical instead of physical, an expression of the same kind of thinking that had gone on before.

"Quite a long time ago, I had proposed to them that a Declaration of *Interdependence* would be the only thing that the world would be impressed with today.

"An interesting development was that M. Carey Thomas, the first woman president of Bryn Mawr, in her latest years when the League of Nations was being formed, had written a Declaration of Interdependence of the World. President Wolford brought it out, and the committee asked me to lead them in the writing of the new Declaration of Interdependence."

Perhaps the most exuberant welcome Bucky received was a front page story in the *Philadelphia Inquirer* on November 1, 1972; it really went overboard in an amusing way. The headline was:

"MAN OF TOMORROW IS OURS TODAY": "Buckminster Fuller a Modern Day Ben Franklin"

"He has been called a visionary, a prophet, a genius and . . . a crackpot. . . . He is a scientist, humanist, inventor, poet and engineer.
"And now, Philadelphia—ready or not—he's here. . . .

"Luring the 77-year-old Fuller away from Southern Illinois University is regarded in academic circles as a coup roughly of the same magnitude as the Philadelphia Eagles acquiring last year's entire Pro Bowl team for a couple of seventh-round draft choices. . . ." Possibly a slight exaggeration!

CHAPTER XXI

THE CRESTING WAVE

IT is a very extraordinary thing, as Bucky says, how happily the Fullers have fitted into the life of Philadelphia. He remembers the first time he ever came to the city in the autumn of 1917 when he was taking the *Inca* from Boston to Hampton Roads. The day before, he had sailed down the East River under Brooklyn Heights and, in answer to his ship's whistle, Anne had run out and waved to him from the lawn of her father's house. At Philadelphia, he had docked at the Navy Yard, not far from where he now lives, and walked up Market Street toward the center of the city. It was a holiday and everyone seemed to be out in the streets. "It was like Mardi Gras in New Orleans," Bucky says. "Perhaps because of my uniform, girls were grabbing me and kissing me all the way up Market Street. I was not too excited by it as I had just been married to Anne."

In October 1972, with the help of Doctor Meyerson, Bucky found a lovely home for Anne and himself; an apartment on the thirtieth floor of one of the tall new buildings which have been built on Locust Street down by the Delaware River, where the old junky warehouses and hovels had been cleared away by the urban renewal program. The many-windowed drawing room seemed to float high above the renascent city like a balloon—you could almost feel its buoyancy. The shipping on the Delaware gave Bucky the feeling of being in touch with all the oceans of the world. To the north he could look over the whole city with Independence Hall in the foreground, surrounded by trees and green lawns and fountains playing, and the rosy brick of the refurbished eighteenth-century houses glimpsed through the leaves.

Do not think that because Bucky is such a futurist he has no feeling for historic places and antiquities. He loves beautiful old things, like Margaret Fuller's ladderback chair and Monroe Hewlett's cobalt blue porcelain Fu dogs, which fit into that modern room as well as they did in the Carbondale dome-house. And he has such a romantic attachment for historic places and such a strong belief in their educational value that, in his Utopian tomorrow of world-around mobility, he plans certain oases of antiquity, where people will be living just as they did long ago. Oxford might be one of these, or a French village clustering around a chateau-fortress on the Loire, or perhaps, a Roman villa on the Tyrrhenian Sea, complete with its farm buildings and yoked oxen pulling the kind of plowshare Cincinnatus beat his sword into, and iron-tired chariots for transportation.

Bucky and his family: Bucky, Anne, Allegra holding cat (Gemini), Jaime, Alexandra holding Mustachio, Bob Snyder's head between Jaime and Alexandra, 1963.

These special places would be kept free of anachronisms so that young people—and old for that matter—could come and look, or even live for a while, and learn at first hand what life had been like in other times; and perhaps gain a sense of serenity and continuity.

So his view of Independence Hall means a great deal to Bucky; even as did the flat prairies of Illinois, where he says: "You got that Abe Lincoln feeling. That was a great experience, too."

Of Philadelphia Bucky says: "This is a center of intellectual life, like Boston. And like Bostonians, the people here are ready to move toward new design. If you build a better boat or design a better sail they will get it. If a thing works, they want it."

Anne also loves Philadelphia, which has many of the things she missed so greatly in Carbondale.

Bucky and Alden at Camden, September 1972.

Bucky has as many strikingly original ideas about the future of education as he has on all the other strategies for achieving success in Universe. Indeed, when he was first at Carbondale, he gave a long discourse to the planners of the new campus at Edwardsville that was published as a paperback book called *Education Automation: Freeing the Scholar to Return to His Studies.*[1] Now, in the congenial and inspiring atmosphere of Science Center, he has enlarged and refined the ideas expressed in that discourse.

Bucky says: "The essence of what the people here are saying to me is that they realize that an education revolution is really coming. This is an old educational complex—it could not be more so—where scholars have been thinking very cogently about the great changes that are taking place, in contradistinction to the relatively new educational institutions where they have not had long enough to sense the changes that are really imminent. So, realizing that the educational revolution is coming, the trustees, the presidents, faculty, students et al.—the community—is really saying, in so many words, 'We would like you to lead us in our accommodation to the great educational revolution. What should we really do?'"

Bucky believes that universities as now organized will become obsolete in ten years. Those that are still operating then will be "very great studios." "You will not find on the campus professors who are just there to earn a living while they do research. Those people will have been given fellowships to go elsewhere and do their studies.

"But the people who are really interested in education will be there; and they will be producing really extraordinary documentaries."

Bucky points out that under the present system the student who wants to get any kind of special information on a particular subject often finds it necessary to spend two years qualifying himself to ask the professor, who is the authority on that subject, the questions he wants answered. And he is just not willing to wait that long anymore.

"Quite clearly, with electronic call-up and so forth it is perfectly possible to have every single subject expounded by the greatest minds in that particular field. There will be these great documentary studios where the experts in a given subject, professors, graduate students, and technicians are participating in the making of these very, very good videos with sound tracks in two or three major languages. If the leading authority does not happen to have very good diction, some other man may read what he has written, supplemented by an enormous number of pictures.

[1] *Education Automation* by R. Buckminster Fuller, Southern Illinois University Press, 1962. (Published in paperback by Doubleday & Co., Inc.)

"It could possibly take a year or two years to make a particularly good video on any given subject. When completed it will be put in cassettes and will be call-upable by computers all around the world by means of the interlinking ability of those computers. With a communication satellite relay system anyone anywhere is going to be able to call up any program visually from any place on the planet within ten years. The documentaries will be there, and just as the student goes to an encyclopedia today and feels his way into finding what he wants, the students of tomorrow will be able to feel their way through the call-ups until they get right on to the subject they do want, and then hear it and see it explained by the greatest living authorities.

"This is the way the educational system is going to go."

Bucky believes that even for young schoolchildren—especially for young children—the living pictures of television are a far more effective means of communication than books and blackboards and teachers explaining things that even they may not properly understand. In *Education Automation* he wrote:

"I have taken photographs of my grandchildren looking at television. Without consideration of the 'value,' the actual concentration of a child on the message is fabulous. They really 'latch on.' Given the chance to get accurate, logical, and lucid information at a time when they want and need to get it, they will go after it . . . in the most effective manner." [2]

Bucky believes that even with the present idiotic programming, television has made it much harder for parents to indoctrinate their children with outworn, bigoted mores and ideologies, and has vastly improved the spoken language of all classes.

There can be little doubt about his major thesis: that undergraduate and graduate students would profit enormously if, instead of listening to some hack professor mumbling through a lecture he has given a hundred times before, they were presented with a brilliant exposition by experts, graphically illustrated with technologically perfect pictures or diagrams. Of course, it would be frightfully expensive with all those satellites, computers, and intraplanetary linkages and call-up systems; but in Bucky's world of plenty, by wide use and savings in unit costs we could easily afford it.

Naturally, the heads of the consortium sponsoring Bucky would like him to stay in Philadelphia much more than his program allows. He

[2] Ibid.

has explained to them that most of his current itinerary was worked out long before they invited him to be associated with them, but he pointed out that the way he carries on his work, living as he does on the cresting wave of knowledge, and operating, as he feels he must, without submitting to the manacles of patronage, working always on his own initiative, he is bound by the obligation to undertake the tasks that need to be done. He is still committed to the concept that nature ecologically does have intersupport. "The tree," he says, "is quite unaware of exchanging gases with the mammals; and the honey bee is quite unaware of his tail cross-pollenizing the vegetation, which can't procreate otherwise. We have then this beautiful design of nature where the individual participants are usually working on local drives quite unaware of the comprehensive integration of the effect of their efforts. I, too, must work in that blind way. My 1927 commitment was very much predicated in the idea that nature does have a synergetic or a precessional ninety degrees resultant to work, and that if I did commit myself to work that needed to be done for the evolutionary support of humanity and to the advantage of humanity, and assuming that the universe had some very important purpose in designing human beings and inaugurating the extraordinary design of the ecology of life on board of our planet led by the human beings that have minds, I said, 'It all seems very purposeful.' I would say that if I really committed myself to participating as competently as I know how I would not have to worry about how to get support, because if I was really making the right contributions, I would be supported completely indirectly."

So it has happened. Bucky pointed this out to Martin Meyerson and Harris Wolford and the others, and explained that the magnitude of his operations had now reached the point where he was required to earn about $200,000 a year to support them, and this could only be done by his world-around lectures. "Furthermore," he said, "these lectures are part of what I am trying to do. Talking to audiences of fifteen hundred or two thousand people at a time in different parts of the world enables me to communicate my ideas and give them coinage. I find it very appropriate. It is all a part of the developing work. I have no agencies to promote me. It all has to come from the spontaneous invitation of somebody or some group of people.

"So I said to the Philadelphians, 'I can't possibly unhook this from the responsibility I have for being able to pay my bills, but also to be able to accommodate this demand for the communication of ideas.' "

However, Bucky does see another way. In line with his Education Revolution he told the Philadelphians, "I would be interested in doing more of these documentaries on my own, and to help you toward doing the right ones. I have made many tapes and some videos, and the World Game is the very essence of the way I do my own. If you can arrange to get support for the development of this kind of programming—the video cassettes—if you can get enough funds to pay for my time, I would be glad to be here more."

Meyerson said to him, "I realize that this is a very risky thing for you to do, but I am going to ask you please to stop making any engagements for 1974, or to cut them down to a minimum. You know me, and I'm going to use all my capabilities to try to make it possible for you to stay."

There it rested.

In June 1972, a group of Bucky's friends and admirers organized the Design Science Institute, a tax-exempt foundation whose purpose is to "encourage, stimulate and advance the philosophy and works of R. Buckminster Fuller on a worldwide scale." It is headed by Doctor Glenn A. Olds, former United States Ambassador to the United Nations who became president of Kent State University after "the troubles" there. Among Doctor Olds's eminent cofounders of the Institute are Norman Cousins, Martin Meyerson, Mrs. Walter Kaiser, John Rendelman; M. W. Whitlow, president of the East Dubuque Savings Bank, who ever since he met Bucky in Wichita days has helped to manage his erratic finances, William M. Wolf, president of Wolf Computer Co., and Frederick J. Close, Chairman of the Board of Alcoa. The institute's World Advisory Council consists of Arthur C. Clarke of Columbo, Ceylon, originator of communication satellites; Constantino Doxiadis, Margaret Mead, Doctor Jonas E. Salk, and President Jerome Wiesner of MIT.

Herman Wolf, who long since made up with Bucky—though not with Anne and Allegra—and unselfishly devotes his time to helping him, is the institute's secretary. Bucky is, of course, its chief consultant.

The basic objective of the institute, as he defines it, is to promote reform through design revolution: "Political revolution, per se, commonly takes from one to advantage another. Yet total success for humanity could eliminate war." This can be accomplished only by "shunting the high priority air-space electronics industry from preoccupation with killingry to preoccupation with livingry." [3]

Bucky gave the back of his mind to both great contending political ideologies long ago in a single trenchant paragraph. He says that they both operate under the false Malthusian doctrine of inevitable scarcity. The free enterprise system solves the problem by "ruthless, but often polite decimation of the unsupportable fractions [of humanity], or leaving the unsupportable fractions to their unhappy fate." On the other hand he calls socialism, "the theory of austerity for all and sharing of the inadequacy with slow mutual approach to certain, untimely demise." [4]

"Livingry," then, is Bucky's purpose for the institute and not hopes for any self-glorification or spurious immortality. The other founders hope that it will serve that purpose and also preserve his ideals and creative thought for posterity.

Financing the institute has been something of a problem because of Bucky's integrity which forbids him to become beholden to any great "patron" such as the Ford or Rockefeller foundations. With his charming belief in the essential goodness and common sense of "Earthians," Bucky apparently expected millions of dollars to be contributed in small amounts by ordinary people all over the world. Thousands of dollars have been donated in small, unsolicited contributions, but Bucky's expectations were too high. The hope of the trustees is for large, no-strings-attached donations at which he cannot cavil.

Meanwhile, the institute serves as a bona fide foundation into which Bucky can pour his own large contributions to the service of mankind to which he pledged himself so long ago.

Though the institute, per se, has not generated wide public support, Bucky's personality and inspiring message have never been so universally acclaimed. He said, "In terms of public response and enthusiasm for my philosophy and the general principles I have discovered, the last three years have equaled all the twenty-five years preceding them."

And he added somberly, "When people accept your leadership and trust you it is a great responsibility. I have found that in order to fulfill the commitments I feel toward them, I have had to work perhaps beyond my capacity. Often after my evening lectures, I have had to work until five or six o'clock in the morning answering letters or trying to solve some mathematical problem that I felt could not wait."

[3] *Earthians' Critical Moment,* Buckminster Fuller, Design Science Institute, 1972.
[4] *Education Automation.*

In November, 1972, Bucky's horrendous schedule finally caught up with him. He suffered a physical collapse in California and was taken to a hospital with a suspected heart attack. It was nothing but sheer exhaustion.

Bucky says: "I just had to sleep. I slept while they were poking things into me and making tests. I even fell asleep under the X-ray machines. For all my willpower I could not stay awake. When I had slept enough I was perfectly all right and started off again."

Try as they might, the doctors could find nothing organically wrong with him. There was a sporadic action of his heart which troubled them a little. But Bucky said to them: "All my life I have experienced this thing of my heart dancing. It means nothing." And they were forced to believe him.

Another physical eccentricity is that sometimes a nerve in his neck is pinched and the supply of blood to his head is impeded. Bucky says: "That, too, I have had forever. When I start feeling a bit queer, I just shake my head hard, and I feel the blood rushing back, and in a moment, I am back to normal."

The collapse in California has made Bucky slightly more cautious, but very slightly. He says: "The trust of people inspires me so greatly that I must go on. *And I Can.*"

The enormous adulation Bucky receives from the young is another thing he knows he must be cautious about. Long ago in Romany Marie's he found people trying to make him a guru, and now he sometimes faces the same situation. The weak and the neurotic see him as a father figure and seek his psychic support. "It would be easy," he says, "to build an organization of weaklings, but that I will not do. People must believe in my principles and my ideals—not in *me*. For I am a very ordinary person."

Though much emphasis is put on the fervor of Bucky's youthful admirers, he has exercised an almost equal influence on mature people in high places. Scientists, architects, engineers, industrialists, philosophers, anthropologists, astrophysicists, monarchs, professional pundits of press and television, poets, and even despised politicians have not only been inspired by his unorthodox creative thought but have given him their warm personal affection. It is not so surprising that they should be stimulated, even a little awed, by the coruscation of ideas that pour like the gleaming particles of a comet's tail from his radioactive intellect. But mental brilliance is seldom an endearing quality; there must be something more. And there is.

It is Bucky's need to be loved, and his eagerness to return such love in lavish, overflowing abundance. For he believes in love as the most important principle of Universe, more important even than intuition. His heart is so full of love that he pours it out, mixed with loyalty, on all who are related to him, and on anyone who has been in any way kind to him, or even on comparative strangers who have only been a little appreciative of something he has done for them; and, of course, on anyone in trouble.

His brother-in-law, Roger Hewlett, best expressed this endearing quality of his when he said: "Bucky will do anything, including inventing geodesic domes, to make you love him. I think that is why he charms the great and the famous and the powerful, like Indira Gandhi.

"They hear about this man of great genius, and they meet this man of utter simplicity—not to mention his fascinating talk. And they are completely beguiled by him, because his wish to be loved shines out all over him." [5]

All sorts of people all over the world are constantly writing about Bucky, usually about his inventions, more often now about his philosophy, which pleases him far more. But they little know of Bucky who have not seen him on Bear Island, where he becomes again the supersensitive little boy who found his greatest youthful happiness there.

In the summer of 1972, Bucky was late getting to Bear Island. He likes to arrive by the first of August, but he had been delayed by the last Doxiadis cruise, and then a month spent in India's torrid summer, working with frustratingly evasive people on the airport buildings. He was close to exhaustion when he arrived.

Physically the island had changed very little with the passing years. The Big House stood, gray and gentle, half hidden by the trees planted when Bucky was a boy. Low, lichen-covered stone walls marked off the different fields. Deliciously pure cold water was still drawn in buckets from the wells; and soft rainwater from cisterns fed by pipes from gutters along the gabled roof was dipped out for washing. The only comparatively modern additions were a rusty jeep, which required very skillful driving because it had no brakes, and a small propane gas stove and refrigerator that stood in the kitchen of the Eating House facing the old iron, wood-burning stove, circa 1906. A small token dome was anchored on the abandoned tennis court.

5 Roger Hewlett to the author.

But Bucky's fame had inevitably altered the island's ambience. Eminent men and women, whom he had met and drawn there by his optimistic viewpoint and unorthodox thinking, were anxious to see him about this or that great enterprise. Teen-age children, who had won his easily given affection, wanted only to sit near his feet and listen to his wisdom. Bucky's uncontrollable hospitality was extended to them all. Of course, Allegra and his beloved grandchildren, and nieces and nephews, and children of old friends, and all Hewletts were always welcome. It made quite a crowd.

To Rosey, whose idea of Eden is that bitter, lonely winter on the island, it had become too much. She had married lawyer Alphonse Kennison and now had grown children of her own, who also loved Bear Island. So she had retired as Bucky's official hostess and built a charming, shingled cottage for her family a few hundred yards from the Big House. She often came for the cocktail hour, but no one went to Rosey's cottage unless they were specifically invited.

Her place as hostess of Bear Island had been taken by Bucky's niece, Leslie Larned,* who had married Richard Dana Gibson, a fine artist and typical New Englander, even though his ancestry was New York State. Leslie has that rare Massachusetts combination of intellectuality and sturdy competence. Clad in a cotton dress, sensible shoes, and an old straw hat, she looks like a pretty, eighteenth-century Puritan housewife as she hauls water from the well.

Leslie keeps the Big House shining, sweeping the floors, making the beds, seeing to it that the Victorian pitcher-basin-and-slop-jar sets in the bedrooms are always clean and fresh; conversing with the guests in whatever rarefied realms of thought they care to soar to; and never, never, never letting their numbers discombobulate her. Bucky calls her "My right-hand niece."

In the safe little harbor floats the Fuller fleet—*Intuition,* the flagship, all dark blue elegance with shining brightwork; Leslie's and Rosey's smaller sloops; the fast cabin cruiser *Alice* for meeting guests; *Lichen,* the twenty-foot utility "stink-pot," as Bucky calls motor-driven workboats; the sixteen-foot fiber-glass sloop *Sandrasan* for the grandchildren's delight, and four dinghies to service them.

Bucky's late arrival that summer of '72 caused unusual congestion. Everyone had to be there for the last two weeks of the summer holidays

* Her mother, Bucky's sister Leslie, had died in 1953. Woolly had died in 1963.

Allegra Fuller Snyder, 1972, aboard the Intuition.

—Anne, Allegra, Bucky's grandchildren—Alexandra, just entering her sophomore year in college and Jaime, about to start as a freshman— Leslie and Richard Gibson and their fourteen-year-old son George, who was in Bucky's old quarters in the attic of the Big House, now partitioned into rooms. Rosey, Alphonse, and their son Oliver were in the cottage, and there was a heavy turnover of distinguished visitors and eager students.

There were, of course, no servants, but two college girls had volunteered to cook for the company. They were Claire Fahnestock and Lucy de Chatenard, both from well-to-do families who worked, not for the wages Bucky paid them, but for the privilege of listening to him expound the secrets of Universe. Remarkable girls they were, completely refuting any theory of the younger generation going soft. Working with the small propane stove, pumping water for dishwashing with a hand pump connected by a hose to the cistern, sleeping, if at all, in unheated cabins, they turned out two good meals a day—breakfast and dinner at night—for up to twenty-eight people, all for love of Bucky.

Usually, Bucky's month on Bear Island was a time of complete relaxation surrounded by the people he loved most; his spirit healed by the omnipresence of his chosen element, the sea. Not that he stopped thinking out loud—for he could never do that. But his thinking there was serenely happy, a syntropic ordering of thoughts he had been too pressured to pursue to their ultimate conclusions.

Not that year. For he is a man whose time has come in the worldwide recognition of his philosophy, as shown in his Chronofile by the mounting tide of news items, articles, and books about him, and by the ever-increasing calls for him to lecture and to teach his doctrine of success for mankind in Universe from people all around the planet. He is like a surfer riding just ahead of the crest of this enormous wave of popular acceptance. Bucky knew this, and at seventy-seven, he knew that there was a limited time in which to complete his great design.

So that summer of 1972, the pressures followed him even to Bear Island. He had no time for the innocent frivolities of ordinary summers, for young laughter, swimming in the icy bay; good, hard, mind-easing manual work; or even sailing through a dusty nor'wester with all canvas set and the kids soaked with flying spindrift and whooping with joy —he only took *Intuition* out once in the first four weeks.

There was a huge accumulation of mail to be dealt with; there was his masterwork, the compendium of all his mathematical theories—

Synergetic Geometry—to be thought about, refined, edited, and amplified; and a new type of dome to be invented. He had arrived exhausted and he never let up. No wonder his skin looked pale and skull-tight, his eyes wearily distant; no wonder he was unusually short-tempered and intolerant of foolishness. He was not even able to get his short, restorative hours of deep sleep. He said, "Often when I lie in bed, the numbers pour through my brain, multiplying, dividing, square roots and fourth powers, making fantastic patterns that go just to the edge of realizing some unique discovery. I cannot turn them off."

And Bucky said, "Bear Island used to be very remote. Now it's suddenly invadable because there are so many powerboats. People can charter boats, and they are suddenly beginning to come out here.

"I really love human beings, but I do need time to do some thinking, and do some forward work. I live on the frontier of science and design; and you've got to put in, in order to put out.

"So Bear Island is where I try to put in. There are stacks of things waiting that I have not been able to find time to read, let alone getting the new work done. It is a life of great thoughtfulness . . . or should be. You might think I've found nothing while I've been here. But by and large a lot comes in."

The people on the island who love Bucky worried but said nothing —the worst possible thing to do was to imply that he was ailing; it would only have increased the pressure. The less knowing ones *did* increase the pressure with questions and demands on his precious time. The outside world refused to keep its distance, but brought its problems to the island.

Early in September Don Moore arrived. Bucky had met him in Moscow the summer of the Khrushchev-Nixon debate in the modern kitchen Don designed for Whirpool. He is a tall, unflappably energetic man with a vigorous mind and the dextrous hands of a watchmaker. He has studied and worked in the great scientific schools—the laboratories of Princeton, general systems theories at Pennsylvania, communications at MIT, business administration at Notre Dame.

When Don got back from Moscow he found that his assistant, a former pupil of Bucky's, had taken over at Whirlpool, and pushed him out of a job. Bucky, feeling a secondary obligation because his pupil had behaved badly, took Don on as his assistant; and never regretted it.

After a few years Don went on to found a successful business of his own as a science consultant.

"But," says Bucky, "he takes the trouble to come here summers, giving up his vacation to help me. If anything goes wrong on the island —things that I used to fix—Don comes along and takes care of it, because I am physically unable to any more. That in addition to his marvelous help building models and working on designs.

"You ought to know why Don is here. Just pure love for me . . ."

Bucky had continued through all these years to experiment with the tensegrity structures he believes will render the classic geodesic domes obsolete. When Don Moore arrived, he and Bucky began designing a new type of tensegrity sphere, which obviated some of the architectural difficulties of previous designs by introducing rectangular sections suitable for doors and windows without destroying the basic triangularity that ensured the fantastic strength of the structure.

The author happened to be present when, after days and nights of intricate calculations and skillful arranging of short hollow rods (compression members) and clothesline (the tensional element), Don Moore began the final assembly of the 4-foot-diameter model in a field beside the Eating House. Bucky, totally drained by having worked through at least one twenty-eight-hour day without even one of his catnaps, appeared so completely a thing of spirit that he seemed to have ephemeralized himself. As he looked at the jumble of rods and ropes lying in the rough grass, he was unusually pessimistic. "It won't work that way," he said. And began a long scientific discourse on why it was impossible. Don Moore paid no attention; just silently kept on threading ropes through rods and tying knots. Everyone on the island, kinfolk, students, and visitors, stood in the chill wind watching in expectant anxiety.

As Don tied the last knots, made the final connections, and tensed the clotheslines, the tangled heap gradually assumed a spherical shape and stood gloriously erect. Bucky poked it tentatively, then brought real pressure to bear. Instead of collapsing, the sphere contracted visibly and the tensional components distributed the load throughout the structure.

Then everybody got into the act, treating it very roughly, pushing it, throwing it into the air, dropping it on the rough ground, where it bounced like a football—for basically the same reasons. This was no delicate toy but an amazingly rugged structure almost impossible to damage. It worked!

Bucky was beaming. His eyes behind the glittering goggles were flashing signals of triumph. Lines of age and care disappeared miraculously from his face, which was suddenly ruddy with health. In five minutes he had lost five years. "This is very wonderful," he said. "It is pure synergy. It is a new development that will mean something great for mankind, and it is eminently patentable. All of you remember this date— September 10, 1972.

"And it's all due to the stubbornness of dear Don Moore. We'll call it the 'Moore Tensegrity!' "

After that things were fine on Bear Island. Bucky bloomed, becoming stronger, ruddier, healthier every day. The old bounce and gaiety came back to him; he began to have fun again. There was even one more glorious sail on *Intuition,* with the fifteen-knot wind driving her, lee scuppers awash, and the clean, cold spray lashing over her bow. They stayed out so long that black night fell before they reached harbor. One or two aboard wondered how Bucky would find his way home.

But he did, getting his bearings from the familiar lights flashing on the horizon—the twins, Minots' Light and Thatcher's Island Light, and Owl's Head Light low in the southwest, threading his way among islands and reefs with the skill and percipience of a Maine-raised boy who, unseeing those hazards in the darkness, feels their presence and avoids them—by intuition.

So Bucky brought his beautiful sloop foaming through the narrow harbor entrance under the dim lights of Pearl Hardie's cottage; swung her sharply into the wind with canvas slatting, and nosed her gently up to her home buoy in the bravura style of the old salt he likes best to be.

Later that night, he stood, square-built and sturdy, on the cliff-prow of his island ship, feeling the earth turn under him in its designed motion in an ever-moving cosmos. The sky, swept clear by the steady northeast wind, was brilliant with all the northern constellations—the two dippers; Orion, Canis, with Sirius dancing like a puppy; the Great Bear and his cub, and Polaris, "the earth's mooring buoy," pointing the true north. He was fulfilled and happy.

For Bucky has an intimate relationship with the planets and the stars.

INDEX

Page numbers in italics refer to illustrations.